# DEMO
## AUTHOR ...M
# IN THE ARAB WORLD

# DEMOCRACY AND AUTHORITARIANISM IN THE ARAB WORLD

## Nicola Pratt

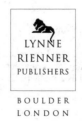

LYNNE
RIENNER
PUBLISHERS

BOULDER
LONDON

Published in the United States of America in 2007 by
Lynne Rienner Publishers, Inc.
1800 30th Street, Boulder, Colorado 80301
www.rienner.com

and in the United Kingdom by
Lynne Rienner Publishers, Inc.
3 Henrietta Street, Covent Garden, London WC2E 8LU

**Library of Congress Cataloging-in-Publication Data**
Pratt, Nicola Christine.
    Democracy and authoritarianism in the Arab world /
Nicola Pratt.
    Includes bibliographical references and index.
    ISBN-13: 978-1-58826-461-9 (hardcover: alk. paper)
    ISBN-10: 1-58826-461-0 (hardcover: alk. paper)
    ISBN-13: 978-1-58826-486-2 (pbk.: alk. paper)
    ISBN-10: 1-58826-486-6 (pbk.: alk. paper)
    1. Arab countries—Politics and government—1945–    2. Democratization—
Arab countries. 3. Authoritarianism—Arab countries. I. Title.
JQ1850.A58P73  2006
320.917'4927—dc22                                           2006021635


**British Cataloguing in Publication Data**
A Cataloguing in Publication record for this book
is available from the British Library.


Printed and bound in the United States of America

      The paper used in this publication meets the requirements
  ∞  of the American National Standard for Permanence of
      Paper for Printed Library Materials Z39.48-1992.

    5  4  3  2  1

*Dedicated to all those who
live and die for peace with justice*

# Contents

# Acknowledgments

ALTHOUGH THESE MAY BE THE first words of this book that you read, for me they represent the final words written for this project, which has taken approximately two years to finish. The relief at finally completing the book is overshadowed by two events that, to a certain degree, bring into stark relief some of the ideas explored here. At the time of writing (May 2006), scores of Egyptian demonstrators are being beaten on the street and detained without trial as the regime attempts to clamp down on the emerging prodemocracy movement. While Egyptians are not strangers to political repression, the scale of the current crackdown is particularly alarming. In many ways, these events prove some of the arguments that I attempt to elaborate here. In other ways, they highlight the apparent futility of writing a book about authoritarianism. When people are being beaten, thrown into prison, tortured, or even assassinated, can the academic justify her pursuit of knowledge, safe in her office or in the library of a UK university?

Also at the time of writing, the UK academics' unions (Association of University Teachers and National Association of Teachers in Further and Higher Education) are in a pay dispute with the university employers, and their members are engaged in action-short-of-a-strike, threatening to keep students from graduating on time this summer. Several universities around the country, including mine, are docking the pay of those engaged in the action, as well as subjecting them to a fair amount of emotional blackmail and pressure. With the prospect of having my pay reduced by a third, the temptation to fold and end my engagement in the action is very tempting. Is the principle of more pay one for which I want to make a personal sacrifice? Or are there greater principles at stake? The long-term standing of academics in higher education? The creation of "pliant" members of staff, for whom anything becomes justifiable in the interests of preventing students from litigating? Or even the principles of collective action? In light of the ideas explored in this book, I begin to understand the significance of the decisions that individuals take at certain moments. One apparently small decision may help to consolidate a longer-term trend. If this book has any significance at all, I hope it is to draw attention to the importance of understanding the longer-term dynamics of the context in which we find ourselves and the decisions that we take in relation to those contexts, so we may prevent the gradual erosion of rights that are essential to a democratic society.

I have a fine collection of friends and colleagues to thank, throughout the UK and beyond. I am particularly indebted to John Greenaway and John Street of the University of East Anglia (UEA) for reading and commenting on all the chapters (in reverse order) and providing me with the support necessary to get this book finished. I am also very grateful to the following people who read and commented on one or more chapters, pointing out factual errors, areas for further elaboration, and conceptual and theoretical problems, and offering vital words of encouragement: Nadje Al-Ali of the University of Exeter, Valentina Cardo of UEA, Salwa Ismail of the University of Exeter, Eberhard Kienle of the University of Aix-en-Provence, Stephanie Lawson of UEA, Agnieszka Pacynzska of George Mason University, Cristina Punter of UEA, Glen Rangwala of the University of Cambridge, David Seddon of UEA, Bob Springborg of the School of Oriental and African Studies, and Sami Zubaida of Birbeck. In addition, two anonymous reviewers provided detailed and thoughtful comments that helped me to revise the initial draft manuscript and, hopefully, to improve it. I have attempted as best that I can to incorporate their comments. However, the responsibility for any errors or lack of clarity is my own.

I owe a debt of gratitude to Paul Jackson of the University of Birmingham for thinking up the title of the book! I would like to express my great appreciation of Rachel Lunness, Melanie Watling, and Kathy Brandish of UEA for support with printing, photocopying, and sending off various drafts of the manuscript and, in general, for being indispensable. I would also like to thank Ziad and Nadia for allowing me to stay in their beautiful apartment while I was using the library at the American University of Beirut. I'm sorry again about the broken ashtray. . . . I am also very grateful to my students at UEA (Introduction to the Contemporary Politics of the Middle East, 2005 and 2006) for giving me the space to think about and discuss many of the ideas here.

This book began many years ago when I was writing a doctoral thesis about the potential for democratization in Egypt. Thinking of that early work, I express a debt of gratitude to Salwa Ismail and to the many individuals in Egypt who were generous with their time in helping me to understand the dynamics of Egyptian civil society. In particular, I thank Gasser Abdel-Razek.

All royalties from the book will be donated to Amnesty International.

*—Nicola Pratt*

# 1

# Reconsidering Democratization in the Arab World

SINCE THE FALL OF COMMUNISM, and with the "Third Wave" of democratization engulfing much of the world (Huntington 1991), academics and activists have been preoccupied with how to promote democratic reforms in the Arab[1] region (Brynen, Korany, and Noble 1995a: 5–6). The 1990s were a time of much optimism about the possibilities for democratization, with arguments that Arab regimes would be forced to open up in response to a more active civil society that included human rights organizations, women's groups, and an array of NGOs (see various authors in Norton 1995 and 1996). In addition, some observers predicted that Arab regimes would have to pursue democratic reforms in tandem with or subsequent to the International Monetary Fund (IMF) and World Bank-sponsored economic reforms in order to maintain their legitimacy in the eyes of citizens (Harik 1992a; Richards 1995; Singerman 1995). Nonetheless, despite the growth in civil-society activity and the implementation of economic reforms, the expected political openings did not emerge in a sustained way.

The failure of democratization to take root has given greater credibility to those within foreign-policy circles who argue in favor of Middle East "exceptionalism," embedded within ahistorical and essentialized notions of Arab-Muslim political culture. Authors such as Bernard Lewis, and others writing within the tradition of scholarship entitled "orientalism," have argued that Arab-Muslim culture is incompatible with democracy because concepts associated with democracy, such as representative government, freedom, and the separation of religion from

1

state, are unknown within Islam and the Arab political tradition (Kedourie 1994; Lewis 1993). In "The Clash of Civilizations?" Samuel Huntington (1993) employs the concept of essentialized cultural difference between a liberal, democratic, secular West versus the "Rest," including the Islamic world, where Western values possess little cultural resonance, to describe the emerging pattern of global politics and conflicts in the post–Cold War context.

This book aims to challenge deterministic and essentializing approaches to theorizing democratic transitions in the Arab world by examining the dynamics of authoritarianism and of opposition to it as a historically constituted political process. This involves an investigation into the development of authoritarian political systems in the Arab world, beginning with the colonial period and continuing through to the present. I argue that authoritarianism is not only determined by the type of regime that is in power and the nature of political relations under that regime. Linked to this, there exists a complex of social relations rooted in class, gender, religious, and ethnic differences. These relations are not only produced as a result of economic and institutional structures, such as the type of development strategy adopted or the structuring of state–civil society relations. They are also constituted by individuals and groups engaging in social and political interactions for the purpose of furthering their interests—whether in support of or against democratization.

These interests cannot be assumed from material circumstances, although these necessarily play a role. In addition, they are shaped by self-identities—such as belonging to a certain national community or to a certain class. Such self-identities are not fixed in stone but have evolved in response to the experiences of colonialism, the anticolonial struggle, and the process of state building in the postindependence period. It is this particular historical experience that is an important factor in understanding the apparent "exceptionalism" of the Arab world with regard to the slow pace of democratic transition.

## Classifying Arab Regimes

Most authors classify Arab countries according to the nature of their regimes: "the radical, populist republics" vs. "the conservative, kin-ordered monarchies" (Ayubi 1995), "socialist republics" vs. "liberal [*sic*] monarchs" (Richards and Waterbury 1990), or "single-party regimes" vs. "family rule" (Owen 2004). Different types of regimes are associated with different types of political institutions, different political cultures, and different relations between regime and societal groups. They are also associated at certain points in their history with different types of political economy.

This book examines the group of regimes that are characterized as radical/populist/socialist/single-party. These are the regimes of Algeria, Egypt, Iraq (prior to March 2003), Syria, and Tunisia, which share a number of features that have led scholars to group them together. First, they have all been, at one point or another, dominated by a single party: the Ba'th parties in Syria and (prewar) Iraq, the Front de Libération Nationale (FLN) in Algeria, the Parti Socialiste Destourien (PSD) (formerly, the Neo-Destour) in Tunisia, and the National Democratic Party (formerly the Arab Socialist Union/National Union/National Liberation Rally) in Egypt. These regimes have co-opted a number of functionally differentiated organizations, such as trade unions, peasant unions, and professional associations, into corporatist arrangements. These have been used to mobilize support for regimes as well as to implement regime policies. Within this system, there has been little room for political or civil-society activity independent of the regime, thereby concentrating formal political power in the hands of the regime. In sum, these regimes have demonstrated the characteristics associated with a common definition of authoritarianism (Linz 2000: 255).

Until the 1970s (or 1980s in the case of Algeria and Iraq), these countries were associated with radical nationalist ideologies and commitment to social and economic transformation aimed at addressing the injustices and underdevelopment that was seen as a legacy of colonial rule. Toward this end, they embarked upon programs of industrialization and agrarian reform, adopting state planning and taking control of the commanding heights of the economy. In addition, they provided extensive welfare benefits, including universal healthcare and education. These attempts at social engineering led them to be described as "radical" and "mobilizing." The term "socialist" has also been utilized to define this period of regime consolidation. While socialist-type policies were pursued and there were attempts to articulate an "Arab" socialist ideology, socialism was used to describe polices conducted out of nationalist and modernizing concerns rather than ideological belief (Ayubi 1995: 198).

In the 1970s, most of these regimes were forced to turn away from their rhetorical commitment to socialism and its associated policies, as a result of economic difficulties, which were compounded by the humiliation suffered by the Arab armies in the 1967 war with Israel. Different phases of economic liberalization were introduced, either voluntarily or as a result of structural adjustment programs sponsored by the international financial institutions (IFIs). Economic reforms were usually accompanied by a shift in foreign policy away from alliances with the Soviet bloc, toward the West and/or the conservative Gulf countries. To different degrees, regimes began to loosen some restrictions on political expression, thereby opening the way for a limited type of political pluralism. In most cases, elections to a national assembly were introduced.

By the 1990s, experiments in limited political liberalization were halted or reversed. In most cases, growing Islamist opposition provided a justification for clampdowns on civil liberties that implicated not only the Islamist opposition but other civil-society organizations as well. In the case of Iraq, the war against Iran in the 1980s afforded a similar opportunity for the repression of any sort of dissent. The situation of blocked political liberalization and restrictions on civil liberties continued throughout the 1990s.

The slow or nonexistent pace of political reform in the Arab world was largely tolerated by external actors, including the United States, until 2001. The terrorist attacks of 9/11 initiated a shift in US foreign policy toward active support for democratization in the Arab world/ Middle East as a means of countering terrorism. Part of the (post-facto) justification for the US-led invasion of Iraq in March 2003 was to bring democracy to the Middle East. With the fall of the Ba'th regime, Iraq was held up as a potential model for democratic reform within the Arab region. For some observers, and despite the ongoing violence inside Iraq, 2005 represented the year when US efforts began to pay off. A series of events appeared to signal a political sea change within the region toward greater democracy (Dickey 2005; Zakaria 2005). This was illustrated by the holding of elections and the drafting of a new constitution in Iraq, the election of a new president in Palestine, municipal elections in Saudi Arabia, the exit of Syrian forces from Lebanon forced by large street demonstrations there, and the holding of the first competitive presidential elections in Egypt.

There are many ways in which such optimism could be qualified— that the Iraqi elections took place in a context of severe violence and the outcome of the constitution drafting contributed to conflict within Iraq; that the Saudi elections were for a limited number of seats, with women being barred from voting; and that Egypt's presidential elections were marred by many irregularities. Meanwhile, Tunisia and Syria appeared to be no closer to political reforms than they were several years previously, and Algeria launched a referendum on a national reconciliation plan that would deny justice to the many victims of atrocities committed during the civil war, while consolidating "oligarchic rule."[2]

The continuing obstacles to political reform—despite the changing political economy, ideological rhetoric, and introduction of elections over time—points to the ability of Arab regimes to adapt and change in order to maintain their authoritarian rule. The longevity of authoritarian rule in the Arab world illustrates that democracy is not inevitable. Rather, there exist significant obstacles to dismantling these regimes. These obstacles are not rooted in a timeless Arab-Muslim political culture, but rather in the dynamics of authoritarianism itself. These dynamics are shaped by the historical context in which authoritarianism has emerged.

## The Basis of Authoritarian Rule: Bringing the State Back In

Authoritarianism is most often defined as a regime type—in terms of personnel, rules of the game, and the structure of the polity (Linz 2000; Richards and Waterbury 1990). As noted above, scholars of Middle East politics have classified different Arab regimes according to certain characteristics: single party vs. family rule; radical vs. conservative. While such typologies can identify differences in policies, political institutions, and ideologies, they neglect to describe or understand the infrastructure that sustains these different regimes—namely, the state.

In examining the nature of the state that has underpinned authoritarian rule, I draw upon the work of three scholars of Middle East political economy—Roger Owen (1992/2004), Simon Bromley (1994), and Nazih Ayubi (1995). They argue that the process of state formation in the Arab world plays a significant role in explaining the nature of politics within Arab states. In other words, authoritarianism is not the product of certain types of regimes but rather emerges from the nature of the states over which these regimes rule.

The starting point for an analysis of the emergence of Arab regimes is the colonial period. Political and economic domination by colonial powers created a particular legacy that shaped the trajectory of state development within the Arab region. Colonial domination, in most cases, created the system of nation-states that exists today in the region. Previously, the Arab lands examined here had been part of the Ottoman Empire. With the exception of Egypt, which had a long history of territorial unity, the creation of a state system imposed new political realities and identities. The legacy of European domination created an impetus for the expansion of postindependence state institutions—including the police, the military, economic enterprises, and the bureaucracy (Owen

2004: 9–11). In turn, state expansion acted to concentrate resources and, consequently, power in the hands of the regimes that controlled the state, thereby paving the way for authoritarianism (p. 27).

Colonial rule, while not initiating the process, certainly increased the pace of the incorporation of the region into the global capitalist system and cemented its subordinate position within this system. This subordination also constitutes a major factor in the development of authoritarianism (Bromley 1994). Postindependence regimes responded to the challenge of economic modernization by initiating heavy state involvement in the economy (e.g., through the nationalization of industries, the redistribution of agricultural land, and control and the direction of trade). The degree of foreign political domination and economic penetration was uneven between different countries of the region, with different political outcomes. Those areas that escaped direct colonial control (Turkey and Iran) or were dependent on the development of a commodity that needed to be sold on the international market (that is, oil in Saudi Arabia and the Gulf states) developed state systems that were *not* anti-imperialist. In these circumstances, indigenous anticolonial/national movements represented a threat to pro-Western ruling groups and were suppressed. On the other hand, in those areas where there was considerable foreign control of the economy (for example, Egypt and Syria) and economic development depended upon indigenous industrialization, state formation took an anti-imperialist direction. In this context, those classes (such as the large landowners) whose interests were associated with colonial rule were politically suppressed. Although the two patterns of state formation differ, through the suppression of certain classes, they have led to the creation of an authoritarian political system (Bromley 1994: 104).

Like Simon Bromley, Nazih Ayubi (1995) also argues that politics in the Middle East has been shaped not only by colonialism and the nature of incorporation into the global capitalist economy but also by the internal social configuration of Middle East societies. The encroaching capitalist mode of production stimulated by colonial penetration was articulated with already existing modes of production, leading to a weak and fluid configuration of classes. In such a context, no one class was able to achieve hegemony. Therefore, the regimes that came to power in the postindependence era were forced to build alliances, through processes of co-optation, in order to maintain their power. This has created states where political relations are structured through corporatist arrangements (p. 25). Corporatism represents a type of state-society relationship that is based on the linking of groups, classes, and individuals to the state through various means (such as patronage, clientelism, welfare measures, etc.), and through various "organizational" modalities (including trade unions and other "mass" organizations) (p. 35).

Under single-party/populist regimes, state corporatism enabled capitalist accumulation (Ayubi 1995: 192). By establishing corporatist structures, regimes politically excluded those social groups that supported the precolonial arrangements, such as large landowners. Simultaneously, regimes used corporatist structures, such as mass organizations, to co-opt and mobilize those sections of society that were necessary for the state's economic development strategy of import-substitution industrialization (ISI), namely the working classes, the peasantry, and the middle classes.

State corporatism functioned to subordinate mass organizations and other groups to the regime. Subordination was achieved by regime control of the selection of the leadership of corporatist organizations and by specifying (through a variety of laws) the limits of their organizational activities—usually defined in terms of national development objectives. Consequently, mass organizations became vehicles for implementing national development policies, such as raising productivity and eradicating illiteracy, rather than as a means of holding their regimes to account. The subordination of corporatist organizations to the regime was legitimized by a populist-nationalist discourse that emphasized the importance of national unity as a means of state building (Ayubi 1995: 206–207). It is no surprise that corporatism, as a system rooted in collaboration between different social groups/classes, should lend itself to a rhetoric of unity rather than pluralism.

The above authors identify the ways in which the emergence of authoritarianism is linked to the process of state building in the postindependence period and, in turn, the ways in which this process depended upon the construction of certain hierarchies of social relations (rooted in the economy and institutions). This process may be regarded in terms of a response to the economic problems created by colonial domination. In the process of ridding their countries of colonial influence, regimes in Egypt, Algeria, Tunisia, Syria, and Iraq repressed large landowners and other groups associated with colonial privilege. Meanwhile, they co-opted workers, peasants, and the middle classes whose productive efforts were deemed essential for national development. The old oligarchy was politically excluded while the popular coalition of forces were mobilized through corporatist organizations. However, this inclusion was structured in a way that suppressed competition and subordinated these groups to the direction of the executive powers. Executive powers were enhanced by the concentration of resources in the hands of these regimes due to the huge expansion of the public sector and bureaucracy. These processes created a system of authoritarian rule.

Yet, state building should not only be seen as a top-down process. In order to succeed, it relies on the participation of ordinary people, who are the basis for the social relations underpinning the state. In other words, the emergence of authoritarianism has not only been shaped by the actions of regime elites in the sphere of state building. It has also depended upon the consent of non-elites in this process, based on some sort of self-interest. For Ayubi, the most important factor in enabling elites to secure the consent of citizens for the building of authoritarian rule was the state's provision of socioeconomic benefits, such as universal healthcare, education, workplace benefits, and subsidized goods and services, enabled by the expansion of the public sector in the early years of independence (1995: 35). The provision of these benefits served to integrate citizens into the state and to lend credence to the populist-nationalist discourse of regimes. In addition, Arab regimes constructed mass-based and functionally defined corporatist institutions, which appeared to include workers, peasants, and other working people politically and to protect and promote their interests within the political system (p. 209). An implicit bargain was struck whereby citizens ceded the exercise of political and civil rights for the consumption of social and economic benefits (Singerman 1995: 245). This socioeconomic inclusion compensated for the limitations on political participation (Ayubi 1995: 33). Simultaneously, it rendered the regime's legitimacy dependent upon its economic performance (pp. 31–32). As soon as this economic performance faltered due to the inherent contradictions of the ISI strategy, regimes were forced to narrow their political alliances in tandem with their economic strategies (p. 219). This led some observers, based on the writings of transition theorists such as Guillermo O'Donnell and Philippe Schmitter (1986), to anticipate that Arab countries would be obliged to pursue democratic reforms as a means of maintaining widespread political support (for example, Ayubi 1995: 410; Richards 1995).

Yet, this democratic transformation has not occurred and poses a problem with regard to understanding political processes in terms of socioeconomic factors. Here, I turn to the writings of Antonio Gramsci (d. 1937), who attempted to understand why capitalism continued to survive in the first quarter of twentieth-century Italy, despite the existence of the objective economic conditions that would support a transition to communism. Gramsci argued that exploitative relations were underpinned by "a complex of moral injunctions that make these relationships seem right and proper to all parties in the exchange" (Femia 2001: 139). In other words, for Gramsci, capitalism is not only a particular structure of economic relations of production but also a system of meanings that normalize those relations. This system of meanings is not imposed upon workers by the owners of capital. Rather, workers also participate in producing a culture—in the broadest sense of the term—in which capitalism is normalized (Eagleton 1991: 114). This consensus concerning the "commonsense" nature or naturalness of existing relations of power, despite their oppressive or unequal nature, is termed "hegemony" (Boggs 1976: 39).

Similarly, authoritarianism continues to exist as a hegemonic system despite the existence of objective economic factors (namely, economic deterioration since the 1970s) that would appear to undermine authoritarianism and support a process of democratization. This, I argue here, indicates that authoritarian rule is not only underpinned by socioeconomic structures but also by a culture (in terms of a socially produced system of meanings) that normalizes it. By this, I do not mean to invoke essentialized and ahistoric notions of an Islamic-Arab culture or mentality. Culture should be seen as ever-changing and shaped by historical processes. It represents a social practice of "meaning-making" in which actors make the world in which they live intelligible (Clarke et al. 1976: 9–74; Wedeen 1999). These meanings do not exist only in people's heads but are realized in the ways that people live their lives—in the choices that they make, and in their everyday behavior. As a system of meanings constructed through social practices, culture is produced, reproduced, amended, and even revolutionized in the context of chang-. ing historical conditions.

## The Culture of Authoritarianism: Hegemony and Civil Society

For Antonio Gramsci, "culture" represents one of the noncoercive mechanisms by which rulers win popular consent for their rule (1971: 258). The operation of culture in normalizing the relations between the rulers and those who are ruled is illustrated by Marsha Pripstein Posusney's 1997 study of Egyptian workers in the postindependence period. She argues that workers believe themselves to be embedded within a reciprocal relationship with the state, in which the latter provides socioeconomic benefits in exchange for workers' contribution to national development as a patriotic duty (rather than in compensation for the withdrawal of political rights). This is demonstrated by the logic of workers' protests, which have tended to favor lock-ins and demonstrations over all-out work stoppages, in order not to disrupt their contribution to national production. The object of their demands has been the restoration of their living standards when these have fallen, rather than new rights, such as the freedom to form an independent union or to strike. Pripstein Posusney characterizes this belief in a reciprocal relationship as the "moral economy" (1997: 4–6).[3] The operation of the moral economy suggests that workers have identified themselves as members of a particular national community. It is within the cultural (or ideological) framework of "nation" that workers perceive their rights as guaranteed. When workers believed that the terms of the moral economy had broken down, they sought to restore these terms through their protests rather than to construct a new framework of demands based on political and civil rights.

The above examination of workers' protests demonstrates that the hegemony of authoritarianism should not be reduced to its economic and institutional dimensions. The cultural dimension of hegemony prevents the establishment of a straightforward causal relationship between economics and political demands. As Pripstein Posusney's study demonstrates, workers have not simply abandoned their belief in the ideological validity of the reciprocal relationship underpinning authoritarianism as soon as economic benefits have been withdrawn. Similarly, we should not assume that society will demand political and civil freedoms in compensation for the loss of socioeconomic benefits. Individuals may support the maintenance of the existing hegemony on the basis of an established reciprocal relationship, which is ideologically as well as materially based. This suggests that hegemony is not a zero-sum game in which the dominant group exercises power at the expense of those who are dominated. Rather, the "dominated" contribute to and participate in their domination through their belief in the validity of the system.

The need for regimes to win the consent for their rule signifies that ordinary people must continue to believe in the system for it to work. This belief is demonstrated through the continuous participation of ordinary people "in the system," as well as by their political actions. In the above case, those workers' actions and demands that reaffirm the validity of the reciprocal relationship underpinning authoritarianism also operate to reproduce authoritarianism, even as they challenge the regime in power. Consequently, challenges to the regime should not be equated with challenges to authoritarianism.

Where regimes have faced challenges to their rule, they have often resorted to coercion in order to suppress opposition movements, demonstrations, and other protest activities. Yet, according to Gramsci, coercion alone is insufficient to maintain hegemony. Prolonged coercion entails high costs to regimes. At the most obvious level, this would appear to mean that coercion, for the most part, is threatened in order to deter people from transgressing the consensus that maintains regime hegemony. Yet, this would amount to stating that society is coerced into accepting the consensus underpinning authoritarian rule. This is contrary to the essence of hegemony as principally a noncoercive form of leadership. As Terry Eagleton argues, "the coercive institutions of a society . . . must themselves win a general consent from the people if they are to operate effectively" (1991: 114). This suggests that, although Arab regimes may be characterized as "fierce" (Ayubi 1995: 449), this level of coercion is not necessarily contested by the majority of society. Indeed, coercion is ultimately rendered ineffective as soon as it ceases to be seen as legitimate by a critical mass within society.

If the maintenance of regimes in power depends upon the existence of a consensus that sees authoritarianism as natural, how is such a world view created and diffused? In this respect, the role of civil society is key as the arena in which hegemony is naturalized (Boggs 1976: 39). For Gramsci, civil society represents the "trench systems" of the state—the position from which the battle for the hearts and minds of citizens is conducted (Femia 2001: 140). It includes those institutions, such as religion, trade unions, and the education system, that are not directly involved in production (such as economic enterprises) nor directly responsible for the exercise of political power (such as the government, the state bureaucracy, or the courts) (Gramsci 1971: 56, n. 5). This is a sphere not merely of organizational actors, but of ideas and culture, in its widest sense. It consists of the spaces in which ideological struggle takes place—such as the media, debating salons, places of worship, and community hall meetings (Cohen and Arato 1994: 429) in addition to the family/private sphere. It is within civil society that projects of anticolonial struggle, national modernization, women's emancipation, and the nature of national identity and culture have been formulated and debated, thereby contributing to their diffusion within the wider society.

This notion of civil society differs from liberal conceptions of the term. Writers within the liberal tradition, such as Alexis de Tocqueville, see civil society as the range of institutions beyond the state that act to counterbalance state power and prevent despotic rule (Kaviraj 2001).

On the other hand, for Gramsci, civil society is an intrinsic part of the modern state (the state = political society + civil society [Gramsci 1971: 262]). Regime domination of civil society under authoritarianism does not destroy civil society. Rather, civil society under authoritarianism continues to exist but does not necessarily behave or resemble civil society in liberal democratic systems. Indeed, in the countries studied here, civil society has played an integral part in state building through the incorporation of individuals into the state as citizens. This has been achieved on several levels. Most obviously, trade unions, peasant unions, as well as other mass-based organizations have institutionally linked individuals to the state and served as a conduit for the state's provision of socioeconomic benefits. More significantly, civil society has played an essential role in supporting a national modernization project that has served to ideologically justify individuals' membership in the nation-state.

The project of national modernization was central to the demands of anticolonial nationalists across the Arab world—whether secular, Islamist, communist, or feminist—and regarded as essential to ensuring national sovereignty in the postindependence period. This project was formulated as a response to the legacies of colonial domination, which include not only the political, military, and economic domination of the region, underpinned by the West's superior material resources, but also the attempts at moral and cultural domination, underpinned by Western discourses about the Orient as the inferior "Other" (Said 1978). "Modernization" was seen to depend upon achieving and maintaining national sovereignty, while national sovereignty was a precondition for modernization to occur. National modernization meant the complete freedom from colonial domination—political, economic, and technological—thereby enabling the new nation-state to participate in the international system on an equal footing with the West.

While the project of national modernization was widely supported and, in the early years of independence, gave many people a sense of dignity, it also contained an illiberal logic that paved the way for the establishment of authoritarianism. Most significantly, national modernization led to the creation of "new social hierarchies and a field of social struggle" (Beinin 2001: 8–9) that privileged the interests of the collective (the nation-state) over the well-being of the individual and, in the process, consolidated authority in the regime as the head of the nation-state. Although nationalist leaders proclaimed new rights and benefits for citizens, these were intended to mobilize the people's moral and political support for political independence and their labor for the purpose of national development (for a comparison with India, see Chatterjee 1986:

153). Within the national modernization project, the working classes, peasants, and women represented not only agents of modernization but, simultaneously, objects of modernization—individuals and groups whose "traditional" practices had to be eliminated for the good of the nation, in order for modernization to occur (Beinin 2001: 8). Such attitudes helped to sustain a sense of paternalism in which workers, peasants, and women were clearly subordinated to those who claimed to speak on their behalf—that is, national elites, the middle classes, and the intelligentsia. Mass-based organizations channeled people's efforts toward the goal of national modernization and enabled new regimes to politically direct civil society. Such measures were seen as necessary for protecting the nation against the internal and external enemies of national modernization—that is, "feudalists" and "imperialists." Dominant political discourses of populist-nationalism operated to fuse regime interests with the interests of the people and, thereby, to disguise the new social hierarchies evolving as a result of national modernization. More significantly, the project of national modernization created a realm of the possible in which citizens, for the most part, consented to authoritarianism in the national interest.

A consensus within civil society supported the aim of national modernization as an objective of nation-state building. However, in the process of ensuring the success of the national modernization project, authoritarianism was normalized. Even as civil-society actors objected to the authoritarian manner in which national modernization was pursued, for the most part they have remained committed to this project. This commitment has been strengthened not despite, but because of, the military defeat of the Arab regimes in 1967, ongoing economic difficulties, and the continuing military, political, and economic dominance of the West. Yet the social and political relations created by national modernization continue to sustain authoritarianism and serve as an obstacle to democratization. Overturning authoritarianism involves contesting the national modernization project of the postindependence era and conceptualizing a counter-hegemonic project.

## Democracy as Counter-Hegemony

In the same way that Gramsci was interested in how subordinated groups/ classes could overturn the hegemony of capitalism, this book is concerned to explore the potential for overturning authoritarianism. Toward this end, civil society is not only considered the terrain upon which regimes secure consent for authoritarian rule but also as the trenches in which social forces could establish their "war of position" against the hegemony that underpins that rule (Gramsci 1971: 229–238). A "war of position" represents an attack not only on the "outer edifices" of the system of rule (for example, the regime, its policies, and its institutions) but also an attack on the ideological complex that underpins that rule (Boggs 1976: 53). By this, I refer to the necessity of challenging a whole range of established ideas and practices—what Terry Eagleton refers to as "culture" in the widest sense—that structure the social relations buttressing authoritarianism (1991: 114). The contestation of dominant ideas and practices paves the way for the formulation of an alternative or "counter" hegemony.[4]

In the case of the Arab regimes examined here, I identify the project of "national modernization" as the most significant element securing hegemony in the postindependence period. Until the late 1980s, national modernization represented the major objective of civil-society actors. This has gradually been replaced by the objective of democratization. For most civil-society actors, democratization entails the introduction of political reforms to enable real alternation of power and political competition. Although a multiparty system and an elected national assembly have nominally existed since the 1970s, in the case of Egypt, Syria, and Iraq,[5] and since the 1980s, in the case of Tunisia and Algeria, this system has not led to an alternation of power. The political opposition that is officially sanctioned has been consistently excluded from power by the absence of free and fair elections. Meanwhile, a substantial element of existing political opposition within these countries, namely Islamist movements, has been prevented from participation within electoral politics as recognized political parties. The experience of these countries demonstrates that multiparty elections do not necessarily lead to democracy and may, in fact, help to strengthen authoritarian regimes. Consequently, prodemocracy groups have focused most of their attention on demanding reforms that will guarantee those rights and freedoms necessary for free and fair elections and a real alternation of power to occur, such as freedom of the press, of expression, of association, and of assembly.

The development of support among many civil-society actors in favor of individual rights and freedoms represents a significant step in the war of position against authoritarian rule. The attention to the rights and freedoms of individuals brings into question the notion of national unity, which forms a major element in the national modernization consensus underpinning authoritarianism. In so doing, it opens new spaces for a plurality of opinions to be represented. It challenges the relationship between regime and society that subordinates the interests of the latter to the policies and programs of the former. Yet, calls for democratic reforms, while a step toward overturning authoritarianism, do not necessarily represent a wholesale attack on the interplay of economic, ideological, and institutional structures that underwrite the hegemony of authoritarianism.

A war of position against authoritarianism would entail the elaboration of a counter-hegemonic project that not only embraces the institutional and legal framework of (liberal) democracy but also eschews other assumptions that help to maintain authoritarianism as a system (and not only as a regime). Here, I identify one particular assumption that is prevalent among many civil-society actors and that is central to the project of national modernization underpinning authoritarianism: national difference.

The discourse of nationalism that dominated the anticolonial struggle and the postindependence period is predicated on the idea of national difference between "us" and "them," where "them" refers to the "West" as former colonizers and as the most powerful states in the international system. The concept of national difference depends upon the construction of an identity and culture that is exclusive and different from those of other nations. This logic entails recourse to "essences" that deny difference *within* nations (Chatterjee 1993). In order to maintain a fixed, monolithic identity, nationalist discourse must construct ideological boundaries that are policed, both literally and discursively, to maintain unity in the face of the "Other." Foreign influences over national culture and identity are seen as a means for the West to undermine the nation. Consequently, ideas and practices perceived as coming from abroad, such as human rights and women's rights, are often condemned. Indeed, some human rights violations may be justified on the grounds of protecting the essence of the nation against cultural imperialism (Pratt 2005).[6]

Ideas about gender roles and identities and ethnic/religious identities are fundamentally linked to the construction of a national identity. In constructing a national essence, certain roles and identities become prescribed and others proscribed in order to construct national "authenticity." For example, in Algeria, Egypt, Iraq, Syria, and Tunisia the promotion of women's participation in the public sphere has been symbolic of national modernization. Constitutions proclaimed equality between men and women with regard to their public roles. Women were encouraged to join the work force through the expansion in state-sector employment, which granted women generous maternity leave and provided crèche facilities (Hijab 1988). While women's visibility in the public sphere became symbolic of national modernization, simultaneously, female modesty in dress and sexual behavior has been regarded as representative of a nation's morality and cultural purity, while women's roles within the private sphere, as mothers, wives, and sisters, are seen as essential to the production of national culture (Kandiyoti 1991; Chatterjee 1993). Toward this end, women's rights within the home, as defined by Islamic-inspired family law, have evolved very slowly and enshrine inequality within the domestic sphere. This division between women's rights in the public and private spheres has acted to limit women's ability to participate publicly. This apparent contradiction may be explained by the attempts of state elites to control women's sexuality for the purpose of national processes. As potential mothers of the future generations of the national community, women's sexuality is central to the reproduction of the collectivity. Consequently, with whom women have sex and/or choose to father their children is often the object of a variety of legislation and subject to public commentary. For example, nationality laws in many countries prevent women from passing on their nationality to their children.[7]

In this sense, gender roles and identities have been an integral part of the imaginings of the national community and its myth of common origins. Women's bodies have constituted the terrain upon which different strands of national identification processes have been reconciled. On the one hand, women's public participation represents the nation's modernity "on the outside." Simultaneously, the image of women as good wives and mothers represents the nation's "authentic" "inner essence" that distinguishes "us" from "them" (Chatterjee 1993). Within this context, the continued existence of Islamic codes that enshrine strict gender roles and relations as the basis for family law may be represented as a means of affirming Middle East countries' "authentic" Islamic roots (Hijab 1988).

In the case of ethnicity, "Arabness" has constituted the predominant marker of national identity. Arabism began as a cultural-linguistic movement in the early twentieth century and later became fused with nationalism in the struggle against colonialism and imperialism. Pan-Arabism grew as a political movement following the Suez Crisis of 1956, thereby helping to make Arabness a central component of national identities. This was the case even as the political aims of Arab unity were downplayed and/or disregarded. The postindependence constitutions of Algeria, Egypt, Iraq, Syria, and Tunisia all mention the Arab identity of the state's citizens or the state's membership of an Arab community. At a popular level, there is evidence of strong support for the concept of an Arab identity (Hinnebusch 2003: 59).

To different degrees in different contexts, Arabness has become closely associated with Islam. This is partly due to the fact that the majority of Arabs are also Sunni Muslims. In addition, the majority of elites in Arab countries are Sunni Muslim (the exception is Syria, where the regime is largely Alawite, and postinvasion Iraq, where power is largely divided between a Shi'ite and Kurdish majority). Moreover, despite being largely secular, Arab nationalism has drawn upon Islamic symbols (such as historic figures), while Arab nationalist intellectuals, such as Michel Aflaq, have seen Islam as a cultural heritage shared by all Arabs (Tibi 1997: 205).

The articulation of Arabness with national identity has been coun- terproductive to the construction of a project of citizenship. Arabness, as an ethnic identity and strongly associated with Islam, has become so dominant as to be regarded as the norm. Within this context, non-Arabs and also non-Muslims are often, implicitly or explicitly, subordinated within the nation. Certain ethnic and/or religious communities may face legal discrimination because of the failure of the state to recognize these social differences or because of state regulations that apply differentially to certain religious groups. For example, laws making Arabic mandatory in the Algerian education system were meant to displace French as the language of instruction. However, they served to marginalize the Berber language and identity within Algeria. Meanwhile, Coptic Christians in Egypt do not enjoy freedom of religion due to rather stringent regula- tions governing the building of churches. Throughout the region, Arab Jews have been regarded with suspicion and often subject to de facto discrimination, as they have been connected with Zionism and the establishment of Israel in 1948. Their status within Arab countries has been rendered vulnerable by a general failure of civil society to promote territorial belonging regardless of ethnicity, religion, or ideology.

National identity (not only in the Arab world but universally) has been mobilizing, at different times, in resistance to political, military, and economic interference by outside powers. History demonstrates that anti-imperialist actions, such as Egypt's nationalization of the Suez Canal and the struggle to regain Arab lands from Israeli occupation, serve to buttress feelings of national unity against a dangerous "Other." It is not only that the mobilization of national identity underwrites military action against the external enemy. It is important to note that the flip side of this process entails the strengthening of those ideas and structures that suppress social differences and dissent (the "enemy" within). In this way, relations of oppression and repression are reproduced within nation-states in the name of national unity.

The question of economic development represents another important part of the hegemony of authoritarianism. State-led modernization strategies have given way to IMF and World Bank prescriptions for economic liberalization and deregulation (also justified by the rhetoric of enabling national modernization). The state's gradual (although not complete) withdrawal from the economic sector has left those groups once protected by state largesse, namely public-sector workers and peasants, particularly women, vulnerable to the market. Meanwhile, the Arab world still suffers from serious developmental issues (*Arab Human Development Report* 2002). Unsurprisingly, there exists opposition to market reforms and the IFIs that promote them. There has been an almost near consensus across the political spectrum that the economic and social rights of working people represent one of the most important pillars of national modernization in the postindependence era and that these must be protected. Toward this end, activists in the Arab world have joined with those beyond the region in what is commonly called the antiglobalization movement. Calls for an end to neoliberal economic reforms are usually tied to support for continued state intervention in the economy, including state ownership of industries. Meanwhile, the IFIs and multinational corporations are held up as the enemy of national development. Yet, it is this economic model (state-led and nationalist) that helped to consolidate authoritarianism in the postindependence period (while simultaneously failing to engender sustained development). Both state-led modernization and neoliberal globalization entail the construction or reconstruction of structural socioeconomic and political inequalities within nation-states (Rai 2002). The emergence of new modes of thinking about economic organization is a necessary part of Arab (or any other) countries being able to negotiate a path that avoids the pitfalls of either of the currently existing models. On the one hand, this may not be totally achievable without fundamental changes to the global economic system. On the other hand, the emergence of a civil society that promotes alternative thinking about economic organization is a necessary precondition for the establishment of an alternative model (and language) of "modernization." Transnational forums, such as the World Social Forum, may represent the beginnings of such a process.

In light of the above discussion, I argue that the dismantling of authoritarianism depends on a war of position that addresses in new ways questions of national identity, anti-imperialism, gender relations, accommodation of ethnic and religious identities, as well as questions of economic organization and "modernization." In this way, democratization represents a project not only of advocating political reforms but also a new world view that breaks down the dichotomies of us/them, authentic/foreign, and state/market that have helped to sustain the unequal relations of power that underpin authoritarianism. The establishment of democratic rules and institutions, without attempts to articulate a counter-hegemonic project, may simply lead to a transition away from authoritarian rule toward a "grey zone" that is not authoritarianism but is not democracy either (Carothers 2002).

## Organization of the Book

This chapter presents a conceptual framework for understanding the chronology of state–civil society interactions presented in the rest of the book. In the course of writing this narrative, I draw upon the many excellent studies—within various disciplines—that have been written about the region. This is supplemented by my own primary research among civil-society actors in Egypt. Indeed, it is the process of conducting research in Egypt that led me to formulate this framework. I hope that this book will contribute to a reinterpretation of the emergence of authoritarianism in the Arab world as a means to better understanding the potential for democratization. In particular, I aim to draw attention to the role of civil society in helping to consolidate and maintain authoritarian rule, in addition to its role in attempting to formulate democratic alternatives and the process by which it may shift between these roles.

Chapter 2 examines the period from World War I to the 1960s, which I characterize as the initial phase of constructing and normalizing authoritarianism. This is the time in which the modern state system was created, nationalist movements emerged upon the terrain of civil society to struggle against European rule, and independence was won. It also includes the early years of nation-state building following independence. The aims of the nationalist struggle for national sovereignty and modernization were embodied within the process of nation-state building. State-led development, the building of a coalition of popular forces against the old oligarchy that had become powerful under colonial rule, in addition to resistance to imperialism, were all regarded as necessary for nation-state building and

were articulated through populist-nationalist discourses of various ideological currents. Support for these objectives was strengthened by the
growing popularity across the region of Arab nationalism, following the
Suez Crisis of 1956. However, within this logic of nation-state building,
new hierarchies of social and political relations were constructed and
normalized. Civil society became subordinated to the regime and state
resources became concentrated in the hands of the regime. This contributed to the consolidation of authoritarian regimes.

Chapter 3 examines the period from the 1960s onward, in which the
postindependence political order experienced crisis and movements in
opposition to regimes began to emerge. The failure of import-substitution
industrialization as a development strategy, coupled with the defeat of
the Arab armies in 1967, called into question the ability of Arab regimes
to deliver on the promises central to pan-Arabism—that is, national
modernization. In response, regimes abandoned much of the rhetorical
commitment to the Arab "socialist" policies associated with the early
phase of state building. The introduction of *infitah* (literally, "the opening up" or "open door" policy) ushered in new political and economic
alliances between regimes and private capital, both domestic and foreign. This was accompanied by foreign-policy shifts toward the United
States and varying degrees of (nominal) political liberalization. Simultaneously, this period witnessed a series of student protests, workers'
strikes, growing opposition from Islamist movements, and other forms
of contentious politics emanating from civil society. These protests
sought to challenge the ability or legitimacy of regimes to deliver on the
promises of national modernization. Despite these challenges, for the
most part, civil-society actors continued to support the political and
economic objectives of the postindependence era, such as national economic self-reliance and anti-imperialism, as essential elements of the
state-building process. In many cases, they called on regimes to restore
their commitment to these objectives through political or ideological
renewal. Indeed, despite an adjustment in the rhetoric of regimes, there
was no real abandonment of the state-led development strategy, while
the 1973 war helped to maintain the anti-imperialist credentials of
regimes. Consequently, the demands of opposition movements of the
1970s and 1980s, rather than challenging authoritarianism, contributed
to its reproduction by continuing to normalize the social and political
hierarchies that underwrite it.

Nevertheless, Arab regimes are cognizant of the threat to their authority posed by the emergence of civil-society activism beyond corporatist
structures. Chapter 4 outlines the way in which regimes have attempted

to deal with the growth in contentious politics, while responding to continuing economic deterioration. These two processes represent a challenge to the economic and institutional elements of authoritarianism. A similar pattern across the region is perceived, whereby regimes initially attempt to liberalize the political system in order to co-opt dissent and to share out the responsibility for the introduction of necessary austerity measures—in the hope of offering political freedoms in compensation for the withdrawal of socioeconomic benefits. Following this, the deepening of the economic reform process has been accompanied by political "de-liberalization," in which regimes have increased their repression of civil-society actors in order to stifle opposition to economic liberalization. However, recognizing that coercion alone is unable to guarantee their continued survival, regimes have also attempted to manipulate public culture as a means of normalizing the new social and political hierarchies resulting from economic liberalization and political de-liberalization, as well as enabling the co-optation of new constituencies of support. In most cases, this has served to intensify the contestation among civil-society actors over public culture as a crucial terrain for the formation of national identity. This has had various implications for regimes and the authoritarian systems that they head.

While the emergence of contentious politics failed to bring an end to authoritarian rule, nevertheless it represented the beginning of a process of formulating alternatives to authoritarianism. Chapter 5 examines the emergence of debates between diverse civil-society organizations—including Islamist groups, human rights groups, and women's rights groups—that, in various ways, challenge the hegemonic project of postindependence state building and national modernization. These debates address issues that include the role of the state, the nature of national identity, and the role of women. They touch upon questions of religion, ethnic and religious diversity, and tactics in the struggle for democratization. In questioning previously held political and ideological beliefs, these discussions represent attempts at formulating a war of position against authoritarianism. In this sense, it is the desire of civil society to continue these debates, rather than the existence of civil society or a prodemocracy movement per se, that constitutes the essential ingredient in the dismantling of authoritarianism. This is not a linear process and it may be disrupted as well as strengthened by the actions of civil-society actors themselves, the regime, and/or international actors.

Chapter 6 examines the emergence of transnational links between civil-society actors within the Arab countries and those beyond the region as a potential resource in the strengthening of movements for democratization. Three case studies are examined: the Islamist move-ment(s), the Palestinian solidarity movement, and the antiglobalization/ antiwar movement. On the one hand, transnational movements, due to their very nature, may challenge the nationalist discourses that underpin authoritarian hegemony, in addition to providing new outside pressures for regimes to politically liberalize. Indeed, the growth of the Egyptian political reform movement "Kifaya" may be seen as an outcome of these processes. On the other hand, transnational movements may represent an internationalization of discourses that strengthen authoritarian rule, such as socially conservative Islam or Arab nationalism. Consequently, trans-national links should not be perceived as essentially a route to democra-tization. Rather, the development of a war of position against authoritar-ianism must address the historical roots and dynamics of that system if it is to succeed. While transnational civil society has a role to play in that process, its formation is not a substitution for the process itself.

Finally, the concluding chapter draws together the main arguments of the book and considers how these impact upon the potential for democratization in the region. It underlines the way in which authoritar-ianism operates through material, institutional, and moral-ideological means. In particular, widespread adherence to the project of national modernization has helped to construct and normalize the hegemony of authoritarian rule. Authoritarianism must be challenged on all fronts as a prerequisite for democratization. The role of civil society in formu-lating a counter-hegemonic project is central to this process. This chap-ter draws out the implications of my arguments for both theorizing about democratic transitions and for policymaking/strategies for pro-moting democracy building. In particular, I argue that by focusing only on reforming formal political institutions and encouraging pluralism within civil society, current mainstream approaches toward democrati-zation will fail in dismantling authoritarianism in the region.

## Notes

1. I use the adjective "Arab" to designate those countries where Arabic is spoken by the majority of citizens. Simultaneously, I recognize that many peo-ple living within these countries do not consider themselves ethnically Arab nor do they speak Arabic as their first language. Moreover, the term "Arab world" is used more as a shorthand expression and not to suggest that those countries where Arabic is spoken by the majority constitute a monolithic, cultural bloc.

2. Bassam Bounenni, "Tunisia: Information Summit and Freedom of Expression," *Arab Reform Bulletin* 3, no. 8, October 2005, http://www.carnegie

endowment.org/publications/index.cfm?fa=view&id=17580&prog=zgp&proj=z drl,zme#information, accessed 1 May 2006; Daho Djerbal, "Algeria: Amnesty and Oligarchy," *Arab Reform Bulletin* 3, no. 8, October 2005, http://www .carnegieendowment.org/publications/index.cfm?fa=view&id=17580&prog=zg p&proj=zdrl,zme#amnesty, accessed 1 May 2006; Sami Moubayed, "Syria: Reform or Repair?" *Arab Reform Bulletin* 3, no. 6, July 2005, http://www.carnegie endowment.org/publications/index.cfm?fa=view&id=17183&prog=zgp&proj=z drl,zme#syria, accessed 1 May 2006.

3. This concept was first articulated by E. P. Thompson (1971).

4. For a development of the concept of "counter-hegemony," see Boggs (1984). Gramsci used the term "integrated culture" to refer to the same concept.

5. I refer to Iraq before the fall of the Ba'th regime in 2003.

6. For a discussion of the process of constructing national difference between the West and Asia with similar effects, see Lawson (1998).

7. After decades of campaigning, this law was amended in Egypt in 2004 to allow Egyptian women to pass on their nationality to their children but still subject to significant bureaucratic processes. See Maria Golia, "Egypt's New Nationality Law Doesn't Bar Discrimination," *The Daily Star,* 19 May 2004, http://www.dailystar.com.lb/article.asp?edition_id=10&categ_id=5&article_id= 3931, accessed 2 May 2006.

# 2

# The Normalization of Authoritarianism

THIS CHAPTER SEEKS TO EXPLAIN the emergence of authoritarian political systems in Algeria, Egypt, Iraq, Syria, and Tunisia. A key factor in this process was the role played by civil society, as the arena in which the nature of the political community was debated. These debates occurred during the struggle for independence from colonial occupation, followed by the process of state building in the postindependence era. In the course of these developments, civil society actually contributed to consolidating the authority of postindependence regimes and, hence, the normalization of authoritarian rule.

In the immediate postindependence period, the authority of regimes was built upon their adoption of the demands of anticolonial movements for national modernization. The achievement of these demands provided great legitimacy to ruling regimes in the eyes of their populations. Simultaneously, the process of pursuing national modernization contributed to the construction of relations of power that underpin authoritarianism. In supporting the objectives of national modernization, civil-society actors have found it difficult to resist becoming subsumed within corporatist structures. Moreover, the discourse of national modernization, diffused by civil society, has normalized these inequalities of power. In this regard, civil society has been essential to the reproduction of authoritarian rule.

## The Emergence of the State and
## Civil Society Under Colonial Rule

### *The Nature of Colonial Rule*

The current system of states in the Arab region was established as a result of growing European domination from the late nineteenth century onward. This process of domination was completed after World War I with the collapse of the Ottoman Empire. However, the region had been gradually losing ground to Europe from the eighteenth century onward. European penetration of the Ottoman Empire began in the 1700s as the Europeans gained control of the East-West trade routes and captured the economic surplus essential to the Ottoman Empire (Bromley 1994: 48–49). This commercial penetration expanded as European ambassadors and consuls used their influence to further the commercial interests of their citizens and the major political interests of their countries (Hourani 1991: 268). European merchants were granted a large degree of autonomy within the empire through the establishment of European-controlled special courts and the granting of trade concessions. Alongside this, European governments were granted rights of protection over indigenous non-Muslim communities, including their economic activities (Bromley 1994: 51–53). Attempts by the Ottomans at "defensive modernization" in response to European encroachment only succeeded in accelerating European penetration by plunging the empire into debt to European banks, thereby giving Europeans even more leverage and, in some cases, leading to European control over domestic finances (pp. 54–55).

On the edges of the Ottoman Empire, some European powers gained direct control of areas. Britain occupied Aden from 1839 and there was a considerable British presence in the Gulf (including Abu Dhabi, Dubai, and Sharja) based on formal agreements with the rulers of the ports there. Algeria was conquered by the French between 1830 and 1847, while Tunisia and Morocco[1] became French protectorates in 1883 and 1912, respectively. Britain invaded Egypt in 1882 but did not declare it a protectorate until 1914. Soon after this, in 1922, Egypt was granted nominal independence.[2] In 1911, Italy conquered Libya. At the end of World War I, the Ottoman Empire collapsed and Britain and France had taken control, in various forms, of the former Arab provinces. Syria and Lebanon became French mandates, while Trans-Jordan, Palestine, and Iraq became British mandates. Only North Yemen and Saudi Arabia escaped direct European control.

The Arab region differs from other parts of the formerly colonized world in that only Algeria, Aden (South Yemen), and Libya were, technically speaking, "colonies" (Owen 2004: 7). Nevertheless, the pattern of European control established—whether in the form of colonies, protectorates, or mandates—may be characterized as "colonial" (p. 9). This pattern of control not only created a system of nation-states, but also transformed socioeconomic structures and established new political and administrative institutions, thereby having a profound impact upon the trajectory of politics (Alavi 1972: 59).

As part of their political domination of the region, the European powers drew boundaries to demarcate a number of nation-states. These states were either comprised of a number of former Ottoman provinces—such as Iraq and Syria—or were based on existing administrative entities, such as Egypt, Tunisia, and Algeria. National boundaries were consolidated through their policing, in addition to other legal and symbolic mechanisms, including the establishment of nationality laws and the signing of treaties to guarantee right of passage between states (Owen 2004: 9–10). National bureaucracies were established in capital cities. These central authorities were responsible for issuing standard rules and regulations, to be applied equally (in theory) to all citizens within the national territory (p. 10).

On the one hand, the Europeans established institutions that were rooted in the liberal-rational notions existing within their own societies—that is, citizenship, rule of law, rational administration, meritocracy, among others. On the other hand, they employed mechanisms for the political control of the colonial states that often contradicted or undermined these liberal-rational notions. For example, the liberal parliamentary system, established by the colonial powers in Egypt, Syria, and Iraq in the inter-war years, became largely discredited due to the actions of the colonizers and their allies in the political elite. Parliaments were viewed as having little decisionmaking power. Rather, decisions were made in London or Paris, subject to the vagaries of national politics in Britain and France (Owen 2004: 14). The limited power possessed by parliaments was often the subject of executive abuse. In Egypt, the monarchy controlled parliament through election rigging, the gerrymandering of electoral districts, and the creation of several palace-dependent parties to do its bidding (Baaklini, Denoeux, and Springborg 1999: 223). When parliamentarians expressed opposition to colonial interests, parliament was suspended, as in Syria in 1933 (Khoury 1987: 393–394).

Another example of how the policies of the colonial administrations undermined liberal notions concerns the law and legal systems. Instead of creating an undifferentiated citizenry, laws were established that recognized religious, national, and other social differences. Foreign residents throughout the region enjoyed economic and social privileges that set them apart from indigenous residents (Hourani 2002: 297). In Egypt, the Europeans established a separate legal system for foreign residents that not only adjudicated cases for the British, but also for Jewish, Armenian, Greek, and Italian residents of Egypt. The existence of separate legal systems and courts for different religious communities provided a de facto continuation of the millet system that had existed under the Ottoman Empire, in which each community governed its own religious, social, and educational affairs.

Moreover, the colonial powers often used social differences—whether religious, ethnic, tribal, or class—for political reasons, thereby politicizing these differences. In Iraq, the British rendered tribal leaders central to their strategy of political control. Tribal authority was strengthened by confirming tribal law and extending jurisdictional rights to tribal leaders, in addition to granting economic privileges. In return, tribal leaders were expected to deliver the political compliance of rural populations (Batatu 1978: 87ff). Rather than socioeconomic and legal transformations associated with colonial rule diminishing the importance of tribes, colonial policies toward tribal leaders reincorporated tribes as institutions of administration, thereby transforming their political role (Dodge 2003: 83ff). Simultaneously, British policies contributed to the shift away from localized identifications to wider communal identifications (Sunni, Shi'a, and Kurdish) (Fuccaro 1997: 562).

Part of the European justification for colonialism was to develop these countries so that they could repay debts owed to Europe and accrued during the nineteenth century (Pappé 2005: 42). Toward this end, the British initially encouraged small farmers but this gave way to a policy of encouraging the further development of commercial agriculture, particularly cotton growing, for export to the British cotton industry (Ayubi 1995: 91). The growth in commercial agriculture was accompanied by the growth in private property of agricultural lands and, in some cases, a concentration in ownership. In Egypt, 50 percent of Egypt's cultivatable land came to be owned by approximately 2 percent of the population (Vatikiotis 1991: 8). To different degrees, concentration of land ownership also occurred in Syria and Iraq (Richards and Waterbury 1990: 147–148). In Algeria and Tunisia, patterns of land tenure were also affected by the physical occupation of the land by French settlers. The best agricultural lands were either confiscated or bought by the settlers and cultivated for the purpose of wine and wheat exports (Beinin 2001: 57). In the case of Egypt, Iraq, and Syria, these economic developments created a "local oligarchy" of large landowners that became the lynchpin of colonial domination (Ayubi 1995: 91; Hinnebusch 2001: 21; Tripp 2000: 69).

Indigenous industrialization was greatly stifled by the policies pursued by the colonial powers. There is evidence that some of the surplus generated from agriculture was invested in industry (Davis 1983; Tignor 1984). However, economic policies tended to favor the colonial powers and to deny economic independence to countries under their control (Owen 2004: 14). Mass-produced European goods flooded the markets of Arab countries, leading to the disintegration of local industry and artisans, such as the Syrian textile industry (Owen 1981: 3–9). Meanwhile, the emergence of the light industry and transport sectors in cities was largely the result of European investment and generally served the needs of trade with Europe (Ayubi 1995: 91; Beinin and Lockman 1987: 8–10). The trade and financial sectors tended to be dominated by minorities, such as Armenians, Christians, and Jews, who were also seen to be closely allied to the colonial powers because of arrangements for the European protection of these groups (Hourani 2002: 326; Ayubi 1995: 173).

The transformation of Arab economies during this period created socioeconomic inequalities based on access to land, finance, and other privileges that the colonial powers endowed upon their allies. Poverty increased, illustrated by the appearance of slum belts around large cities for the first time (Pappé 2005: 45). Investment in education, health, and public works was minimal, since the large proportion of national budgets was allocated to police and security (Owen 2004: 10–11, 13). The vast majority of people continued to be illiterate, with education confined mostly to the offspring of the indigenous elites whom the colonial authorities wished to co-opt (Richards and Waterbury 1990: 123).

European rule also brought with it the seeds of its own destruction. During this period, new ideas and technology were introduced and new social formations and social identities emerged. These developments contributed toward creating a *national* political field, which structured political action in new ways (Zubaida 1989: 145–146). This field was constituted by the establishment of national political institutions, such as parliament and a secular legal system, as well as the growth in European-style education and the spread of print communication, which facilitated the discussion of national political events (Hourani 2002: 271–278). In addition, the political field comprised the emergence of new political vocabularies of "nation, nationality and nationalism, of popular sovereignty, democracy, liberty, legality and representation of political parties and parliamentary institutions, as well as various ideological pursuits of nationalism, Islam and socialism" (Zubaida 1989: 146). What Sami Zubaida calls a "political field" corresponds to the sphere of intermediate associations and ideological struggle that characterizes "civil society." This emerging national civil society was animated by already existing social groups (such as the rural notables), as well as newly emerging social classes (namely the urban middle class/intelligentsia and the working class). Their activities upon the terrain of national civil society played a major role in ending colonial rule.

### The Evolution of National Civil Societies

National civil societies emerged with the establishment of the modern nation-state system in the region and they were shaped by the circumstances under which that system was established—that is, colonial domination. The activities of the groups and organizations constituting civil society were, for the large part, motivated by the objective of ending colonialism and were framed by a discourse of nationalism. Nationalist ideas had a widespread impact on society in the Arab region in terms of mobilizing and politicizing a wide sector of the population, including the urban lower and middle classes and students (Khoury 1987: 627; Vatikiotis 1991: 333).

Social changes that were already under way before colonial rule provided a backdrop for the emergence of new spaces and forums for the development of national civil societies. The growth in cities, mechanized transport, and print media provided new opportunities for people to meet and exchange ideas. Men and women no longer lived entirely within a quarter but sometimes traveled to their place of work or to visit members of the extended family in other parts of the city (Hourani 2002: 337). National print media appeared in Arabic, as well as English and French, and provided a forum for political debate, as well as translations of the works of European thinkers (Pappé 2004: 187, 188).

Social, economic, and demographic changes during the inter-war years provided the basis for the growth in mass politics. The transformation of land tenure patterns, together with population growth, provided an impetus for urbanization. Landless and dispossessed peasants migrated to the cities in search of work and many found jobs in the new industrial and transport sectors. They contributed to the formation of a working class. The earliest signs of working-class organization were seen in Egypt and date back to before World War I (Beinin and Lockman 1987: 83ff). Syria and Iraq both began to experience trade union activism between the wars (Farouk-Sluglett and Sluglett 1983; Longuenesse 1996). In Tunisia and Algeria, the first trade unions were formed by French workers, followed by indigenous workers in 1924 in Tunisia and in 1956 in Algeria (Ahmad 1966).

Meanwhile, a new stratum of students, teachers, lawyers, journalists, and other professionals, such as white-collar employees and lower- and middle-level government functionaries, grew as the beneficiaries of the modern education system that was gradually spreading (Yapp 1996: 18). These individuals constituted the membership of the professional associations, women's groups, and intellectual/cultural clubs that emerged under colonial rule (p. 19). These included, among others, the Committee for Spreading Modern Culture, the Syrian Woman's Awakening Society, and the Egyptian Bar Association (Botman 1988: 11; Reid 1981; Thompson 2000: 94ff). While established to pursue nonpolitical or professional objectives, these groups formed part of the nationalist movements of their countries and were often concerned with reforming social and political life.

The establishment of parliaments provided an important subject matter for commentary—whether in the press, literary salons, or other forums where political debate took place. Despite the manipulation of parliaments by the colonial powers, members played a role in mobilizing public opinion against colonial rule (Baaklini, Denoeux, and Springborg 1999: 15). The landowning classes and rural notables, whose strength increased under colonialism, formed the core of this new national politics in Egypt and Syria and, together with ex-Ottoman administrative elites, in Iraq. Out of the limited political pluralism of the inter-war years, there emerged political parties or groupings calling for an end to British influence (in the case of Egypt and Iraq) or, at least, for self-rule (in the case of Syria) (Ayubi 1995: 106–107; Khoury 1987; Tripp 2000: 65ff). The Wafd Party in Egypt probably represents the most successful such grouping to emerge. It became a mass party, promoting a secularist concept of citizenship and calling for Egyptian independence from British rule.

### Nationalist Movements

National civil societies in Arab countries, like their counterparts in many other parts of the world, were important arenas for the growth of anticolonial nationalist movements (Chatterjee 2001: 174). Civil society was created within the public sphere that arose with the colonial state but, simultaneously, represented an expression of the frustrations associated with the limitations of the colonial modernizing project (Chatterjee 1993: 10). Civil society became the terrain upon which nationalist movements sought to construct a counter-hegemonic project in resistance to European rule. The principal aims of this project were to capture the state from the colonial powers in order to ensure modernization and achieve equality within the international system of states.

Until the 1930s, a liberal outlook predominated within nationalist movements (Hourani 1983). However, from the 1930s onward, growing socioeconomic inequalities and opposition to the corruption of the European-created political system led to radicalization among certain social groups (Hourani 2002: 403; Moore 1965: 27–32; Vatikiotis 1969: 315ff; Ruedy 2005: 131ff; Yapp 1996: 65–66, 81–82, 94). The failure of Arab armies to stop the creation of the State of Israel in 1948 gave further impetus to this trend (Ismael 1976: 12).

Obviously, each group had a different ideological outlook (for example, liberal/Islamist/communist), employed different rhetoric, and had different constituencies. Nevertheless, they shared many common themes. As Israel Gershoni describes, radical nationalist movements tended to be characterized by their propagation of "populist nationalism combined with socialist elements," their employment of "nativist rhetoric," and their hostility to "ethnic interlopers (Greeks, Italians, French, British, and in some cases Christians or Jews)" (1997: 17–18). They (as with other anticolonial movements) accepted the modernizing logic of nationalism, which sought to capture the material advancement of the Europeans (Hourani 1983: 345–346). They called for industrialization, the development of infrastructure, and the extension of education (Khoury 1987: 401; Richards and Waterbury 1990: 122–123; Vatikiotis 1991: 330–331). They often supported the establishment of a strong military and, in some cases, developed paramilitary-style groups (Thompson 2000: 191ff; Tripp 2000: 61–62; Vatikiotis 1969: 330).

Social inequality, lack of economic development, and political domination were issues that were intrinsically linked in the minds of nationalists. As Antoun Sa'adah, founder of the Syrian Socialist National Party (SSNP), wrote in 1949: "Our national struggle, O workers and farmers, is against two enemies: against domestic feudalism and capitalism backed by foreign feudal and capitalistic forces" (cited in Sharabi 1966: 113). An end to European control was regarded as essential in enabling the Arab countries to embark upon the path to modernization. In addition, there could be no freedom without freedom from foreign domination.

The struggle against colonialism was not only a struggle over the "material domain of the outside"—the economy, the state, and science and technology (Chatterjee 1993: 6). An essential aspect of nationalist thought was the distinction between the "material" and the "spiritual." While the superiority of the colonialists in the "material domain" was recognized and was to be imitated, their influence was resisted with regard to the "spiritual," which represented "an 'inner' domain bearing the 'essential' marks of cultural identity" (Chatterjee 1993: 6).

In the Arab world, nationalist movements and thinkers put forward competing conceptions of the basis for this cultural identity—either ethnic, religious, based on territorial location, cosmopolitan, or a mixture of these. The most influential identification in the region has been that of Arabism. In the pre–World War I period, Arabism represented an anti-Ottoman movement. However, it then metamorphosed into a number of anticolonial parties and associations in the inter-war period (Choueiri 2000: 83–100). It constituted the foundation for pan-Arab nationalism, which was most famously elaborated by Sati' al-Husri. For al-Husri, the Arab nation was rooted in the shared language and history of the Arab people. For many proponents of pan-Arabism, including al-Husri, pan-Arabism was separate from Islam, although Islam had contributed to the historical achievements of the Arabs (p. 121). The secular nature of Arabism made the doctrine particularly attractive to Arab Christians, such as Michel Aflaq, founder of the Arab Ba'th group in Damascus in 1943. Yet many of the symbols of pan-Arabism were Islamic (Barnett 1998: 60). In multiethnic, multireligious Iraq, pan-Arabism only gained widespread support, beyond the Sunni Arab urban middle and lower-middle classes, after the Suez Crisis in 1956 and the emergence of Gamal 'Abdel-Nasser as a regional hero (Farouk-Sluglett and Sluglett 1991: 1415).

Arabism competed with territorial identifications—Egyptian and Iraqi nationalism, as well as the pan-Syrian nationalism of the SSNP (which deemed Syria to be all the former eastern Ottoman provinces). Territorial nationalisms could be secular, such as the Egyptian nationalism of the Wafd, which claimed "Religion is for God and the Homeland is for All," but also religious, such as the Association of 'Ulema, who claimed "Islam is my religion; Arabic is my language; Algeria is my fatherland." Islamist identification, such as that of the Muslim Brotherhood, was often intermingled with territorial nationalism, in that Islam was presented as the means of renewing the nation-state (Hourani 2002: 347; Sullivan and Abed-Kotob 1999: 42). More cosmopolitan conceptions of identity were promoted by communist activists across the region, many of whom came from minorities. Yet, cosmopolitanism disappeared with the demise of the liberal era of politics, and some communist parties experienced debates over the desirability that minorities, particularly Jewish activists, be considered leaders of nationalist struggles (Beinin 1998: 144–145).

These different imaginings of the nation were all subject to the same logic, which was to construct a national identity and culture that was modern but not Western (Chatterjee 1993: 6). The sphere of culture, morality, and spirituality, as well as the "inner domain" of women and gender relations, became objects of nationalist struggles and debates. Religious, cultural-nationalist, and women's groups were active in condemning so-called foreign habits, such as the consumption of alcohol and state-licensed prostitution. Meanwhile, different trends within society were involved in debates over the significance of women's role and the nature of the family as principal pillar of the nation (Badran 1991: 208–209; Badran 1995; Hatem 1993: 38–42; Hourani 1983; Jayawardena 1986: 48–56; Khoury 1987: 609–610; Philipp 1978; Thompson 2000: 143; Vatikiotis 1991: 330–332).

The nationalist assertion of moral values not only constructed national difference from the Europeans. It also reversed the binary division created by European writers and colonial administrators. Europeans used science and reason to demonstrate that the peoples of the East were "slothful, preoccupied with sex, violent, and incapable of self-government" (Kabbani 1986: 6; also Said 1978). This gave colonialism a moral raison d'être and was intrinsic to the colonial enterprise (Kabbani 1986: 6; Said 1978). A reversal of this binary division enabled nationalist movements to present themselves not only as the expression of the nation's morality but also of its superiority over that of the Europeans, and therefore its ability to govern itself.

### Nationalism's Discontents

Nationalist movements constructed a unified identity (based either on Arabism, Islamism, or territorial patriotism) for the purpose of achieving political independence and national modernization. While this represented a powerful means of uniting people against colonialism in order to achieve independence, it also comprised antidemocratic tendencies. Nationalist discourse acted to erase social differences, yet, simultaneously, it constructed new hierarchies of social relations by privileging one identity over others.

Arabist and Islamist notions of identity have clear exclusionary implications for many people within the region. These include non-Arab groups such as the Kurds (in Iraq), Berbers (in North Africa), and Turkmen, Assyrians, and Armenians (in the former eastern Ottoman provinces), in addition to non-Muslim groups such as Jews and Christians (throughout the region), and Alawis and Druze[3] (in Syria), among others. Even territorial patriotism has often implied the exclusion of non-Arabs or non-Muslims—particularly, indigenous Jews. Such implications became clear following the partition of Palestine and the creation of Israel in 1948 (Beinin 1998).

Not only can nationalism lead to the exclusion from the polity of those that are not deemed sufficiently "authentic." In addition, nationalism establishes hierarchies of power relations that have implications for social groups who are included within the conception of the national collective. This has been particularly evident in the case of the working classes, peasants, and women. Nationalist discourse co-opted the activism of these groups, thereby helping to create a legitimate space for them in public life. Yet, simultaneously, nationalism subordinated their demands to the objectives of nationalist movements (Beinin 2001: 98). This had the effect of constraining the recognized demands of these groups, as well as limiting their autonomy. To illustrate this point, I examine the case of workers and women.

Workers and their organizations played a role in the struggle against colonialism in the Arab countries studied here (Ahmad 1966; Beinin and Lockman 1987; Farouk-Sluglett and Sluglett 1983; Longuenesse 1996). In general, workers organized themselves and engaged in collective action against the foreign owners and managers (including colonial state officials) who were in charge of the industries and companies in which they worked. Their demands were social and economic, yet because they were directed against the foreign-dominated state and economy, this brought them into alliance with the political nationalist movements (Beinin and Lockman 1987: 16–17; Longuenesse 1996: 105–107). In this way, the emergence of working-class activism mirrors the emergence of other types of civil-society activism, in that it was linked to the struggle against foreign political and economic domination. By linking their activism with the nationalist struggle, workers' organizations were also able to achieve widespread legitimacy within society. The fusing of working-class demands with the struggle against colonialism meant that nationalist leaders were obliged to address the demands of workers' organizations, thereby raising the need for social as well as political reform within the nationalist struggle (Beinin and Lockman 1987: 455; Longuenesse 1996: 107).

Yet the above characteristics of workers' movements also constituted a weakness. First of all, working-class organizations often became subsumed within the nationalist movements or subject to control by various political currents, thereby losing their independence (Beinin and Lockman 1987; Bellin 2002: 91–92; Davis 1994; Longuenesse 1996). Second, the social and economic demands of workers' organizations became linked to the struggle against colonialism, thereby blurring the lines between class demands and national political demands (Ahmad 1966: 156–157; Beinin and Lockman 1987). Consequently, nationalist leaders (of various currents) were able to gloss over potential tensions between class-based demands and the nationalist movement (Beinin 1994). Among Arab nationalists, there was a general enmity toward the idea of class struggle, which was seen as being divisive (Choueiri 2000: 141). Communists were programmatically committed to the emancipation of the working class, yet their adoption of a staged approach, whereby national emancipation necessarily preceded social emancipation, also led them to disempower workers (Beinin 2001: 141).

Women's participation in civil society also expanded due to participation in their countries' nationalist movements (Badran 1991; Jaya-wardena 1986). Women were active in anticolonial and anti-Zionist nationalist politics through street demonstrations, organizing petitions, and public debates (Badran 1991; Philipp 1978; Thompson 2000). In Algeria, women were involved to a substantial degree in the armed struggle against French colonialism as both civilians and combatants and also experienced terrible torture at the hands of French interrogators (Lazreg 1990: 767). In addition to supporting demands for national independence, many women organized in order to bring about reforms to improve the status of women. From the early 1920s onward, women's organizations called for equal political rights with men, reform of the personal status laws, and extending work and education to women (Babal 2006; Badran 1993: 135–136; Brand 1998: 202–203; Thompson 2000). In addition to organizing as women, they were also involved in the various political parties/currents and student and workers' movements (Abdalla 1985; Babal 2006; Badran 1991; Botman 1988; Thompson 2000).

While nationalist politics opened up new possibilities for women's public participation, it also set a limit upon the agenda for women's rights. Qasim Amin and Tahar al-Haddad represented a trend within national movements that called for women's emancipation as a necessary part of national liberation (Hourani 1983). However, nationalist arguments for reforming the most obvious aspects of women's oppression, such as their lack of access to education, early marriage, and polygamy, were promoted not in terms of respecting women's rights as individual human beings but in terms of their negative impacts on the family and, consequently, future generations of the nation (Ahmed 1982; Baron 1991; Philipp 1978). Meanwhile, in Egypt and Syria, woman's suffrage was opposed by many (though not all) nationalist leaders (Philipp 1978; Thompson 2000: 119–120, 123, 147).

The Janus-faced nature of nationalist leaders with regard to women's rights was due to the nature of gender relations being implicitly linked to defining the cultural essence of the nation. Nationalist leaders often valorized the gender status quo as a means of asserting national identity. For example, in Algeria, the Front de Libération Nationale (FLN) publicized women's participation in the war "as evidence of their freedom and dignity under Islam, as validation not of any fundamental change in women's position but of the strength and diversity of their 'traditional' roles as defined by religion and custom" (Tucker 1999: 112).

In other words, within nationalist discourse, women were not regarded as the bearers of equal rights with men, but rather as symbols of national progress, liberation, and identity. Any improvement within their position was legitimized by the needs of the nationalist struggle or as reward for their participation in this struggle (Baron 1991; Lazreg 1990: 770; Philipp 1978). Attempts to go beyond the framework of nationalist discourse to promote women's rights, through reference to "feminism" or "communism," were denounced as European infiltration and a threat to the nation. In order to counteract these accusations, women activists generally framed their demands within the discourse of nationalism or Islam (Ahmed 1982; Badran 1993: 135; Botman 1988: 22–26). This practice served to limit the potential of women activists to challenge the patriarchal logic of nationalist discourse.

From the above discussion, the emergence of national civil societies was both a result of and a response to socioeconomic and political conditions under colonial rule. The intrinsic link between civil society and (anti)colonialism shaped the discourse, strategies, and objectives of civil-society actors. On the one hand, anticolonial nationalism mobilized civil society for the objectives of national independence and modernization. Nationalist leaders were forced to address issues of social inequality in response to active workers' and women's movements. On the other hand, nationalist discourse reproduced hierarchies based on social difference. The demands of women and workers were subordinated to the ultimate objective of achieving national independence. Meanwhile, for the sake of unity, significant communities within Arab countries were excluded from visions of the polity on the basis of their ethnic or religious affiliation (that is, either non-Arab or non-Muslim, or a combination of both). The inequalities inherent within nationalist discourse are significant in understanding civil society's contribution to the construction of authoritarianism in the postindependence era.

## Civil Society and Postindependence Nation-State Building

### The End of the Old Order

The onset of postindependence nation-state building differs between Arab states. Egypt, Syria, and Iraq followed similar stages: nominal independence accompanied by the continuing influence of the Europeans and growing radicalization of nationalist movements; the discrediting of existing oligarchies in the wake of the partition of Palestine in 1948, followed by army coups that deposed the elites that had dominated parliament under colonial rule. Socioeconomic developments also supported these political changes. Growing social inequalities, the expansion of the urban middle and working classes, and the spread of education all fueled opposition to the traditional political-economic oligarchy, which was associated with European influence. Civil society represented the terrain upon which opposition to colonial rule was organized. However, it was the execution of military coups that formally ended European influence and the political order associated with it.

Egypt was granted nominal independence in 1922 but the British retained a political and military presence until the army coup, or "revolution" of 1952, which deposed the monarchy and brought the Free Officers' regime to power (Vatikiotis 1969: 264–373). Constitutional government was suspended in 1952, a republic was declared in 1953, and official withdrawal of British forces was negotiated in 1954 (pp. 374–393). In the same year, Gamal 'Abdel-Nasser came to power and would embody the dream of Arab nationalism until his death in 1970 (Hourani 2002: 351).

Iraq was the first Arab country to join the League of Nations at nominal independence in 1932. A series of military coups failed to unseat British military presence in the country. In the end, widespread opposition to the government's signing of the Baghdad Pact in 1955 (a Western-led security pact to contain Soviet influence), coupled with admiration for Nasser's challenge to the West during the 1956 Suez Crisis, triggered a military coup in 1958, thereby deposing the monarchy and ushering in the leftist government of 'Abd al-Karim Qasim (Tripp 2000: 77–147).

French troops were forced to evacuate Syria in 1946 and the country became an independent republic, led by the existing class of notables. The army, which had become highly politicized and factionalized, staged a series of coups following the Palestine disaster, in an attempt to depose the oligarchy and establish modernizing regimes (Hinnebusch 2001: 28–41). Nasser's success during the Suez Crisis led to a struggle between competing political trends, resulting in 1958 in the victory of the Arab nationalist trend and unification with Egypt (the United Arab Republic). This experiment was cut short by another coup in 1961 and the establishment of a conservative government that attempted to reverse some of the Arab socialist policies introduced during unification. Finally, in 1963, one political trend managed to capture the army, and a coup brought the Ba'th Party to power and reimposed Arab socialist policies (Hinnebusch 2001: 41–45).

A long and bloody war for Algerian independence was fought from 1954 to 1962. By the end of the war, the FLN became the undisputed leader of the armed revolt against the French and represented not only a military organization, but also an embryonic state, with its clandestine schools, local authorities, and police, among other institutions (Tlemcani 1986: 65). On gaining independence, the FLN took power and the first president was Ahmed Ben Bella. He was deposed in 1965 by Boumédienne (a member of the FLN leadership), who died in 1979. Unlike in Algeria, the French handed over power peacefully in 1956 to the leaders of the Tunisian nationalist Neo-Destour Party, headed by Habib Bourguiba—who retained power until 1987.

## The Project for National Modernization

On coming to power, postindependence nationalist regimes experienced internal challenges, instability, and uncertainty. Moreover, none had clear political programs, except to rid their countries of European influence and the inequalities associated with it. They were often welcomed by the majority of society as purging politics of the old oligarchy and paving the way for full political sovereignty and the pursuing of socioeconomic reforms necessary to modernize the country. The consensus in favor of, what I term here, a national modernization project was developed by civil-society actors during the struggle against colonialism, and this consensus provided a framework for the policies of ruling regimes in the postindependence era. During the anticolonial struggle, national independence was seen as prerequisite for national modernization. In the postindependence period, continued resistance to foreign military, political, and economic influence was seen as necessary for protecting the national modernization process. Toward this end, civil society supported anti-imperialism and the building of national unity, on the basis of a shared national identity. Simultaneously, the introduction of populist welfare measures represented a strategy for building national coalitions that would strengthen national unity. In addition, the reform of women's position was advocated as both a symbol of modernization and as instrumental in the process of modernization. These elements of national modernization—anti-imperialism, national identity construction, populism, and reform of women's position—are explored below in relation to different countries. In each case, the desire to achieve these objectives, as part of the modernization project, contributed toward normalizing authoritarianism in the postindependence period.

### Egypt: The Importance of Being Anti-Imperialist

The Free Officers presented themselves as the embodiment of the nation's aspirations for socioeconomic development, socioeconomic justice, and freedom from British domination. Indeed, various political groupings within the nationalist movement—Wafdist, Muslim Brethren, and communists—supported the Free Officers' coup as necessary for bringing about political and social reforms (Gordon 1992: 9–10). Yet, unlike Syria and Iraq, the military was not captured by a dominant political trend, and the ideology of the Free Officers reflected general views of the time of nationalism and social reform (pp. 12, 39). The Arab "socialist" policies that would later characterize the Nasser regime, and become typical of Iraq, Syria, Algeria, and Tunisia as well, were not initially apparent in the actions of the Free Officers in the first few years of their rule. The period 1952–1955 was characterized by a substantial degree of uncertainty and instability, as the Officers attempted to consolidate power (Gordon 1992).

The first three years of the Free Officers' regime saw the repression of all political parties and forces, as well as trade unions and other independent civil-society organizations. Simultaneously, some measures were enacted to reflect the demands of the nationalist movement. Central to the Free Officers' program was land reform, which, with some difficulties, was pushed through in the first few months following the coup (Gordon 1992: 62–67). Land redistribution, together with other measures, contributed to improving the condition of peasants and also broke the power of the landowning class who had comprised the old oligarchy (Beinin 2001: 132). General hopes in the progressive character of the coup led some communists (the Democratic Movement for National Liberation) and the Founding Committee for a General Federation of Egyptian Trade Unions to support the Officers, even after the army brutally suppressed striking workers at the Kafr al-Dawwar textile factories in August 1952 and implemented the death penalty for two of the alleged ringleaders (Beinin and Lockman 1987: 421–431). Following this incident, the new regime issued a law withdrawing the right to strike and limiting trade union pluralism. However, the regime conceded to long-standing workers' demands, such as guaranteeing job security and improving work conditions. These measures were effective in winning the support of a significant number of trade unionists and workers (pp. 432–433). The negotiation of the evacuation of British troops from Egypt was finally concluded in 1954 and represented a boon for the Free Officers in resisting opposition from the Muslim Brotherhood (Vatikiotis 1969: 389).

The turning point for the new regime came in 1955–1956. Events in those years enabled the new regime to establish its anti-imperialist credentials and, consequently, to gain significant authority, even in the eyes of its political opponents. First, in response to the creation of the Baghdad Pact, which was interpreted as the West's attempt to retain influence in the Middle East, the regime sought out alternative political and military support (Hinnebusch 2003: 22–24). Nasser's attendance at the Bandung Conference and the signing of an arms purchase agreement with Czechoslovakia in 1955 signaled a shift in foreign policy toward strident anti-imperialism (Vatikiotis 1969: 390–391). Second, and related to the regime's foreign-policy shift, the United States, followed by the United Kingdom and the World Bank, withdrew the offer of a loan to build the Aswan High Dam. The dam represented the centerpiece of the regime's modernization strategy by enabling an increase in land under agricultural cultivation and the generation of hydroelectric power (p. 392). Denied funding for the High Dam, Nasser declared the nationalization of the Suez Canal in July 1956. In retaliation, Britain, France, and Israel launched what would be known as the Suez crisis (or Tripartite Aggression) against Egypt (pp. 392–393).

The Suez Crisis constituted a landmark event in consolidating the Egyptian regime and, in particular, the leadership of Gamal 'Abd al-Nasser. Nasser was perceived by many within the Arab world as the political victor against imperialist aggression. Suez increased his standing, not only at home, but throughout the region (Hourani 2002: 368). Many of those who had been political opponents of the Free Officers were brought onto the regime's side as a result of 1956 (Beattie 1994; Gordon 1992: 196–197). The historical significance of the event is reflected in its retelling through the medium of the film, *Nasser 56*. Produced in Egypt and released in 1996, the film was greeted with popular and critical acclaim, demonstrating the degree to which the event represents a "golden era" in Egyptian history (Gordon 2000).

Suez also represented a turning point in the evolution of the "Arab socialist" policies associated with Nasser. In the aftermath of Suez, the Egyptian government sequestered and then nationalized all foreign establishments, thereby beginning the path toward economic etatism (Clawson 1981: 99; Richards and Waterbury 1990: 195; Beattie 1994). This trend culminated in the nationalization of all firms and state control of the economy (Vatikiotis 1969: 397). In 1960, Egypt embarked on its first five-year plan, marking the introduction of an import-substitution industrialization (ISI) strategy.[4]

The adoption of ISI and state control of the economy served a number of functions for the process of nation-state building at both the material and ideological levels. First, ISI, with its emphasis on industrialization, represented the motor of national modernization. Second, by seeking to reduce foreign imports, as well as foreign investment, in the economy, ISI also represented a strategy of national self-reliance and a challenge to the Western-dominated international economy. Third, it was a principal engine in the expansion of the state bureaucracy and the co-optation of citizens into the state, thereby contributing to the process of state building (Ayubi 1995: 298, 320). In particular, the logic of ISI led the regime to make populist concessions to the middle and working classes, peasants, and farmers. In order for ISI to work, these classes had to cooperate with state economic plans, to contribute to national production through their labor, and to participate in the economy as consumers. Consequently, the ISI model privileged the "popular" sector over other social groups, while discursively constituting the idea of a "popular" coalition of working people (workers, peasants, the middle classes, the military, the intelligentsia, and domestic capital) (Ayubi 1995: 205–206, 209). In order to mobilize a populist/ISI coalition, the regime implemented socioeconomic welfare benefits (universal healthcare and education, guaranteed employment, workplace rights, subsidies on essential food and services, and rent controls, among other measures) and undertook a radical land reform program in the countryside (Abdel-Fadil 1975 and 1980; Richards and Waterbury 1990: 152–184; Ayubi 1995: 217; Pripstein Posusney 1997: 47–48, 59–60, 70). The social mobility, income redistribution, and improvement in the condition of the majority of the population achieved as a result of these measures should not be underestimated (Mabro 1974). The material and ideological benefits of state-led modernization for the majority of citizens facilitated their integration into the nation-state and, consequently, helped to consolidate regime authority.

Citizens were not only co-opted into the process of nation-state building through their participation in national modernization but also through the "corporatization" of civil society. A number of civil-society organizations had been banned or their boards stuffed with regime appointees in the first years of the Free Officers' rule in order to stymie opposition. However, Nasser (like other populist leaders) came to realize the significance of organizing the populist coalition for ISI through the creation of sociopolitical organizations, which could then be incorporated into the state (Ayubi 1995: 209). Toward this end, a number of organizations were created and others were brought under state/regime tutelage. The regime finally conceded to long-standing trade union demands to form a national federation and, in 1957, the General Federation of Egyptian Trade Unions (GFETU) was established (Pripstein Posusney 1997: 40ff). The number of agricultural cooperatives was rapidly expanded by the government during the 1950s, and in 1961, they were brought under the supervision of the Ministry of Agriculture (Vatikiotis 1969: 399). Party pluralism was replaced by a single party—the National Union until 1963, then the Arab Socialist Union (ASU). The ASU provided a mechanism for the regime to mobilize support for its policies from the unit of the village upward, as well as via functional categories, such as worker, farmer, and professional members (pp. 402–403).

On the one hand, corporatism may be seen as a mechanism for regime control of civil society. Civil society sacrificed its political independence in return for certain material benefits. The national federations, such as GFETU, were subordinated to and significantly constrained by the executive ('Adli 1993). Meanwhile, the single party overlapped considerably with the government (Owen 2004: 134) and was responsible for screening all candidates for election to the national assembly—half of whom, after 1964, were either members of executive-controlled trade unions or agricultural cooperatives (Baaklini, Denoeux, and Springborg 1999: 224–225).

On the other hand, corporatism also enabled the voicing of interests. For example, the establishment of a trade union federation was welcomed by the workers' movement as strengthening their voice in national affairs (Pripstein Posusney 1997: 64). The ASU gathered many of the different trends constituting the pre-1952 nationalist movement, who felt they could make an impact on the ideological direction of the regime (Baaklini, Denoeux, and Springborg 1999: 225; Beattie 1994: 129). Moreover, members of corporatist organizations received moral benefits. Workers and peasants were deemed to play a special role in the modernization of the state and were publicly praised for their contributions to economic development (Pripstein Posusney 1997).

Many of those who participated in corporatist structures believed in the state-led modernization project of Nasser's regime—even if they did not support the regime itself. As one former student activist and current human rights activist told me: "I was involved with the debates within the Nasserist youth organizations but from the outside. I argued against

Nasserism but I was still assimilated in the dream of Nasserism."[5] Similarly, communist activists supported the regime's policies on state-led development and anti-imperialism, even while they criticized the regime itself (Ismael and el-Sa'id 1990). Meanwhile, some civil-society activists were directly co-opted into the regime. For example, former Muslim Brotherhood member Sheikh Baquri became minister of religious endowments (Gordon 1992: 197). Aminah al-Sa'id, former member of the Egyptian Feminist Union, dissolved in 1956, helped serve the state's drive to mobilize women (Badran 1995: 249). Whether these individuals allowed themselves to be co-opted out of pragmatic interests or out of ideological commitment is unclear. However, the apparent consensus for the regime's policies, if not the regime itself, suggests that "corporatism was a bargain, not an imposition" (Pripstein Posusney 1997: 64).

The "bargain" struck between civil-society organizations and the regime was instrumental in consolidating the authority of the latter and its authoritarian nature. Corporatism established control over civil society and enabled the regime to co-opt major political and social forces and to disseminate its vision for society. Those that refused to be co-opted, such as the Muslim Brotherhood, were repressed. The regime was able to present its actions as being in the nation's interests since it addressed the most significant demands of the pre-1952 nationalist movement—for liberation from foreign influence as a means of achieving political sovereignty, national modernization, and social justice. In particular, the events surrounding the Suez crisis provided the regime with the moral legitimacy to represent the aspirations of the people. As former Free Officer and now head of the leftist Tagammu' party, Khaled Mohi El Din, remembers: "Regardless of my assessment of Nasser's attitude toward democracy, neither I nor anyone else can deny that the people overwhelmingly supported him and his achievements and did not pause even for a moment to consider the issue of democracy" (Mohi El Din 1995: 238).

Independent political/civil activism (that is, outside corporatist structures) was delegitimized as threatening national interests and divisive to national unity (Abdel-Malek 1962: 318; Mohi El Din 1995: 233). In this way, the enemies of the regime were transformed into the enemies of the nation, while the interests of those who constituted the popular coalition, such as workers, were subordinated to national interests. Meanwhile, the rapid expansion of the state-led economy and welfare provision enabled the rapid growth of the state bureaucracy and, with this, the capacity of the regime to control the population.

The process of negotiation between civil society and the regime was far more conflictual than the above account would appear to argue (Abdel-Malek 1962; Gordon 1992; Beattie 1994). Yet, despite the conflicts and struggles that characterized the early years of the postindependence era, a consensus emerged in favor of national modernization and anti-imperialism above all else. In the words of a former student activist and medical doctor who volunteers in a human rights organization: "We had felt that at last Egypt is controlled by Egyptians and we can build the economy and develop. We believed in pan-Arabism as a strategy for development of resources. After the new type of colonization in 1948 [that is, the creation of Israel], we felt that we could regain Palestine. The price was to follow the leader and sacrifice democracy."[6]

The strident anti-imperialism and anti-Zionism of the Nasser regime, coupled with its commitment to national development in the form of ISI and the building of a populist coalition, echoed the desires of many civil-society actors (as well as society in general). Egypt's challenge to Britain, France, and Israel during the Suez Crisis represented a crucial element in consolidating the Nasser regime's popularity and political leadership of the Arab world. In addition, it contributed to the wave of Arab nationalism that swept through the region during the 1950s, triggering army coups in Syria and Iraq and (unsuccessful) attempts at Arab unity (Hinnebusch 2003: 159–163).

## Algeria: National Liberation and Arab Identity

Despite the intra-elite rivalry, which characterized the FLN in the immediate postindependence period, there was considerable consensus over the nationalist-populist direction of the new regime (Tlemcani 1986: 73ff; Bennoune 1988: 95–98). The Tripoli Programme, which outlined the regime's platform in 1962, prioritized the achievement of economic independence, through nationalization of the economy and appropriation of all foreign-owned land and capital. National planning was deemed necessary to eliminate the vestiges of colonial rule (Bennoune 1988: 95). "Autogestion" (self-management) was decreed as a response to the massive exodus of Europeans following independence. However, workers' self-management, with its veneer of populism/socialism, soon evolved into state management, justified by the failure of autogestion to address the country's economic problems (Bennoune 1988: 106–108; Tlemcani 1986: 95–105). The public sector was further expanded through nationalization and the adoption of ISI, based on the growth of heavy industry (Bennoune 1988: 120ff; Tlemcani 1986: 111ff). In the agrarian sector, the regime implemented land redistribution, land reclamation, and modernization of farming methods in order to increase production and feed into industry (Bennoune 1988: 176ff; Tlemcani 1986: 124ff). Agricultural coopera- tives and workers' assemblies were established, ostensibly to enable mass participation in decisionmaking but, in practice, they became mechanisms for implementing regime policy, principally controlled by the bureaucracy (Tlemcani 1988: 156). Civil-society groups formed before independence (such as the trade union federation, peasants' union, and women's union) were already subordinated to the FLN as part of the national struggle and this subordination was institutionalized in the postindependence era (Zartman 1963: 58; Entelis 1980: 116). In turn, the FLN, due to its historical evolution as a front for various political factions, was subordinated to the bureaucracy and the military in polit- ical decisionmaking, while symbolizing the essence of the "revolution" (Entelis 1980: 111–116).

The populist-socialist character of the structures created after 1962, in addition to the huge expansion of the public sector, helped to stabi- lize the regime and consolidate its authority. Alongside these develop- ments, the new regime also engaged in the construction of national identity on the basis of the Arab-Muslim character of Algeria. Indeed, the populist-socialist policies were intrinsically linked in official dis- course to Islam through the ideology of "specific socialism"—that is, the Islamic source of Algerian socialism and its nationalist nature (Cheriet 1992: 10). This process served to unite the disparate elements of the FLN (particularly, to co-opt the Association of 'Ulema), retain the sup- port of other Arab countries and the Arab League, mobilize popular sup- port for national modernization, and provide ideological legitimacy to the new regime (Nouschi 1993; Entelis 1980: 105–106).

The significance of Islam in nationalist politics may be traced back to the formation of the Association of 'Ulema in 1931. Through their Quranic schools and scout movement, the association promoted an Algerian nationalism rooted in reformist Islam, as opposed to the assim- ilationists led by Ferhat Abbas and the "collaborationism" of the Sufi mystic orders. Although the association was not a dominant force within the wartime FLN, it succeeded in making Islam an integral part of Algerian nationalism. "The Ulama laid the foundations of a national ideology in Algeria by transforming puritan Islam into a modern value system . . . This was no religious fanaticism, but the expression of a ris- ing political community whose ideational representations were extracted from an Islamic world view, probably the only thoroughly integrated and internalized legacy shared by the vast majority of Algerians" (Cheriet 1992: 11).

The construction of Arab-Muslim identity was pursued through the Arabization program and the emphasis of the Islamic character of Algerian socialism. The Arabization program was declared as early as 1962 and aimed to make Arabic the official language of Algeria and the medium of instruction in schools. Due to the domination of French in the school system before 1962, Arabic instruction was increased gradually (Bennoune 1988: 222–223). Egyptian schoolteachers were imported in order to contribute to this effort (Nouschi 1993: 127). The Arabization program was not only about changing the language of instruction but was also perceived as a means to combat the influence of Western culture that had evolved under French rule, thereby enabling a "renaissance" of indigenous culture (p. 128).

The role of Islam in Algerian identity evolved over a longer period in the postindependence period. Initially, there were splits within the regime over the role that Islam should play in public life, reflecting the different currents comprising the FLN. On the one hand, several tendencies possessed a secular outlook. On the other hand, the Association of 'Ulema regarded Islam as the essence of Algerian identity and anticolonial resistance, while Boumédienne, rival to Ben Bella in the period immediately following independence, attacked the socialist policies of the new regime on the basis that they were contrary to Islam. As a result, Ben Bella was obliged to declare Islam the official religion of Algeria in 1962 and to state, on several occasions, that Islam and socialism were not "irreconcilable doctrines" (Ottaway and Ottaway 1970: 181–182). Nevertheless, on deposing Ben Bella in 1965, Boumédienne received the full support of religious leaders and conservative groups (p. 190). Islamization was pursued in a more coherent fashion under Boumédienne (Nouschi 1993: 125; Entelis 1980: 105). The first minister of religious affairs was Tawfiq al-Madani, a former leader of the Association of 'Ulema (Vatin 1983: 111). It was under Boumédienne's rule that the concept of "Islamic socialism" was articulated and stipulated as the basis of Algerian society. Official discourses promoting modernization and "socialist" policies "were transmitted by means of a religiously influenced vocabulary" (p. 110). Meanwhile, religious institutions were nationalized and public religious observance was incorporated into official life (Ruedy 2005: 224–225; Vatin 1983). The Islam promoted by the state was the reformist Islam of the Association of 'Ulema.

The construction of an Arab-Muslim identity was part of the rejection of colonial rule and influence over Algeria. The French had attempted to extinguish Arab-Muslim identity, which was seen as a barrier to the French "mission civilitrice" (Lazreg 1990: 757–759). Religious institutions were supervised by the Directeur des Affaires Indigènes (Vatin 1983). School instruction was in French and the curriculum prioritized French "culture" and "values." Meanwhile, Arabic was taught only a couple of hours per week as a second language and sometimes as an extracurricular activity (Heggoy and Zingg 1976). The greatest disruption to Algerian culture was French attempts to quell peasant resistance in rural Algeria, which entailed the destruction of whole villages and the appropriation of land, and resulted in a huge disruption to family and kinship networks (Bennoune 1988: 39ff; Lazreg 1994: 99–106).

The Arab-Muslim identity propagated in the postindependence period was portrayed as a restoration of the culture extinguished by the French (Nouschi 1993: 127; Lazreg 1994: 167). The "nationalization" of Islam, through state-governed institutions and appropriation of Islam into official rhetoric, coupled with the Arabization of education, served to construct a national identity for Algerians. The discourse of "specific socialism" (the combination of modernization with Islam) represented regime measures as "modern" on the inside and "traditional" on the inside. Yet, Algerian culture before and under colonial rule was by no means identical to the Arab-Muslim identity promoted in the postindependence period. Prior to independence, Algerian Islam was heavily shaped by Sufi practices, including the veneration of saints (*marabouts*) and pilgrimages to shrines. Meanwhile, the vast majority of people spoke an Algerian dialect of Arabic and Berbers spoke their own language (Nouschi 1993: 113). In the postindependence period, an austere, orthodox version of Islam was promoted, based on the teachings of the Association of 'Ulema, while the Arabization program focused on the introduction of "modern standard" Arabic (Nouschi 1993; Vatin 1983). The emphasis on a certain form of Arabic and Islam reflected regime concerns to dismantle "traditional" power structures in order to make room for the "modern" in an attempt to reorientate Algerians toward national modernization. Simultaneously, official discourses invoking Arab-Muslim heritage served to "anchor" Algerians in the midst of rapid socioeconomic change. In other words, despite its nationalist-populist appeal, the construction of Arab-Muslim identity in the postindependence period represented the marginalization of cultural practices associated with the majority of Algerians and the bolstering of a "modernizing" elite. In this way, attempts to formulate a Algerian national identity in order to affirm Algeria's new sovereignty served to incorporate the majority of Algerians in subordination to the regime, while excluding potential political rivals, such as the predominantly francophone Berbers, as well as those religious groups that did not subscribe to official interpretations of Islam and those sectors that resisted the regime's modernizing thrust.

## Syria and Iraq:
## Populism and Modernization in Divided Societies

Syria and Iraq share a tumultuous and violent postindependence period. The Syrian Ba'th Party assumed power in 1963 and the Iraqi Ba'th in 1968, after both countries had experienced a series in military coups. The installation of Ba'thist regimes, through army coups, occurred in the context of a widespread upsurge in radical nationalism in the 1950s, boosted by Nasser's victory in the Suez Crisis (Hinnebusch 2001: 47; Hopwood 1988: 41; Tripp 2000: 142–143; Davis 2005: 82–83). This political turmoil was partly due to struggles between the major political groupings of the period—Ba'thists, communists, Nasserists, pan-Arabists, nationalists, and socialists—as well as personal rivalries (Hinnebusch 2001: 41–45; Tripp 2000: 148–192). In multiethnic/multireligious Iraq, different conceptions of the polity (pan-Arab vs. territorial nationalist) became highly politicized and took on a sectarian hue, thereby representing a significant challenge to the consolidation of postindependence regimes.

The instability, violence, and ideological disputes that marked the 1950s and 1960s in Syria and Iraq before the Ba'th came to power obscure some of the political continuities over this period with regard to the main objectives of these regimes. A key feature of this continuity was the commitment to national modernization and anti-imperialism (Lenczowski 1966: 34–35). These features were displayed by the military leaders that sought power through coups from 1949 onward in Syria, as well as the regime of 'Abd al-Karim Qasim, who came to power in Iraq in 1958 (Farouk-Sluglett and Sluglett 2001: 76–78; Hopwood 1988: 34–38; Tripp 2000: 163–167). These instances of military intervention "served to break the political backbone of the traditional ruling class and to transfer a growing share of power to new groups and parties" (Rabinovich 1972: 5), such as the Ba'th and the communists.

The Ba'th Party originated in Syria in 1943 and a branch was established in Iraq around 1950 (Farouk-Sluglett and Sluglett 2001: 90). The emergence of the party was part of the upsurge in radicalism after World War II and it played a role in nationalist politics in Syria and Iraq before taking power in the 1960s (Hinnebusch 2001: 30–36; Farouk-Sluglett and Sluglett 2001: 90–92). In the Syrian parliamentary elections of 1954, the Ba'th Party won 22 seats out of 142, to become the third-largest political grouping, after the Independents (a collection of landowners, businessmen, tribal and minority leaders, and heads of powerful families) and the People's Party (a pro-Hashemite group with a regional base in Aleppo and Homs) (Seale 1965: 175–182). This represented an "unprecedented achievement" for a modern radical party in the Arab world and reflected the growing support for the party among students, the intelligentsia, and the trade unions and the waning of power of the traditional oligarchy (Rabinovich 1972: 12–13; Seale 1965: 179).

The Ba'th doctrine was populist–pan-Arabist, demonstrating hostility to the established oligarchic political order. It believed in an Arab renaissance (the meaning of *ba'th*), through an end to injustice and feudalism and the unity of the Arab region, which they considered as artificially divided by imperialism (Hinnebusch 2001: 30). The party's official program in 1947 called for state-led development, social welfare services, labor rights, the regulation of the private sector in the national interest, and agrarian reform (p. 30). The appeal of the ideology in Syria was its ability to "bridge the class and sectarian cleavages which divided Syrians" (p. 31). In Iraq, Ba'th ideology was challenged by the ethnic and religious inclusiveness of the Iraqi Communist Party, and Ba'thists only succeeded in gaining power through a military coup (Farouk-Sluglett and Sluglett 2001: 91; Davis 2005: 129–147).

After the victory of the radical wing of the Syrian Ba'th Party, the regime embarked upon a "revolution from above" (Hinnebusch 2001: 52ff). The new regime moved quickly to reduce ceilings on land ownership and to increase the pace of expropriation and redistribution (Ahsan 1984: 306). Simultaneously, it embarked upon a program of sweeping nationalization. By mid-1965, the state controlled banking and insurance, energy, most of the import trade and at least three-quarters of export trade, about one-third of road transport, and most of industry, excluding small workshops (Ahsan 1984: 306). The regime also initiated new infrastructure projects, such as the Euphrates Dam, and widened access to education.

A significant factor in the regime's ability to galvanize support and consolidate its rule was its ability to build mass support in rural areas through the creation of the General Federation of Peasants, established in 1964. The union aimed to mobilize the rural residents for the purpose of modernization by circumventing the traditional local power structure and "recruiting and organizing a wholly new village leadership from the mainstream peasantry" (Hinnebusch 1990: 198). A union branch was established in most villages with the help of already existing village party activists, of which there were a significant number (p. 268). Peasants were attracted to joining through a mix of ideological commitment to the Ba'thist principles of antifeudalism and nationalism, as well as material incentives, such as land redistribution and access to cheap credit (p. 199). Those who remained outside the union framework included peasants in areas not yet reached by organizers; those who were apathetic; or those who were hostile to the Ba'th or sympathetic to other political currents, such as the communists (p. 200).

The creation of the peasant union facilitated the implementation of the regime's modernization policies. As Ray Hinnebusch states, "Without such political penetration [of the villages], the regime could not have put down roots, spread its message, or established its village institutions with any efficacy" (1990: 269). Most importantly, the creation of the peasant unions and the implementation of land reform and other modernizing policies, broke the power of the traditional landlords and urban merchants, who exploited the peasantry through their monopoly of land and credit, as well as political power. The peasant union served to shift power to the hands of younger and poorer members of village communities, contributing to an improvement in the living conditions of these groups and to their social mobility. To some degree, by replacing dependency on large and powerful families with dependency upon the regime and its state institutions, Ba'th policies contributed to removing the material bases for sectarian and other social cleavages within villages, thereby contributing to nation-state building. In examining the histories of several Syrian villages in different parts of the country, Hinnebusch often finds that the political activism of local Ba'th members at the village level generated new forms of cross-sectarian or cross-family association in opposition to the existing powerful families, who traditionally drew on sect-based loyalty to boost their authority, while state penetration resulted in protection for minorities and women's rights (pp. 224, 229, 234, 246, 254). In other words, the peasant union, buttressed by tangible improvements to rural life, did not only exist at the level of the regime's populist-nationalist rhetoric but also played a significant role in nation-state building, which, in turn, helped to consolidate Ba'th rule. Simultaneously, it created a new framework for politics based on populist-nationalism, which was barely challenged by the regime's political opponents, such as the communists, Nasserists, and political Islamists.

In Iraq, political rivalries were more bloody and protracted than in Syria. This not only affected the nature of the regime but also the nature of many civil-society actors. Regimes were violent and those civil-society groups allied to a political current often demonstrated similar intolerance for their political rivals. For example, between 1958 and 1963, under the regime of Qasim, rivalry between the Iraqi Communist Party and the Ba'thists and their allies reached lethal levels (Batatu 1978: 859ff). By the time the Ba'th finally seized power in 1968, many Iraqi civil-society organizations had been destroyed (as they had been associated with the communists), or had become appendages of the state. In addition, in the lead-up to the Ba'th coup, the Iraqi regime was embroiled in a war with Kurdish parties and the economy was in disarray (Davis 2005: 143; Farouk-Sluglett and Sluglett 2001: 101–104). No doubt, a large part of the population craved political stability.

In the wake of the 1968 coup, the Iraqi Ba'th Party implemented several measures that sought to increase the welfare of the majority of Iraqis, such as land redistribution in favor of peasants, electrification of villages, the introduction of state marketing boards that removed peasant dependence on middlemen, subsidizing of essential food items, raising the minimum wage for unskilled public-sector employees, and extending social security. Although the initial impact of these measures was limited, "that some of [the peasants and urban laborers], at least, have come to regard the regime as their champion cannot be disputed" (Batatu 1978: 1096). The regime was able to pay for these significant increases in public expenditure through the nationalization of the Iraq Petroleum Company in 1972, which "was greeted with . . . universal enthusiasm," and provided the Ba'th with a huge amount of legitimacy (Farouk-Sluglett and Sluglett 2001: 147; also, Batatu 1978: 1097). The huge rise in oil prices after 1973 drastically increased revenues to the state, enabling a generous extension in social welfare benefits and improved socioeconomic conditions for the majority of the population—including the Kurdish north and Shi'ite south—in addition to an immense source of patronage power for the regime (Farouk-Sluglett and Sluglett 2001: 229ff). Moreover, the nationalization of the oil industry finally enabled the regime to co-opt the Iraqi Communist Party (p. 147).

Oil wealth was also used to sponsor cultural production. The number of official publications greatly expanded, international conferences and festivals were hosted, and new museums were opened (Davis 2005: 156). The regime financed the Project for Rewriting History and the creation of a new Iraqi identity, based not on pan-Arabism but on pre-Islamic Mesopotamian heritage. The construction of an Iraqi-centered national identity was reconciled with traditional Ba'thist notions of pan-Arabism by declaring that Iraq was destined to lead the Arab world through its illustrious heritage (Baram 1991). This took the form of the cultivation of folklore, the introduction of ceremonies, names, and symbols dating back to pre-Islamic times, into the administrative, political, and cultural life of the country and an official drive to encourage Iraqi archeological research (Baram 1991; Davis 2005). This cultural project had important political and ideological ramifications. "By positing a definition of political community that ostensibly incorporated all elements of Iraqi society, the Ba'th sought to eliminate political dissension by symbolically offering everyone limited political and cultural space" (Davis 2005: 157). This happened as, simultaneously, the regime became more sectarian in character (Batatu 1978: 1078ff).

The cases of Iraq and Syria demonstrate how the nationalization of the economy and the extension of populist welfare measures enabled regimes to consolidate their authority, even under adverse conditions. These measures not only responded to widespread desires for social justice but also contributed to state building as well as nationally integrating socially fragmented societies. As heads of the nation-state, regimes benefited from nation-state building processes. However, simultaneously, many ordinary citizens also benefited. In Syria, the building of mass-based organizations not only enabled the state to penetrate the countryside and, thereby, to dominate it. These organizations were an important agent in facilitating the implementation of modernization policies and contributing to the construction of universal citizenship. In Iraq, the nationalization of the oil industry not only gave the regime a populist-nationalist veneer and helped it to bring the communists into a coalition government. Simultaneously, it financed significant welfare benefits for ordinary people, as well as the construction of an Iraqi identity that, at least on the surface, was inclusive of all sectors of society. The benefits that regimes brought and their achievements in nation-state building contributed to their authority, even while political opponents were brutally repressed. In both cases, civil society, albeit created by regime measures, played a crucial role in these processes. Even where these participants were not ideologically motivated, nonetheless, ordinary men and women initially *consented* to participate in the mass-based organizations and the Project for Rewriting History.

## Tunisia: State Feminism and Modernization

The Neo-Destour Party came into being in 1934, under the leadership of Habib Bourguiba. It led the nationalist movement and was committed to national independence and modernization via grass-roots organization and mobilization (Entelis 1980: 38). In 1954, groups of guerrillas, or *fellaghas,* began to operate in the countryside, attacking French troops. By June 1955, the French granted autonomy to Tunisia, followed by full independence in 1956. The monarchy was abolished in 1957, as the first act of the newly elected national assembly (p. 132).

As in Egypt, the first few years of independence were characterized with some degree of conflict and instability while the new regime, headed by Bourguiba, attempted to eliminate rivals and consolidate power (Entelis

1980: 129–133). The Union Générale Tunisienne du Travail (UGTT), an important element of the nationalist movement, played a central role in this process of regime consolidation. First, the UGTT's backing of Bourguiba against his rival, Salah Ben Youssef, secured Bourguiba's leadership. Second, Bourguiba engineered a split within UGTT leadership in order to guarantee the supremacy of the Neo-Destour over the trade union (Bellin 2002: 93–95; Entelis 1980: 131–132).

The chronology of regime consolidation in Tunisia also bears other similarities with Egypt. Functional groups within the nationalist movement (representing workers, peasants, and small businessmen), together with newly created groups, were corporatized, while independent political parties and associations were forbidden (Bellin 1995: 127–128). Political plurality was portrayed as divisive and detracting from the project of building a modern nation-state (Bellin 1995: 127; Charrad 2001: 210). Anti-imperialism was significant in enhancing the popularity and legitimacy of the new regime, following regime demands for an evacuation of the French military from the port of Bizerte in 1961 (Entelis 1980: 134). Following this, the Bourguiba regime embarked on a (short-lived) "socialist" experiment. It expropriated foreign-owned land, pursued radical agricultural reform, and adopted state-led economic planning and ISI as a means of generating economic development and modernization (Bellin 2002: 21). In 1964, the Neo-Destour was renamed the Parti Socialiste Destourien (PSD).

An important factor in the consolidation of the Tunisian regime has been its image as a (relatively) benign, modernizing dictatorship. It is often overlooked that women and gender play a central role in the construction and diffusion of this image. While formal commitment to enhancing women's condition and participation (otherwise known as "state feminism") is a hallmark of all the radical, single-party regimes during this period, the Tunisian case stands out because women's emancipation and integration into the economy were prioritized by the regime and reforms toward this end are perceived as being some of the most radical for the region (Moghadam 1993: 56, 252).

Prior to independence, the Tunisian Islamic reformer Tahar al-Haddad advocated the emancipation of women as necessary for modernization. His writings helped to instigate the establishment of the first Tunisian women's association, the Muslim Union of Tunisian Women (UMFT), by educated urban elite women such as Bchira Ben M'rad, who sought to renew Islam and demonstrate its positive contributions to improving women's status (Sadiqi 2005: 653–654). Despite his respected position as a scholar of the Great Mosque of Zitouna, his views were perceived as controversial at the time. Many nationalist leaders, Bourguiba included, denounced the ideas proposed by al-Haddad (Moore 1965: 31). In resisting the French colonizers, nationalists deemed it necessary to postpone any talk of reforming personal status laws in order to protect national culture (Charrad 2001: 217–218). Nevertheless, reformist thinking found expression in postindependence reforms. Merely five months following independence, in 1956, Bourguiba introduced a unified civil code regulating family law—the Tunisian Code du Statut Personnel (CSP). This abolished polygamy, forced marriage, and male repudiation, raised the legal marriage age, and placed all personal status matters under the jurisdiction of civil courts (Brand 1998: 207–208; Charrad 2001: 224–231).[7] The abolition of polygamy represented the most far-reaching reform of personal status law in the region. Other measures in favor of women included support for family planning, promotion of girls' education, and legislation ensuring women's right to work and equal salary in the workplace (Brand 1998: 209). In addition, women were given the right to vote and to stand for election in 1957. These measures were buttressed by Bourguiba's public declarations of his opposition to arranged marriages and veiling and support for women to participate in public life (Marshall and Stokes 1981: 637; Moore 1965: 55).

The regime sought to promote its project of women's emancipation through the creation of the Union Nationale de la Femme Tunisienne (UNFT) in 1958. The UNFT was created by merging the women's cells of the Neo-Destour Party and the UMFT. However, Ben M'rad was pushed out of the new organization. Activists in other women's organizations, such as the Communist Party–affiliated Union des Femmes de Tunisie, were harassed. Yet, "the euphoric atmosphere following the liberation . . . led many women to join the UNFT" (Brand 1998: 203), while others were persuaded by the regime's promulgation of the CSP of its "recognition of the role played by women in the struggle for independence."[8] The UNFT's function was to "educate" women to support and to implement the regime's modernization program. The union encouraged women to vote, taught them about their new legal rights and duties, and carried out welfare projects (Moore 1956: 56). In addition, it campaigned against practices that were seen as hindering modernization, such as visiting saints, tombs, and the increasing dowry level (Brand 1998: 204).

State feminism served to consolidate the regime on a number of levels. First, the promulgation of a relatively progressive personal status code enabled the regime to break the power of kinship and tribal solidarities in society, thereby dismantling potential sources of opposition and ensuring national unity (Charrad 2001: 232). Second, the (relatively) progressive nature of the law and other reforms in favor of women's participation were symbolic of (and instrumental for) the regime's modernizing thrust (pp. 219–220). Third, the adoption of state feminism and the sponsorship of the women's union helped to build a female constituency for the regime, as representing their interests. The latter would later prove effective in defeating the Islamist opposition movement in the 1980s (Brand 1998: 244–245).

Civil society played a significant role in laying the ground for the success of state feminism. Anticolonial nationalists, such as Tahar al-Haddad and the UMFT, provided a framework for conceptualizing women's rights in the postindependence period—that is, women's rights were instrumental in renewing Islam and, therefore, in contributing to the goals of national modernization. Consequently, the needs of national modernization determined the content of women's rights. In the postindependence period, the newly acquired women's rights were propagated by the UNFT, which had branches throughout the country (Brand 1998: 206). There existed no challenge to this conception of women's rights until the emergence of an Islamist movement and independent women's organizations in the 1970s.

## Conclusion

Colonial rule had long-term implications for the political, economic, social, and cultural development of the Arab states studied here. The injustice and indignities suffered shaped the aspirations of nationalist movements across the region for freedom from foreign domination and an end to social injustices. The inability of indigenous elites to meet these aspirations during the inter-war years led to a radicalization of nationalism and a discrediting of the parliamentary systems established by the Europeans. The major objectives of nationalist movements were not only to rid their countries of foreign influence, but also to erase the privileges of the landowning elites who were associated with colonial rule and to set their societies on a path of national modernization.

In understanding the normalization of authoritarianism in the postindependence period, it is necessary to appreciate the degree to which radical nationalism was vindicated. Radical nationalist regimes in Algeria, Tunisia, Egypt, Syria, and Iraq successfully rid their countries of colonial influence, challenged imperialism, broke the political and economic power of traditional indigenous elites, promoted economic development, and improved the living conditions of working people. Simultaneously, they eschewed liberal democracy and established new hierarchies within these societies.

Although there were calls for the establishment of parliamentary democracy and an end to the military's role in politics, these voices were either co-opted or driven out of the public domain. Other regime opponents, such as the Muslim Brotherhood in Egypt, were brutally repressed. Their demands possessed little validity within a discursive framework that prioritized the goals of protecting the achievements of national modernization.

Civil society played a role in the normalization of authoritarianism through its support for national modernization. Under colonial rule, nationalism became the predominant political framework for the beliefs and actions of a range of civil-society actors, and modernization and freedom from foreign influence became primary goals. This framework, or counter-hegemonic project, became hegemonic in the postindependence period and shaped the discursive field of political action. Even those who opposed the new regimes, such as the Egyptian Muslim Brotherhood and the Iraqi Communist Party, supported the goals of national modernization, albeit from the ideological standpoints of Islam and communism, respectively. Regime commitment to the goals of the anticolonial struggle enabled, in some cases, the co-optation of political rivals and civil-society activists into the government, the newly created mass organizations, and/or regime-directed projects, such as the Project for Rewriting History.

The success of regimes in pursuing the aims of national modernization led to the creation of new social and political hierarchies that underpinned authoritarianism. These hierarchies were normalized through nationalist discourses. Individual rights were legitimately sacrificed (often by regime opponents, as well as regimes themselves) in the name of national interests and protecting "the revolution." Despite the widespread rhetoric of populism and commitment to women's "emancipation," workers, peasants, and women were subordinated to the goals of national liberation and modernization. The articulation of Arab-Muslim conceptions of identity as the basis of national inclusion served to exclude non-Arabs and non-Muslims from the polity. Meanwhile, improvements in the welfare of citizens, the establishment of heavy industry and large infrastructure projects, resistance to imperialism, and the ending of "feudalism" (although often partial) helped to give ideological credibility to the regime. The increased role of the state in the economy and in the protection of the "gains of the revolution" led to a huge concentration of resources within the hands of ruling regimes that, even as their legitimacy faltered, were able to be deployed to prevent significant challenges.

Despite objections to the dictatorial methods employed by regimes to achieve the aims of the hegemonic project, it was difficult for civil-society actors to oppose them because they, themselves, supported these aims. Moreover, regimes were able to utilize the increased resources under their control to monopolize and reconstruct civil society for their own ends. The incorporation of trade unions, peasant unions, women's unions, and professional associations within corporatist structures eliminated any room for action independent of the regime and secured the final nail in the coffin of democracy.

## Notes

1. Morocco was previously not part of the Ottoman Empire.
2. Independence was nominal because, in reality, the British retained considerable influence within Egypt through various mechanisms, including the high commissioner, advisers with the Egyptian government, and command of the Egyptian army (Yapp 1996: 56–57).
3. Although Alawites and Druze consider themselves to be a branch of Islam, they are not recognized thus by mainstream Sunni and Shi'a Islam.
4. ISI was first adopted by Latin American countries and Turkey, in the inter-war period. The strategy is based on the notion that countries could develop by substituting products that they import with locally produced alternatives. It entails the establishment of domestic industries for the production of goods, protective barriers to protect infant industries and prevent competition with foreign goods, and a monetary policy that overvalues domestic currency (thereby rendering local goods cheaper than imported goods). The strategy also relies on the extraction of capital from the agricultural sector in addition to mass consumption of domestic products (Richards and Waterbury 1990: 26–27).
5. Interview with the author, Cairo, 21 June 2000.
6. Interview with the author, Cairo, 27 March 2000.
7. It should be noted that the CSP does not grant women equality with men in family law. Rather, the CSP aims to strengthen the nuclear family at the expense of the extended family and male kin. As such, it only represents progress in women's rights to the extent that a woman is no longer beholden to her male kin in making decisions about her future and is no longer threatened by the prospect of her husband taking another wife or divorcing her without limitations (Brand 1998: 208; Charrad 2001: 219).
8. Noura Borsali, "L'Union des femmes de Tunisie (U.F.T.): Nébiha Ben Miled, Gladys Adda, Sofia Zouiten et Neila Haddad," *Réalités* online, 9 March 2006, http://www.realites.com.tn/index1.php?mag=1&cat=&art=14795&a=detail1, accessed 20 July 2006.

# 3

## Challenges to Authoritarianism

BY THE 1960S, ALGERIA, EGYPT, Iraq, Syria, and Tunisia had all achieved independence and one-party political systems were firmly installed. As discussed in the previous chapter, these regimes developed similar politicoeconomic characteristics as part of the state-building process: the integration of civil society through corporatist institutions, dominated by the executive, and an import-substitution industrialization (ISI) strategy, fueling the growth of a large public sector. This was accompanied by strong rhetorical commitment to populist and anti-imperialist nationalism.

These elements of the postindependence political economy enabled nation-state building but also created new social hierarchies that underpinned authoritarianism. In particular, the consensus surrounding the project of national modernization, developed by civil society in the struggle against colonialism, contributed to creating a discursive framework where the subordination of the welfare and rights of ordinary citizens to those of the national collective was deemed legitimate and even natural. Simultaneously, the increased role of the state in the political and economic life of the nation concentrated resources in the hands of those groups that had captured the state, enabling regimes to dominate civil-society organizations through corporatist institutions. The expansion of corporatized mass organizations enabled regimes to mobilize support for their national modernization efforts and to marginalize concerns for democracy.

Authoritarianism appeared to be a coherent system in which the economic, the institutional, and the ideological reinforced one another. State provision of welfare benefits was coherent with populist nationalism and contributed to building corporatist institutions. Populist nationalism accorded with corporatist institutions and the establishment of a large public sector for social-justice ends. ISI was also presented as a logical outcome of national self-reliance and anti-imperialism. This system achieved hegemony not only through the executive's domination of political life, but also through a consensus that the goals, if not the means, of national modernization were legitimate.

However, from the late 1960s onward, fault lines began to appear in this postindependence consensus. This was a result of adjustments to the political economy, which undermined the "socialist" gains of the postindependence period. In addition, the 1967 military defeat at the hands of Israel led to much soul-searching about the ability of Arab nationalist regimes to meet the aspirations of the public for freedom from imperialism. With the economic and the ideological pillars of the authoritarian system brought into question, the continued existence of the consensus supporting the postindependence political order appeared to be in the balance.

## The Crisis

Egypt and Tunisia were the first to experience economic problems. In Egypt, the First Five-Year Plan (1961–1965) resulted in external and domestic deficits (Richards and Waterbury 1990: 196). Consequently, in 1965, the regime introduced obligatory salary deductions for public-sector employees to contribute to a savings plan. Several factories were closed and some prices and taxes were increased (Waterbury 1983: 93–97, 409). In Tunisia, the First Four-Year Plan (1965–1968) managed by Ahmed Ben Salah, secretary of state for national planning, created a series of balance-of-trade deficits, together with a shortage of capital for investment. Meanwhile, measures to cooperatize agriculture were deemed a failure and highly unpopular among the regime's small landowning constituency (Bellin 2002: 23, 95; Richards and Waterbury 1990: 203). By the end of the 1960s, Syria was also experiencing economic difficulties, illustrated by a shortage of foreign exchange and poor agricultural production (Hinnebusch 2001: 59).

Algeria and Iraq did not face economic difficulties until much later. In Algeria, state-owned heavy industries in the metals and hydrocarbon sectors were the centerpiece of the country's industrialization strategy adopted after independence. However, concentration of investment in this sector was to the detriment of the agricultural sector, causing regional disparities in development and encouraging rural-to-urban migration. By the late 1970s, approximately two-thirds of cereals consumed were imported, while rapid urbanization created a severe housing shortage (Bennoune 1988: 212, 237ff). Meanwhile, poor management of state-led industries and lack of competition led to inefficiency and low productivity (Richards and Waterbury 1990: 252–253). Iraq's state-led development strategy was given a boost by the nationalization of the petroleum industry and the quadrupling of oil prices between 1972 and 1975 (Ayubi 1995: 362). Huge oil revenues helped to offset the problems of the inefficiency and mismanagement of state-owned industries. It was not until the war with Iran during the 1980s that Iraq was forced to address these problems through the encouragement of private-sector growth (Richards and Waterbury 1990: 256–257).

Problems of fiscal crisis, trade deficits, inefficiencies in production, and sectoral and regional inequalities were inherent within the state-led ISI strategy. ISI relied on the two contradictory processes of investment (in production) and consumption (of welfare goods and services) (Cooper 1979). ISI led to inefficiencies in production and investment allocation and neglect of the agricultural sector, and exacerbated the need for hard currency to pay for imported industrial inputs, thereby leading to fiscal problems. As domestic productivity fell, so did the state's revenue-raising abilities. Continued investment in the public sector to meet consumptive demands depended upon finding other sources of financing. In the cases of Algeria and Iraq, oil revenues succeeded in mitigating the structural problems of the ISI development model. However, in Egypt, Syria, and Tunisia, where domestic revenue-raising abilities were limited, the only alternatives were to either borrow massively from abroad or to implement austerity measures (Bellin 2002; Cooper 1979; Hinnebusch 2001: 127).

The problems engendered by the ISI strategy were not only economic. As already noted, this model of economic development was inextricably linked to state building and regime authority. Once regimes were forced to reduce their distribution of socioeconomic goods and services, the basis of their authority was brought into question (Cooper 1982). This was most manifest in Egypt and Tunisia, where workers and peasants protested against the regime's failure to meet the terms of the moral economy. In Egypt, the village of Kamshish was the scene of an important peasant rebellion, demonstrating the discontent with the slow pace of land reform. In 1966, Salah Husayn Maqlad, who had campaigned vigorously for the rights of Kamshish peasants, was assassinated

by the Fikkis, a family of large landowners who had previously controlled the village. The authorities' enquiries into evasion of land reforms by feudal landlords never resulted in real punishment of those
responsible—including those who assassinated Maqlad (Hussein 1973:
232–236). In July 1967, the first desequestrations of land were announced
and, in 1969, a court upheld Muhammad al-Fiqqi's right to evict former
tenants who occupied his land (Beinin 2001: 135).

Similarly, workers also demonstrated their discontent with their
regimes' failure to protect their standard of living. In Egypt, a number
of strikes erupted at the end of 1966 in response to deteriorating economic conditions and there were cases of workers evading disciplinary
measures, slowing down work, and even breaking machines (Hussein
1973: 234–237). In Tunisia, a devaluation of the dinar in 1964 to correct
the trade imbalance led the Union Générale Tunisienne du Travail
(UGTT) to override its policy of counseling wage restraint (for the sake
of national development) and instead to demand wage rises to compen-
sate for loss of earnings (Bellin 2002: 95–96). These demands were not
addressed. In the end, the union leadership could not stem the rising discontent of rank-and-file workers and a number of wildcat strikes took
place in 1969 (cit. in Beinin 2001: 137). Algeria also experienced an increasing number of wildcat strikes throughout the 1970s (Tlemcani 1986:
181–183).

The political and economic problems caused by the ISI strategy
were magnified for Egypt and Syria following the defeat of their armies
(in addition to Jordan's) at the hands of Israel in the June 1967 war. Following rising tensions in the region, on 5 June, Israel attacked Egypt in
response to the closing of the Straits of Tiran (one of Israel's shipping
routes). Within the next few days of fighting, Israel managed to occupy
Egypt's Sinai Peninsula, the Egyptian-controlled Gaza Strip, Jordanian-
controlled Jerusalem and the West Bank, and the Syrian Golan Heights.
A cease-fire agreement was reached on 11 June. During the war, the Arab
armies sustained massive losses in comparison to Israel, demonstrating
Israel's military superiority. The heaviest casualties were inflicted upon
the Egyptian army, who lost between 10,000 and 15,000 soldiers—in
comparison to the deaths of 338 Israeli soldiers on the Egyptian front.
In addition, the war caused approximately 300,000 West Bank Palestinians to flee to Jordan, while the remaining 600,000 were subjected to
occupation.

A contributing factor in the escalation of Arab-Israeli tensions that
resulted in the 1967 war was the growing strength of radical Arab nationalism and the competition between Egypt and Syria over the leadership

of the radical "Arab bloc" within the region (Hinnebusch 2003: 163–168; Kazziha 1990). Nasser, in a bid to maintain his leadership of the radical Arab states, attempted to demonstrate that the Arab nationalist regimes were able to regain Arab lands from Israeli control, thereby asserting Arab sovereignty. Moreover, it was hoped that by achieving regional leadership, the regime could divert attention away from the economic problems experienced from the mid-1960s (Johnson 1972). In other words, the 1967 war was not about the security of the Arab states per se but rather about maintaining the ideological dominance of pan-Arabism and the political dominance of the regimes that espoused it.

Within this context, the defeat was not only military but also political and ideological. As in the 1948 war, the defeat weakened and discredited the regimes directly involved. Israel's capture of Arab lands represented an assault on Arab sovereignty and therefore called into question the moral authority of those regimes that espoused the pan-Arabist ideology and who claimed to defend the ideals of Arab independence and dignity.

As a result, those countries directly involved with the defeat experienced varying degrees of political turmoil. The greatest impact was in Egypt, as the leader of the Arab world. Initially, the regime's position appeared to be secure. When Nasser offered his resignation immediately following the defeat, people throughout Egypt took to the street calling for him to stay in office. Despite the humiliation of the worst military defeat of that century, people still saw Nasser as their only protection against acquiescence to US and Israeli domination of the region and a reversal in the socioeconomic gains of the popular classes (Johnson 1972). Following the show trials of February 1968, in which the military generals were found responsible for the 1967 defeat but given lenient sentences, a wave of protests broke out among workers and students, beginning with the Helwan workers' demonstrations. Their protests, initially calling for the resignation of the military generals, rapidly developed into demands for democratic reforms, such as freedom of the press and a free parliament, as well as calls for the release of those detained during the demonstrations (Abdalla 1985: 152, 189–191, 224–226). It took heavy police intervention to break up the great number of protests that erupted around Cairo (Hussein 1973: 292–297). After the Israeli air force blew up an electric plant in Upper Egypt in December of that year, angry demonstrations broke out throughout the country. In March 1969, Nasser launched the "war of attrition" against the Israelis in a bid to usurp the radical following enjoyed by the Palestinian resistance across the Arab world and to quell the demands of protesters at home (Johnson 1972).

In Syria, where the Ba'th Party regime had made anti-imperialist (including anti-Israeli) resistance a central plank of its radical credentials, the defeat demoralized the party rank and file and split the leadership (Hinnebusch 1990: 137–139). Although not frontline states, Algeria, Tunisia, and Iraq witnessed popular demonstrations against the Arab defeat and the loss of Arab lands to Israel. These demonstrations did not necessarily challenge the legitimacy of these regimes but did bring into question the moral legitimacy of Arab nationalism (Halliday 1987).

## Rethinking Arab Nationalism and the Postindependence Consensus

### The Response of Arab Regimes

The 1967 defeat marked a watershed in the evolution of Arab regimes— even for those regimes not directly implicated in the war. For Egypt, Syria, and Tunisia, it coincided with the appearance of the economic problems associated with ISI. In Syria and Iraq, it caused division within the ruling regimes. In Syria, an internal Ba'th Party coup shifted the orientation of the party. In Iraq, a military coup brought the Ba'th to power. Only Algeria, on the periphery of the Arab regional system, whose regime had direct roots in a successful anti-imperialist struggle and whose oil revenues provided sufficient financing for "Arab socialist" measures, was able to weather the storm until the late 1970s.

By the early 1970s, the regimes of Egypt, Tunisia, and Syria had abandoned many of the policies associated with the state-led ISI development strategy and introduced measures to encourage the growth of the private sector and foreign investment. This shift in development strategy—termed *infitah,* or the "Open Door Economic Policy"—was also accompanied by a transformation in regime rhetoric and domestic coalitions. The Tunisian regime was the first to bring an end to the state's domination of the economy with the removal of Ahmed Ben Salah in 1969. A number of measures introduced from 1972 onward provided incentives for both domestic and foreign (private) firms as engines of export-oriented activities as well as national growth (Bellin 2002: 24–25). In addition, there was a certain degree of denationalization, including the sale of some state economic enterprises, the dismantling of cooperatives established in the 1960s, and restoring titles to previous owners (Harik 1992b: 212). Simultaneously, the regime maintained tariff barriers and regulated the establishment of new businesses to protect local producers from international and domestic competition, thereby ensuring excellent profits for Tunisian business owners irrespective of their efficiency (Bellin 2002: 25–26). The socialist rhetoric of the 1960s was discarded and the official trade union, the UGTT, was brought into the policymaking process through a corporatist triumvirate with the state and business, in return for containing the aspirations of its membership (pp. 99–100).

It was Egypt where *infitah* and the accompanying ideological and political changes made their deepest impact—for Egypt had been the center of radical Arab nationalism for over a decade, was the most populous Arab country, and played a strategic role in the international relations of the region. In 1974, Anwar al-Sadat, Nasser's successor, introduced policies aimed at attracting capital from the newly rich oil states of the Gulf, enticing Western investment in Egyptian production units through joint ventures, promoting exports and the private sector, and improving the productivity and competitiveness of the public sector (Richards and Waterbury 1990: 241). Sadat waited until 1974 to announce these measures in order to capitalize on the more favorable political climate brought about by the partial victory of the Arab armies in the October 1973 war against Israel (Aulas 1982).

These measures, aimed at correcting the country's serious economic problems, necessitated a shift in international alliances away from the USSR and radical Arab regimes toward a closer relationship with the United States and the conservative regimes of the Gulf states (Richards and Waterbury 1990: 241). Sadat's signing of a peace treaty with Israel in 1979 represented a culmination in this process of reorientation and aimed to place Egypt firmly in the Western camp. Domestically, Sadat attempted to build a constituency among the national private sector through encouraging the establishment of businessmen's associations and their access to policymaking circles (Abdelrahman 2001: 149). Simultaneously, labor rights for workers in the newly created joint-venture companies were withdrawn and the official trade union federation (GEFTU) was brought under tighter political control ('Adli 1993: 151–153).

Syria's shift away from radical Arab nationalism and its associated "socialist" measures is associated with Hafez al-Assad, who went on to rule the country for over thirty years. Following 1967, power shifted within the Syrian Ba'thist regime toward the pragmatic stance of Hafez al-Assad (then defense minister) until the latter staged a military coup in 1970 and successfully took power. "Asad's aim was to consolidate the unstable Ba'th state and mobilize Syria for a war to recover the lost territories" (Hinnebusch 2001: 65). Toward this end, he ushered in the "corrective movement." Like Sadat, Assad formed new alliances with the

Arab Gulf states and introduced measures to encourage private-sector growth (p. 65). The validity of these measures appeared to be vindicated by the Syrian army's credible performance in the 1973 war.

Tunisia, Egypt, and Syria all introduced limited political openings in the 1970s in an attempt to expand the regime's constituencies and to co-opt opposition to economic liberalization. Egypt permitted three "platforms" to emerge within the Arab Socialist Union, which were legalized as political parties in 1977 and multiparty elections were held in 1979. Syria introduced a People's Assembly, which included political forces beyond the regime. Meanwhile, Nasserists, communists, and Arab socialists were co-opted into a National Progressive Front and were awarded a share in office, although the Ba'th Party remained dominant. In Tunisia, Prime Minister Hedi Nouira replaced the rhetoric of socialism with that of liberalism (Bellin 2002: 99). A number of resolutions were passed at the ruling party conference in 1971, paving the way for electoral competition. However, President Bourguiba rejected the idea of pluralism and moved to reverse the political openings created by the 1971 party conference, culminating in the expulsion of liberal members of the party in 1974 (Waltz 1995: 69). In 1975, Bourguiba made himself president for life. The limits of political openings were also demonstrated in Egypt and Syria. Sadat moved to stifle opposition to peacemaking with Israel by introducing draconian legislation to criminalize dissent. In Syria, the regime unleashed brutal force upon the (Sunni) Islamist urban guerrilla warfare, which had grown throughout the 1970s, fueled in large part by discontent with the sectarian (Alawite) nature of the regime (Hinnebusch 2001: 98–102), as well as repressing the secular opposition movement (HRW 1991).

Not only was the character of political openings limited. Simultaneously, economic openings were partial. The aim of *infitah* policies was to offset the financial deficits of the state-led ISI strategy—rather than to replace it (Richards and Waterbury 1990: 261). Indeed, the state sector sustained growth from the 1970s onward (Ayubi 1995: 293). The continued domination of the state-led economy was accompanied by the regimes' continued commitment to the provision of many of the popular socioeconomic benefits achieved in the postindependence era. For example, urban protests in Egypt in 1977 against the rising cost of living for the poor and those on fixed incomes led the regime to reiterate its commitment to the postindependence moral economy and to restore food subsidies.

## The Response of Arab Intellectuals

As Arab regimes dismantled some aspects of the postindependence political economy to reflect the apparent defeat of Arab nationalism in

1967, civil-society actors engaged in a reconsideration of the political and social aspirations that Arab nationalism had represented. The defeat of 1967 unleashed a great soul-searching among Arab intellectuals and others who had lived the dream promoted by the Arab nationalist regimes. Everything was questioned—politics, ideology, culture, and religion—in order to understand the reasons behind the defeat. In particular, the Egyptian and Syrian regimes and the ideals that they stood for were the object of critique and criticism (Ajami 1992: 31). In the post-1967 period, various critiques were presented to explain the causes of the defeat and the solutions for building an alternative political order that would restore Arab dignity. Two major trends emerged among Arab intellectuals: secular and Islamist.

The critiques of secular intellectuals tended not to reject Arab nationalist ideology and the socioeconomic model associated with it, but rather to critique the Arab nationalist regimes for not having gone far enough in their radical reforms. The failure to fulfil the ambitions of the revolutionary moment that had gripped these societies since the 1950s was regarded as the cause behind the defeat of the Arab regimes at the hands of Israel. At the root of that failure was the inability of those in power to renew Arab culture. "There was a consensus that the heroes of yesterday had made too many compromises with the past, that they had given in to that frustrating, hopeless body of attitudes and habits, that immutable thing called tradition" (Ajami 1992: 32). For some, a significant element in the renewal of Arab culture was the abandonment of religion. The Syrian poet and writer Adonis argued that Arab nationalist regimes had failed to challenge old beliefs and superstitions and, therefore, people had remained enslaved by these and unable to carry out a revolution of society (p. 36). In his 1968 book, *al-naqd al-dhati ba'd al-hazima* ("Self-Criticism After the Defeat"), the American University of Beirut academic Sadeq al-Azm also blamed the defeat of the so-called revolutionary regimes on their failure to sweep away the past and to create modern citizens, who are able to fight and die for the state. Regimes had failed to integrate Arab individuals into modern state institutions and, consequently, these individuals retained their primary loyalty to their family and clan (Ajami 1992: 40).

While secular-oriented intellectuals blamed the persistence of religion for military defeat, another group of writers believed that the Arabs had lost the war because they had abandoned their religious beliefs. They argued that Islam, unlike imported doctrines such as Marxism, could mobilize people to make the necessary sacrifices to create a great Arab civilization—capable of confronting Israel and the West (Ajami 1992: 61ff). Muhammad Galal Kishk, an Egyptian writer with Muslim

Brotherhood sympathies, wrote in his 1969 book, *al-naksa wa-l-ghazw al-fikri* ("The Defeat and the Intellectual Invasion"), that Islam represented the only authentic body of ideas that could guide a successful revolution and secure victory for the Arabs, as in the case of the Algerian war for independence (Ajami 1992: 67–68).

These intellectual trends reflected a radicalization of civil society that crystalized into different social movements. Some called for a social revolution that would sweep away traditions and enable the Arab world to modernize. Others called for bringing religion back into politics as a means of grounding modernization in indigenous structures. In both cases, "A frightening generation gap developed in the aftermath of the defeat: the language, the symbols, and the world view of the men in power were losing their grip on the young, who were now marching to a different drum" (Ajami 1992: 84).

Despite the different evaluations of the Arab nationalist regimes and the different rationales presented for the defeat, these critiques converged in their aims to restore Arab sovereignty against imperialism and to ensure the modernization of the state. In other words, Arab intellectuals voiced their discontent with the Arab nationalist regimes, rather than the national modernization project upon which they had embarked in the postindependence period. The restoration of this project became an objective of the various tendencies that emerged within civil society after 1967.

## Transformation of Civil Society

Before 1967, civil-society actors in the various mass organizations created by Arab nationalist regimes had, more or less, become closely linked to their regimes through corporatist institutions. This relationship was not only institutional but also ideological, in that civil-society actors often articulated support for the anti-imperialist and populist goals of their political leaders—even if they did not support the leaders themselves. Throughout the 1970s, civil-society actors voiced their opposition to the abandonment of "Arab socialism," the failure of postindependence modernization, the rise in socioeconomic inequalities, and the increasing US hegemony in the region. This provided a new opportunity for civil-society actors to break free of their ideological and institutional adherence to their respective regimes. Within this context, new social movements began to appear. The emergence of contentious politics, in and of itself, represented a serious challenge to Arab regimes. On the other hand, these movements often worked within the discursive framework of the national modernization project and, in this respect, did not necessarily represent a challenge to the social and political relations underpinning authoritarianism.

## The Student Movement

Throughout the Arab world and at various times, students have played a significant role in national political developments through organizing street protests. In addition, university campuses have provided important "incubators" for civil society, as former student activists graduate and go on to participate in other forms of civil activism. In particular, the post-1967 Egyptian student movement represented one of the most radical and sustained movements in the Arab world. As noted above, Egyptian university students were at the forefront of demonstrations against the regime immediately following the defeat. This upsurge in activism was significant in that, until 1967, postindependence university campuses had been devoid of any sort of activities that could be deemed antigovernment. The only student organization permitted was the official student union, affiliated with the regime party (the Arab Socialist Union). Consequently, the widespread uprising of the students after 1967 could be considered a measure of the depth of discontent felt. One member of the post-1967 Egyptian student movement told me: "Nineteen sixty-seven opened our eyes and overturned our ideas. We saw the corruption of the system. My peers died in Sinai without a fight."[1]

For a while, the regime managed to quash the street demonstrations and to weaken the leadership of the student movement (Hussein 1973: 317). However, after Sadat came to power, the students again staged demonstrations that became a focus for national discontent. In 1972, there were massive confrontations between the students and the police over the course of ten days, and other demonstrations by workers and the urban unemployed in Cairo and other large cities. The students were supported by journalists, lawyers, writers, and artists, eighty-nine of whom were expelled from the Arab Socialist Union (Johnson 1973; MERIP Reports 1973).

In addition to demands for civil freedoms, both on and off campus, the students' manifesto focused on the need to resume war with Israel in order to regain Arab territory. The students rejected UN Security Council Resolution 242 (which ended the 1967 war and called for an Israeli withdrawal from occupied lands in return for peace), called for the introduction of a "war economy" to mobilize the country for a new war against Israel, and supported the armed Palestinian resistance. There were also concerns about the need to address the growing social inequalities within the country (Johnson 1972 and 1973). The student movement was restorative, in that it aimed to restore national dignity against the enemy, Israel, and the socioeconomic benefits that large sectors of the population had come to expect. While the demands for civil and political freedoms represented a significant challenge to the authoritarian nature of the regime, they were framed as a means of renewing the system in order to face the enemy (Israel). The tension between these different demands is noted by one former student activist and current youth leader, who said, "Our de facto attitude as students was to defend patriotism *and* democracy. But we lived the contradictions of this because our leaders used patriotism against democracy."[2]

As an indication of the restorative nature of the student movement demands, the October 1973 war went some way to appease the widespread discontent expressed with the post-1967 territorial settlement and led to a weakening of the student movement. The Arab armies failed to liberate the land occupied by Israel. Nevertheless, the war demonstrated that the Arab armies could inflict damage upon Israel, while the oil embargo threatened Western interests. Consequently, the war changed the strategic balance between Israel and the Arab countries and forced the United States to support a negotiated settlement, thereby giving the Arab countries more leverage (Hinnebusch 2003: 175). In addition, the war appeared to revive the notion of Arab unity, as the Arab countries demonstrated unprecedented cooperation in supporting Egypt and Syria. Jordan and Iraq provided military support, while Algeria and the Gulf states provided financial backing (p. 176).

The ebbing of the student movement impacted upon the development of civil society. The student movement had been an impetus for the emergence of a variety of organizations within civil society. Conversely, the disintegration of the student movement led some activists to reassess their engagement with civil society. Some student activists withdrew almost completely from civil activism, feeling disillusioned and disorientated. *Al-infitah,* the shift in international alliances toward the United States, the growth of political Islam, and the failure of secularist ideologies to mobilize people created an "identity crisis" for many of those who had subscribed to leftist-nationalist ideologies (Dwyer 1991: 61, 64). It became clear that Egypt was not on a linear course of development toward the vision of Arab socialism.[3] Many activists "took time out" to read or pursue careers or doctoral studies abroad. Some began to revise their nationalist or Marxist ideas regarding social change in order to incorporate the concept of democracy.[4] For some activists, this revision was a result of their negative experiences of participating in Marxist politics through their membership in underground organizations.[5] For others, the experience of traveling to the "West" enabled them to see liberal democracy in practice and to appreciate it as a superior system.[6]

After the establishment of a multiparty system, some former student activists joined the leftist Tagammu' Party—a coalition of socialists, communists, and Nasserists who were formerly part of the Arab Socialist Union (ASU) and permitted to form a party in 1977. However, many of these young activists were forced out, finding the experience of party membership deeply unsatisfactory. The party's leadership (drawn from a generation that had participated in the ranks of the ASU) was viewed as too conservative and undemocratic. Other former student activists were faced with similar challenges in the professional syndicates. Some women activists found the party hierarchy patriarchal, fellow party members sexist, and that issues concerning women's rights were marginalized.[7]

A resurrection of the question of "national liberation" following the 1982 Israeli invasion of Lebanon revitalized some of the former student activists into public activism. However, rather than working in political parties or under the banner of particular political ideologies, some activists began operating in working-class communities "as a way of re-linking ourselves to the people."[8] Simultaneously, the increasing inability of the state to meet the needs of its population by the mid-1980s, due to severe economic problems, helped to encourage societal demands for "alternative models" of social development. The state's retreat from its socioeconomic role contributed to a reassessment among some activists of their ideas about the role of the state in social change. They became involved in establishing literacy classes, community centers, and other social projects. This approach to public activism represented a change in tactics from the ""grand slogans" and protests of the student movement," which had failed to build a popular movement for reform.[9]

## Political Parties

The initial postindependence phase witnessed the repression of political parties or their integration into the single parties sponsored by new regimes. In the 1970s, some preindependence political parties reemerged or new political parties were formed as a result of the limited degree of political liberalization that occurred (Ibrahim 1995: 40–41). Egypt spearheaded the revival of party politics with the introduction of a multiparty system in 1977, the dissolution of the ASU, and the authorization of five political parties: the regime's National Democratic Party (NDP), the

Wafd, the leftist/Nasserist Tagammu', the Socialist Labor Party, and the Ahrar Party (the latter two being Islamist-oriented). Tunisia and Algeria introduced multiparty elections in 1989.

For the most part, the parties that emerged following the introduction of a multiparty system did not represent existing social currents and were often constituted by ex-members of the ruling parties. For example, the Mouvement des Démocrates Socialistes (MDS) was founded in 1976, and officially recognized in 1984, by a group of liberals expelled from the ruling party in Tunisia in the early 1970s (Waltz 1995: 69–70). Similarly, some of the many parties formed in Algeria were led by politicians associated with the Front de Libération Nationale (p. 96). Of the parties authorized in Egypt after 1977, the Tagammu', Ahrar, and NDP were formed out of the Arab Socialist Union. The NDP was the party of President Sadat, while the Socialist Labor Party was formed by then minister of agriculture, Ibrahim Shukri, on the encouragement of Sadat (Kassem 1999: 42).

The exception to this rule was the Front Islamique du Salut (FIS), the political wing of the Islamist movement, which won a landslide victory in Algeria's municipal elections in 1990 and was on the verge of winning a majority of seats in the legislative elections of 1991, before the army intervened to cancel the process. Islamist groups in Tunisia and Egypt have been prevented from forming political parties but have managed to win seats in legislative elections by standing as independent candidates. While not initially formed as a result of any social trend, the Egyptian Tagammu' Party did manage, for a while, to attract individuals with leftist, Marxist, or Nasserist political sympathies. It was the only political party to oppose Egypt's peace treaty with Israel in 1979 and was part of the widespread opposition within civil society to this, leading to the arrest of a number of party members and security raids on the party's headquarters (Sayed 1989: 38; MERIP Reports 1979). However, as noted above, many young members left the party, becoming disillusioned with its lack of internal democracy.

The experiences of political parties in Algeria, Egypt, and Tunisia demonstrate that political parties have not generally represented a conduit for contentious politics. The aim of political liberalization has been to renew ruling parties and control political opposition within official structures. In the case of Algeria, this backfired. In Egypt and Tunisia, multiparty politics has become completely fettered by electoral engineering in favor of the ruling party, intimidation of the opposition, and legal restrictions on freedom of assembly (see Chapter 4 for further discussion).

Contrary to the North African experience, political parties in Syria and Iraq continued to exist after the revolution and reflected different ideological trends within society (principally, leftist/communist and nationalist). After 1970, leftist and nationalist political parties were integrated into a "united front" with the ruling Ba'th Parties in both countries (Hinnebusch 2001: 66; Tripp 2000: 196). This policy of co-optation enabled regimes to monitor and control the secular-oriented opposition parties. Eventually, they became ineffective as independent political forces and lost their constituencies. This policy was starkly illustrated by the fate of the Iraqi Communist Party—once a powerful force in Iraqi politics with links to many popular organizations. In 1972–1973, the regime "lured" the party into the open through its integration into the National Patriotic Front, only to facilitate its eradication as a mass movement by the end of the 1970s (Tripp 2000: 196–197). Meanwhile, the Syrian and Iraqi Ba'th Parties, once mass-based parties, gradually became mechanisms for the monopolization of civil society and the establishment of sectarian-based patron-client relations (Hinnebusch 2001: 65ff; Davis 2005: 149, 177–178).

## Professional Syndicates

Some of the dissent of the 1970s and early 1980s was expressed through the professional syndicates. Like many other civil-society organizations in the Arab world, professional syndicates predate independence and played a role in their respective anticolonial movements. After independence, they became integrated into regime corporatist structures and their role was limited to representing professional interests. The 1970s was a turning point for the role of many professional syndicates.

In Syria, the bar association, together with the engineers', doctors', and teachers' syndicates, played important roles in the nonviolent opposition movement of the late 1970s, opposing the Syrian invasion of Lebanon and making demands for democratic reforms. In 1978, the Syrian bar association sent a letter to the government requesting that "it respect the rule of law, abolish exceptional military courts, and release all those detained without trial," leading to discussions with Ba'th Party officials during the year (HRW 1991: 86). They spearheaded demonstrations and one-day strikes that, by March 1980, "shook the whole country except Damascus" (p. 12). However, this protest movement was uncompromisingly repressed by the regime. The dissident syndicate boards were dissolved and replaced with proregime, compliant bodies, while scores of the leaders of the original associations were imprisoned and even executed (George 2003: 103–104; HRW 1991: 13–14). Loyal branches of the Peasant Union and Trade Union Federation were transformed into militias and were "encouraged by the president to defend the revolution at all costs"—which, in practice, meant arbitrarily stopping people on the street, detaining them, and even assaulting them with impunity (HRW 1991: 11–12).

In Egypt, certain syndicates were part of the upsurge in criticism of the regime during the 1970s. In particular, the bar association became outspoken in opposing many government domestic and foreign policies and a civil-liberties committee was established to defend the rights of the scores of political prisoners held as a result of their opposition to the signing of the peace treaty with Israel. Several syndicates continued to constitute forums for nationalist/leftist opposition to the Israeli invasion of Lebanon after 1982. However, antiregime activism largely died out as a result of the initial promises of political reform offered by President Mubarak, after Sadat's death.

## Workers' Protests

The 1970s and 1980s witnessed an increased number of workers' strikes and protests, in comparison to the 1960s. Many of these were not led by the official trade unions. While workers had previously engaged in collective action in the postindependence period, the 1970s represented a dramatic upsurge in worker militancy, which often shocked regimes. For the main part, these actions occurred in response to an erosion in the real wages of workers, unmet promises by company management, and/or increasing wage disparities (Tlemcani 1986: 181–183; Pripstein Posusney 1997: ch. 3; Bellin 2002: 98ff).

In Egypt, upsurges in worker protests were recorded in 1971, 1972, 1974–1976, and 1977 (Pripstein Posusney 1997: ch. 3). In addition to economic issues, the January 1975 protest also raised political slogans against Sadat's domestic and foreign policies (MERIP Reports 1975). In January 1977, workers played a key role in the urban uprisings (or "bread riots") that broke out in response to the announcement of the withdrawal of consumer subsidies (Beinin 2001: 157). In Tunisia, several years of strikes and protests culminated in a general strike in January 1978, which became a catalyst for uprisings by the urban poor. Between 100 and 500 people were killed in clashes with security forces that day (Disney 1978). In Algeria, the number of strikes in the state sector increased fifteenfold between 1970 and 1980. In 1977 alone, strikes were recorded among the dockers of several major harbors, the bakery workers of Algiers, rubbish collectors in Algiers and Oran, and the national railway workers (Tlemcani 1986: 182–183).

The dramatic increase in workers' protests illustrated not only their perception of an erosion of their livelihoods, but also of a loss of their status within the postindependence modernization project. *Al-infitah* courted the private sector bourgeoisie and rolled back some of the economic and rhetorical benefits that workers previously enjoyed. Ordinary workers opposed what they perceived as a breakdown in the moral economy constructed in the postindependence period (Pripstein Posusney 1997). They sought to restore the benefits that they had enjoyed, rather than to reform the system. Moreover, their protests followed a well-established pattern: immediate and often violent suppression followed by conciliatory measures by the authorities to address the workers' demands. Meanwhile, the official trade union leadership ultimately remained loyal to their regimes, thereby maintaining the corporatist system established by postindependence regimes (Bellin 2002; Pripstein Posusney 1997; Tlemcani 1986).

## The Islamist Movement

While the existence of political Islamist groups predates 1967, the defeat gave a new impulse to their beliefs. It was argued by some that Israel's military victory derived from its foundations as a Jewish state and, therefore, that the establishment of an Islamic state was necessary to restore the dignity of Arab countries (Ayubi 1991: 59). The reconsideration of pan-Arabist ideology and Arab socialism among intellectuals even led to some left-wing/communist activists, such as 'Adil Hussein in Egypt, eventually joining the ranks of the political Islamists. The growth in the Islamist movement was most apparent on the campuses of universities across the region. As the largely leftist/nationalist–led student movement began to weaken, the political Islamist movement grew in strength. In the case of Egypt and Tunisia, this movement was encouraged by regimes as a countertrend to political opponents among the Nasserists and leftists (Jones 1988; Sullivan and Abed-Kotob 1999: 73). Simultaneously, Islamist movements often provided a mechanism for frustrated youth to express the social dislocation experienced as a result of *infitah* policies (Ayubi 1991: 75). Political and economic changes on the regional level also encouraged political Islamist groups. The rapid increase in oil wealth in Saudi Arabia was used to finance these groups as a means of demonstrating the kingdom's newly acquired political and cultural power within the Arab world. The Iranian revolution of 1979 appeared to provide further evidence of the political power of Islam to confront despotism. By the end of the 1970s in Egypt and the 1980s in Algeria and Tunisia, the political Islamist trend was dominant on university campuses, while nationalist/leftist forces were in retreat.

In Egypt, the Islamist groups that emerged on university campuses after the early 1970s had a more militant outlook than the long-standing

Muslim Brotherhood. In addition to preaching religious observance and adherence to Islamic codes of morality on campus, they were also active in enforcing these codes. They sought to combat the expression of what they perceived as "un-Islamic" behavior, such as the mixing of men and women, parties, films, and music. They also encouraged "Islamic" observance by providing women-only buses to university and encouraging the wearing of the veil as a means of protecting women's modesty. In Upper Egyptian universities, Islamists clashed with Christian and secular-oriented students and faculty. The groups succeeded in mobilizing support by providing much-needed social services to students (Sullivan and Abed-Kotob 1999: 73).

The Islamist movement changed from potential ally to opponent of the regime, criticizing Sadat's visit to Israel in 1977, the signing of peace accords with Israel in 1979, and the offer of asylum to the deposed Shah of Iran. In response, Sadat attempted to clamp down on the movement by withholding funds to the Islamist-dominated student unions and outlawing Islamist student groups (Sullivan and Abed-Kotob 1999: 74). Consequently, Islamist activism was largely displaced from the universities. Some Islamists channeled their activism into the voluntary sector, establishing community centers, health clinics, and charitable foundations (Rosefsky Wickham 2004: 217). Some established underground armed cells in Upper Egypt and the informal settlements that grew rapidly around Cairo in the 1970s (Ismail 2003: 82ff). Others joined the Muslim Brotherhood and spearheaded the Brotherhood's entrance into parliament, the professional syndicates, and the university faculty clubs (Rosefsky Wickham 2004: 218).

The Tunisian Islamist movement also began life in the universities—specifically, the Zitouna university—through the establishment of government-sponsored Quranic study circles. As in Egypt, the Quranic study circles were encouraged by the regime in order to marginalize the leftist/nationalist trends that were opposed to the liberalization of the Tunisian economy after 1969. In 1970, Rachid al-Ghannouchi, who would later head the al-Nahda group, joined one of these study circles "to rebuild the 'Arab–Muslim character' of Tunisian society." Like many of his generation, he blamed Western ideologies of socialism and nationalism for the defeat in 1967 and saw the regime as lacking direction (Dwyer 1991: 41–42; Jones 1988). The teaching in the study circles focused on ethical and religious matters and presented an alternative to the state-sponsored religious indoctrination (Ismail 2003: 142).

In 1974, Islamist activities began to take hold in the university through prayer rooms and mosques. In addition, the state granted permission for the publication of two journals, *al-Ma'rifa* and *al-Mujtama'*.

Like the Islamists on Egyptian campuses, the focus of activity was the prevention of "un-Islamic" behavior, and the group's journals included discussion of issues such as women's dress and loose morals in society (Ismail 2003: 142). The growth of the movement came in 1978, with the regime's brutal suppression of a general strike. Al-Ghannouchi realized that the failure of the Islamists to engage in these events had alienated the movement from a large audience (Jones 1988). In response, the cadres of the Quranic Preservation Society formed a clandestine organization, al-Jama'a al-Islamiyya fi Tunis, which began to give lectures, sponsor conferences, and create activist cells throughout Tunisia. In addition to talking about issues of "morality," the organization also began to engage in discussion of economics and politics (Ayubi 1991: 115; Jones 1988).

In 1981, in response to Bourguiba's announcement of political liberalization, the group renamed itself the Islamic Tendency Movement (ITM) and requested an official license. Simultaneously, the ITM infiltrated the official trade union, the UGTT, and the professional syndicates and built support on university campuses (Ismail 2003: 144; Jones 1988). In response, the regime began to harass the movement's members. In 1981, police arrested ITM members, including al-Ghannouchi. They were released following the bread riots of January 1984. However, the government ordered public institutions not to rehire them. In addition, public observance of Islam, such as praying during working hours and women wearing the veil in universities and workplaces, was officially banned. Al-Ghannouchi was barred from teaching, public speaking, and preaching at mosques and prevented from traveling abroad (Jones 1988). His arrest again in 1987 marked the beginning of a concerted effort by the regime to finally erase the organization (which renamed itself al-Nahda in 1989).

In both the Egyptian and Tunisian cases, the Islamist movement grew out of the disillusionment of young people with their secular-oriented regimes in the wake of the 1967 defeat. Moreover, in the context of *al-infitah* policies, entailing economic opening and foreign-policy shifts toward the West, Islamist movements reflected feelings of disorientation/alienation and a quest for an authentic national identity (Ayubi 1991: 217). Toward this end, their strategy initially focused on attempts to enforce "Islamic" behavior in formerly state-dominated spaces of university campuses, with the blessing of their respective regimes. At a later stage, these groups extended their activities beyond the universities and aimed their criticism at the corruption, despotism, and foreign policies of their regimes, thereby provoking harassment by the authorities. In this respect, Islamism became an oppositional movement, invoking a discourse of cultural nationalism based on the construction of a particular Muslim identity.

On the whole, Egyptian and Tunisian Islamists have sought to work within existing state (corporatist) structures: university campuses, the party system, the trade unions, and the professional syndicates. In Egypt, Sadat's clampdown on the movement led some Islamists to engage in armed movements. Similarly, repression of the Islamists contributed to the development of armed groups in Algeria. In distinction to the Tunisian case, Egyptian and Algerian groups that engaged in violence were able to insert themselves into the informal housing settlements and the informal economy that emerged with the retreat of the state after the 1970s (Ismail 2003: 98ff and 134ff).

### Subnational Challenges

In those countries where regimes discriminated against or refused to recognize certain ethnic/religious communities within the polity (particularly Algeria, Iraq, and Syria), contentious politics often took the form of subnational or communally based challenges to the regime. In the case of Syria and Iraq, where civil-society organizations beyond state-dominated structures became practically nonexistent, the ties of family, kin, and religion often provided the only networks able to sustain any sort of collective action—albeit underground and mostly military in nature.

In Algeria, the failure of the postindependence modernization project to meet the aspirations of the young led to an upsurge in social movements and actions beyond regime control—including protests by workers and women, in addition to the rise of the Islamist movement. Within this context, a wave of protests in 1980 broke out in response to the banning of a seminar on ancient Berber poetry at the university of Tizi Ouzou. These crystallized into the Berber Cultural Movement, which objected to the regime's refusal to recognize Berber culture and also the socioeconomic marginalization of the Berber Kabyle area (Tlemcani 1986: 201–203; see Chapter 4 for more details).

In Syria, the focus of organized opposition to the regime during the 1970s and early 1980s was the Sunni Islamist movement. The Syrian movement differed from those of North Africa in both its origins and its ideological orientation. This is largely due to the social makeup of Syria, where the regime is dominated by the Alawite minority that rules over a Sunni majority. Moreover, the Sunni community is preponderant within the class of private-sector merchants, who resented the expansion of the Ba'thist state from 1963 onward. Within this context, the

Syrian Islamists represented a Sunni-dominated movement in opposition to the Alawi-dominated regime and its economic policies (Ayubi 1991: 87). Its resistance to the regime grew throughout the 1970s and, in 1980, the brotherhood became a focus for antiregime opposition, not all of which was necessarily religiously motivated, in response to "economic troubles, growing inequality, corruption, elite embourgeoisement, and departures from traditional Arab nationalist policies" (Hinnebusch 1990: 277). The Islamists themselves issued a proclamation in 1980 in which they stated their opposition to the "sectarian fascism" of the Ba'th, their support for industrial advancement and development as a *fard kifayah* ("religious obligation"), and their declaration that "the struggle for Palestine is an Islamic cause" (Abd-Allah 1983: 136, 138, 179). After an assassination attempt on the president in June 1980, the authorities clamped down hard on the Islamist movement through the use of extrajudicial killings. The final showdown occurred in Hama in 1982, when government forces destroyed whole quarters of the town and killed thousands in order to put down an Islamist uprising. This marked the end of the Islamist movement in Syria (Hinnebusch 2001: 100–101).

Like the North African Islamists, the Syrian Islamist movement was both a resistance to the secularizing and populist tendencies of the national modernization project as well as an attempt to restore the objectives of this project within an Islamic framework. Simultaneously, it represented an attempt to capture the state away from the Alawite-dominated regime. In this regard, to the degree that the movement called for democratic reforms, this represented a means to the end of ridding Syria of the Ba'th and installing an Islamic state.

The expansion of the Iraqi nation-state from 1958 onward was met with growing opposition from among certain sections of the country. In particular, Kurdish leaders and Shi'ite clerics were resistant to the largely secular and Arab identity of the state. The Kurdish struggle for autonomy gained momentum under the leadership of Mullah Mustafa Barzani and the Kurdish Democratic Party (KDP), after his return to Iraq in 1958. Initial optimism that the new military regime would grant the Kurds autonomy soon dissipated and war between Barzani and the central government raged on throughout the 1960s. Barzani was hostile to the attempts of Baghdad to impose an Arab nationalist identity upon Iraq and politically and militarily control the Kurdish region. Moreover, tribal leaders formed a significant part of the KDP and were alarmed by the announcement of the "socialist decrees" in 1964 (Tripp 2000: 179). After the Ba'th seized power in 1968, there were renewed attempts at meeting the demands of the Kurdish national movement, and in 1970, an agreement was drawn up "in which the government seemed to commit itself to a recognition of Kurdish rights that far exceeded anything that had been conceded before" (p. 200; also Yildiz 2004: 18–19). However, Barzani did not trust the regime and further fighting broke out in 1974–1975. Iran's withdrawal of support for the Kurds led to the end of the war and the disintegration of the KDP in 1975 (Tripp 2000: 211–213). Following this, some leftist Kurdish nationalists regrouped under the leadership of Jalal Talabani (who had previously been a member of the KDP) to form the Patriotic Union of Kurdistan. The KDP soon reemerged and rivalry between the two groups was manipulated by Saddam Hussein in order to contain the Kurdish opposition to Baghdad (p. 229).

Religious Shi'a dissent emerged in the context of the expansion of the (secular-oriented) Ba'thist state. From 1969, the regime moved to bring the Shi'a religious establishment and its educational system under its control. In response, the Shi'ite religious group al-Da'wa al-Islamiyya became politically radicalized. Throughout the 1970s, there were major clashes between the regime and the religious Shi'a movement, leading to a massive clampdown on Shi'a religious leaders, scholars, and their students. This included the regime's ban on the annual ceremony commemorating the martyrdom of Husayn (Aziz 1993). However, rising state revenues enabled the regime to invest huge resources in education, health, and infrastructure that benefited the Shi'a poor and Kurdish areas, thereby helping to prevent the development of mass opposition to the regime within these communities (Baram 1991: 19–20; Tripp 2000: 214).

Neither the Kurdish movement nor the Da'wa Party were concerned with the establishment of greater political openness in Baghdad. Rather, their opposition to the Ba'th is rooted in resistance to the usurping of the authority of Kurdish leaders and Shi'ite clerics to the benefit of the state. In this respect, these opposition movements did not seek to capture the state but rather to halt nation-state-building processes that encroached on their domains of authority. This was a question of constructing social and political hierarchies that maintained the dominance of Kurdish and Shi'ite leaders at the expense of the dominance of the Ba'thist state.

### The Cultural and Intellectual Arena

Novelists, poets, artists, and writers have played a particularly important role in creating contentious politics in those countries (Iraq and

Syria) where repression rendered the emergence of sustained opposition movements almost impossible. Before 1967, the predominant orientation among artists and intellectuals in the Arab world was Marxist/nationalist. The ideas of political and social commitment, inspired by Jean-Paul Sartre, were pivotal to the new generation of writers in the 1950s and 1960s (Jabra 1996; Hafez 2000). These individuals were not only engaged with cultural production as an end in itself but as a means of political and social transformation. Some were members of political movements, while others chose to be the "rebel outsider" (Jabra 1996). However, they overwhelmingly supported the modernization projects of Arab nationalist regimes and they benefited from state expansion of education and sponsorship of intellectual and cultural production.

After 1967, many artists began to explore themes of justice, liberty, and liberation through their works as a critique of ruling regimes (Na'ana 1999: 66–67). In many cases, writers used the mechanisms of surrealism and fantasy to address what was not only a political crisis, but a psychological and intellectual crisis.[10] For example, the novel *Banquet for Seaweed* by Syrian writer Haydar Haydar, first published in 1983, represents a critique of the despotism and corruption of radical Arab nationalist regimes through the form of a love story between a young Algerian woman and an exiled Iraqi communist (Hafez 2000: 128ff).[11]

Writers and creative artists also played a role in the secular-based protest movements in 1970s Syria. In the summer of 1976, eighty-three leading authors, film makers, and other artists signed a petition protesting the war in Lebanon and the Syria-backed massacre at a Lebanese Palestinian refugee camp (HRW 1991: 9). This spirit of dissidence among this section of society was revitalized in 2000, when over a third of those that signed the "Statement of 99," calling for political reforms, were novelists, poets, cinematographers, theater producers, actors, and artists (George 2003: 33, 178–181).

In Iraq, increased oil wealth from the 1970s onward financed the Project for Rewriting History under the Ba'th regime. The aim of the project was to revise understandings of the past in order to justify Ba'thist rule. However, an examination of a selection of texts by Eric Davis finds that, in some cases, writers used readings of history to implicitly criticize the regime of Saddam Hussein (Davis 2005: 226). For example, *The Iraqi Working Class* by Kamal Mazhar Ahmad examines the development of this class only until 1934. Nevertheless, it stresses the autonomy of working-class organizations and their ability to resist the British occupation and the monarchy, thereby implicitly criticizing the loss of working-class autonomy under the Ba'th (pp. 218–219).

Novels, poems, and historical texts have constituted the "hidden transcripts" of resistance to authoritarian regimes.[12] James Scott's conceptualization of the politics of the "dominated" illustrates that individuals are never devoid of agency, even under authoritarian regimes. Moreover, these individual acts of resistance may become the seeds for collective resistance, as in the case of the Syrian "Statement of 99." However, a minimum guarantee of public freedoms over a long period is necessary for "hidden" resistance to authoritarian regimes to develop into collective resistance to authoritarianism.

### The Women's Movement

Independent women's groups emerged within the context of the ideological, political, and economic transformations experienced by Arab countries—including the post-1967 reassessment of dominant ideologies, economic liberalization and economic recession, the retreat of "state feminism," and the rise of Islamism. In addition, the specific experience of women active in the public sphere led them to establish autonomous groups to escape the sexism of leftist/nationalist milieus. Unsurprisingly, early women's groups emerged among women students.

The student movement never raised the question of women's rights and equality in its demands to the regime. This was partly a result of the regime having co-opted the demands of the preindependence women's movement. These demands included rights to political participation and to work. Simultaneously, the state monopolized women's activism through the establishment of corporatist women's unions: l'Union nationale des femmes algériennes, l'Union Nationale de la Femme Tunisienne, General Union of Syrian Women, and the General Union of Iraqi Women. These state-sponsored women's organizations have tended to limit the women's rights agenda to one of enabling women to participate in the social and economic development of their countries. This has tended to focus their activities on social development projects for their "less-educated sisters" in rural areas and working-class neighborhoods.

Moreover, various "progressive" ideological currents in the student movement failed to problematize gender within their political critiques. Both Marxist and nationalist trends assumed that once women were granted equal rights in the public sphere, this would automatically grant them social equality. This position ignored the question of gender inequalities within the private sphere and denied the existence of patriarchy. In addition, both Marxism and nationalism prioritized either the class struggle or the struggle for national self-determination over that of any other struggles, including the struggle for women's equality (Saadawi 1997: 235–241). These positions were largely internalized by women student activists.[13]

The work of Egyptian Marxist-feminist Nawal El Saadawi represented a catalyst for many women in rethinking the position of gender in political struggles (Al-Ali 2000: 76–80; Dwyer 1991: 194). El Saadawi's 1971 work, *al-mar'a wa-l-jins* ("Women and Sex"), represented the first public discussion of issues concerning female sexuality, including female genital mutilation and incest. From the end of the 1970s onward, independent women's groups began to address these previously taboo areas. These autonomous women's groups included the Tahar Haddad club in Tunisia, founded in 1978 and named after a key figure in the early-twentieth-century Tunisian nationalist movement who advocated women's emancipation; the Arab Women's Solidarity Association (AWSA) founded by Nawal El Saadawi in 1982; and the Bint al-Ard association and New Woman group founded by ex-student activists in Egypt in 1982 and 1983, respectively.

The women's organizations that emerged from the end of the 1970s distinguished themselves from state-dominated women's organizations, in addition to existing leftist/nationalist movements, by the issues that they addressed, as well as their style of working. These early groups provided an important springboard for the development of further women's activism in response to threats to women's rights. In particular, the issue of women's position within the home and its codification within personal status laws has been an important focus for independent women's activists.

Nawal El Saadawi was one of the organizers of the Committee for the Defence of Women and Family Rights to protest the amendment of the Personal Status Code in 1985, which would result in a withdrawal of many of the rights previously granted women. For the first time in the postindependence period, women activists from various civil-society organizations, including those of different political orientations, came together to form the committee (NWRC 1996: 27–28). In Algeria, several hundred women protested in 1981 against the government's attempt to introduce conservative amendments to the personal status law. Although an even more conservative law was passed in 1984, these protests, organized outside the official l'Union Nationale des Femmes Algériennes, signaled a new attempt by Algerian women to reappropriate public space for their own demands (Tlemcani 1986: 205).

It is not only that women activists began to address issues concerning women's rights in the private sphere. It is also significant that some women began to make links between women's rights and wider politics. In a 1981 paper that was adopted as AWSA philosophy, El Saadawi argues for the creation of a women's political movement as a means to struggle against patriarchy, which she views as a necessary component of the struggles against capitalist exploitation and imperialism and for democracy (El Saadawi 1997: 241–242). For El Saadawi, the formation of a women's organization was seen as a necessary means to politically empower women (Dwyer 1991: 188–189). The founding of the Tunisian Movement of Democratic Women represented not only an opportunity for raising feminist issues but also for women to engage in autonomous political action (NWRC 1996: 103). Within this framework, some women's rights activists have not only addressed issues concerning women's rights in the strictest sense, but have also been involved in activities protesting Israeli occupation and against the Gulf War. Yet, this has often taken place by "adding women" into already existing political activities in this regard, rather than offering a critique of "male-stream" approaches to these issues.

Another issue of concern to many women activists was the question of internal democracy within organizations. As activists in the student movement and other leftist/nationalist movements, women had not only experienced discrimination but other antidemocratic practices due to the hierarchical nature of these organizations. Instead, some women's groups attempted to establish nonhierarchal organizations where decisionmaking would be based on consensus. In practice, this has not been easy to achieve. In Egypt, younger members of at least one women's organization have rejected the nonhierarchical model and see the benefits of somebody being in charge and taking responsibility (Al-Ali 2000: ch. 6). In Tunisia, the women's collective magazine, *Nissa,* established in 1984, also faced problems of how to practice consensus democracy. Disagreement over the content of articles waged over several editions of the magazine and the women were never able to find a way to resolve these internal differences. These conflicts principally concerned the definition of the relationship between women's issues and politics, on the one hand, and the wider cultural milieu, on the other. The group finally dissolved following the eighth edition of the magazine in 1987 (Dwyer 1991: 201ff).

By the end of the 1980s, independent women's organizations represented a challenge to the postindependence political consensus on a number of levels. The creation of autonomous groups confronted their regime's monopoly over the agenda of women's rights, while the examination of issues pertaining to women's position within the private sphere contradicted the marginalization of these issues in nationalist and leftist circles. While the issue of internal democracy was not easily achieved, the attempt by some women's groups to find a nonhierarchical way of working differentiated them from other organizations within civil society. Finally, the organization of women around issues of international politics rendered visible women's political agency in the public sphere.

## The Human Rights Movement

The establishment of human rights groups in the Arab world has represented a significant turning point in the development of civil society. On the one hand, the emergence of an Arab human rights movement may be perceived as a reflection of the growing international concern for human rights in the postwar period. On the other hand, human rights groups in Arab countries were initially established in response to specific political events within their countries and were embedded within the political order, rather than being "outsiders." The Arab world's first independent human rights group was the Tunisian Human Rights League, formed in 1977. The founding members were a group of liberal politicians who had been ejected from the ruling Neo-Destour Party in the early 1970s and had begun to meet as the Mouvement des Démocrates Socialistes to discuss the need for liberal reforms (Waltz 1995: 134). "By working within a framework intellectually acceptable to the government [that is, a human rights framework] while exposing internal contradictions, Tunisian liberals hoped to force the political system open and reserve a place for themselves within it" (p. 135).

The Algerian human rights movement emerged in response to the repression of the Kabyle (Berber) protests at the beginning of the 1980s. Abdennour Ali Yahia, a lawyer and former government minister, became active in the defense of the Berber activists, leading to the formation of the League of Human Rights in 1985. Miloud Brahimi, part of the country's political elite, formed another human rights league in 1987, following negotiations with the authorities (Waltz 1995: 141–142). While not necessarily linked in any way to their regimes, the Arab intellectuals who created the Arab Organization for Human Rights (in 1983) were a part of the generation that had benefited from the expansion of the nation-state in the postindependence state. They came from different political persuasions but were generally pan-Arabist/leftist in ideological orientation (el-Khawaga 1997: 235; El-Sayed Said 1997: 14–15; Sha'rawi 1994: 238–239).

Many founding members of the Egyptian Organization for Human Rights (EOHR) saw the organization as a continuation and extension of their ongoing civil activism, rather than a break from it. The organization's founding charter portrays human rights as a means to restore national dignity, rather than an end in itself; as an expression of an authentic identity, rather than an embrace of universalism. "While dangers surround Egypt and the entire Arab region, the Egyptian citizen feels the weight of restrictions imposed on his actions, his freedom of expression, his attempt to emancipate his country from all forms of foreign influence and economic, political, and military dependence. Hence, methods should be enacted to reinforce justice, freedom and authenticity of the Egyptian/Arab peoples" (EOHR 1988).

Early interventions by human rights groups in areas such as the defense of striking workers[14] helped to raise the profile of the organizations and to gain wider credibility with leftist/nationalist activists, many of whom regarded human rights as either "a bourgeois construct" or as "an American ploy to further subjugate the Arab world" (Waltz 1995: 225; El-Sayed Said 1997: 14, respectively). Human rights organizations distinguished themselves from other civil-society organizations by presenting a consistent public voice against regime repression. In Egypt, the official trade union condemned the iron and steel workers' strike, while political parties appeared to be ineffective in confronting the government over the arrests of workers.[15] The assimilation of the concept of human rights by leftists and nationalists helped to give momentum to the human rights movement in its early years, by demonstrating that it was not a bourgeois/Western ploy (El-Sayed Said 1997: 14).

The general political climate also boosted the appeal of the human rights movement. The increased political dissent of the 1970s and 1980s provoked increased political repression. Consequently, people of different political/ideological persuasions were brought together in prison. The experience of prison has been formative for many civil-society activists in that it has provided an important opportunity to debate with others. In Syria, one activist thanks Hafez al-Assad for widespread repression of dissidents, as it enabled the formation of a "democratic bloc" of different political trends, including the Islamists (George 2003: 62). The experience of prison is usually accompanied by the experience of torture. The theme of torture (either witnessed or experienced personally) appears in many interviews with human rights activists in the Arab world. For them, torture symbolizes dehumanization in the name of politics and, therefore, ultimately delegitimizes politics.[16]

The story of the late Hisham Mubarak is emblematic of the shifting perceptions of activists during the political upheavals of the post-1967 period. As a student in Cairo, Hisham Mubarak belonged to one of the underground Marxist parties. During the iron and steel strikes of 1989, Hisham, along with other activists, was arrested. Like many leftists at the time, Hisham believed that human rights was a "bourgeois" notion. While held at the police station, Hisham experienced two events that would radically shape the direction of his activism. First, he met a member of the EOHR, who had also been arrested due to the organization's defense of the striking workers. Hisham entered into an in-depth discussion with the board member over the course of their confinement (El-Sayed Said 1998a: 11–13). Second, while in prison Hisham was tortured, leaving him with partial hearing in his right ear. Hisham's experience of torture in prison, together with his engagement in a debate over the concept of human rights, fueled his belief in the necessity of a framework that guarantees dignity for all human beings. After his release, he began working for the EOHR, eventually becoming the executive director in 1991. In 1993, he won the Reebok international prize for human rights and used the money to establish a legal aid center in 1994 (the Center for Human Rights Legal Aid). Tragically, in 1998 he suffered a heart attack and passed away at the young age of thirty-five, but his commitment to the struggle for human rights lives on in the posthumously named Hisham Mubarak Law Center.

## Conclusion

The 1970s and 1980s represented a crisis of the postindependence hegemonic consensus that had developed throughout the 1950s and 1960s. In response to the economic problems of ISI and the military defeat of 1967, Arab regimes embarked upon a process of economic and political adjustments that distanced them from "Arab socialism" and the radical Arab nationalism associated with Egypt's Nasser and the Ba'th Party. In response, students marched, workers went on strike, and professional syndicates sent communiqués calling for resistance to imperialism, the defeat of Israel, political reforms, and more pay. Simultaneously, an Islamist movement was born that also called for resistance against the West and Israel, in addition to a reversal of the moral and cultural decay of the Arab world.

For the most part, the movements that emerged in the post-1967 period sought to restore national dignity and social justice as elements in the successful continuation of the national modernization project. They saw these elements eroded by military defeat, *infitah* policies, peace with Israel, and alignment with the West. On the other hand, the calls for political reforms, women's rights, and human rights constituted a new departure for civil-society activists. Moreover, many of these demands were made outside regime-dominated corporatist structures—through wildcat strikes, street demonstrations, and independently organized groups. For the first time since the colonial era, Arab countries experienced the rise of contentious politics.

According to Adam Przeworski, independent organizations represent a challenge to regime stability because they represent collective projects for an alternative future (1991: 54–55). However, the upsurge in contentious politics did not destabilize Arab regimes—although it alarmed them. Opposition movements were defused through a variety of mechanisms. Most obviously, and to different degrees, regimes repressed public protests and strikes and imprisoned movement leaders, thereby preventing opposition from becoming widespread.

It should also be noted that, in most cases, the demands raised by opposition movements did not threaten the bases of authoritarianism. Calls for war, for Arab unity, the opposition to peace with Israel, and the restoration of the socioeconomic benefits that constituted the moral economy all contributed to reproducing the discourses that normalized the social and political inequalities underpinning authoritarianism, as well as legitimizing the regime's authority in political and economic life. The simultaneous calls for political reforms were implicitly framed as a means of strengthening the nation against the enemy and of resisting imperialism, as the founding charter of the EOHR illustrates. To a large degree, this served to undermine the democratic nature of these calls.

In other words, for the most part, civil-society demands failed to challenge some of the core elements of the hegemonic consensus around the project of national modernization. However, the emergence of a discourse of rights, illustrated by the establishment of human rights and women's rights groups, as well as the activities of some professional syndicates, in addition to the formative experiences of imprisonment and torture, paved the way for a shift in the ideological outlooks of several civil-society activists. The embracing of a discourse beyond the populist-nationalist ideologies of the postindependence period helped to create an environment in which demands for an end to authoritarian politics could be envisioned.

## Notes

1. Interview with the author in Cairo on 27 March 2000.
2. Interview with the author in Cairo on 7 February 2000.

3. Interview with the author in Cairo on 27 March 2000.
4. Interview with the author in Cairo on 13 August 2000.
5. Interview with the author in Cairo on 21 June 2000.
6. Interview with the author in Cairo on 7 February 2000.
7. Interviews with the author in Cairo. Various dates, 2000.
8. Interview with the author in Cairo on 8 January 2000.
9. Interviews with the author in Cairo on 8 January 2000 and 6 June 2000.
10. Charles Paul Freund, "Severed Heads and the Arab World's Foul Predicament," *The Daily Star,* 21 August 2004, http://dailystar.com.lb/article.asp?edition_id=10andcateg_id=5andarticle_id=7570, accessed 23 August 2005.
11. In Egypt, in 2000, this novel became the object of student demonstrations and parliamentary debates, after one Islamist writer deemed the work "blasphemous." See Chapter 4 for further discussion.
12. The concept of "hidden transcripts" is that of Scott (1990).
13. Interview with the author in Cairo on 6 June 2000.
14. Interview with the author in Cairo on 5 February 2000.
15. Interview with the author in Cairo on 13 August 2000.
16. Various interviews with the author, Cairo, 2000.

# 4

---

# Authoritarianism Renewed

---

IN CHAPTER 1, I ARGUED that authoritarianism is rooted in a complex of social and political relations, normalized through a consensus around the objective of national modernization. In the postindependence period, authoritarianism was built upon a moral economy sustained by import-substitution industrialization (ISI), the construction of corporatist structures, and the diffusion of populist-nationalism, in various forms. The failure of ISI, from the mid-1960s onward, together with the military defeat in 1967, brought into question the hegemony of regimes in Egypt, Syria, and Tunisia and led them to introduce *infitah* policies in response. In Algeria and Iraq, structural economic problems were not immediately apparent due to the state's ability to accrue large oil revenues. The *infitah* policies aimed at reorganizing (rather than eliminating) the public sector and encouraging private-sector involvement in the economy. These were supposed to address the problems of the ISI strategy and to engender the economic growth necessary to maintain the moral economy and, thereby, to maintain regime hegemony. Yet, these economic measures contributed toward the growth of contentious politics and the emergence of civil-society actors beyond corporatist institutions, as examined in Chapter 3.

By the latter half of the 1980s, it was clear that the economic reforms, introduced in response to the problems of ISI, were failing to deliver the economic growth necessary for development. Foreign debts grew to unmanageable levels as a result of overborrowing by Arab regimes and overlending by international banks awash with petro-dollars

(Ayubi 1995: 336–337; Henry 1997: 26ff). Inflation increased, eroding the purchasing power of those on fixed incomes (predominantly, state employees); unemployment, particularly among urban youth, was rising; and national income inequalities were widening. In addition, by the 1980s, successive years of underinvestment in urban infrastructure created severe housing shortages and crumbling health and education systems (Hinnebusch 2001: 128–131; Seddon 1986; Tlemcani 1990; Rose 1986; Richards and Waterbury 1996: 257–259; Handoussa 1991; Sadiki 1997: 136–138). A whole generation was becoming excluded from the postindependence national modernization project (Sadiki 1997: 137; Verges 1995). These problems were exacerbated by the collapse in oil prices in the mid-1980s and, in the case of Iraq, by war with Iran.

Unable to continue the state-led economy of the postindependence period, regimes were obliged out of economic necessity, as well as growing international pressure from the International Monetary Fund (IMF) and World Bank, to consider further restructuring of the economy through liberalization measures. Liberalization was preceded by austerity measures to secure short-term stabilization of the economy. These consisted of reducing government spending, increasing interest rates, and devaluing the currency (Pfeifer 1999: 23). In the case of Tunisia and Algeria, austerity measures led to an overnight rise in the cost of basic goods. This triggered widespread street protests and riots in Tunisia (1984) and Algeria (1988). These protests were spontaneous and led predominantly by unemployed youth and students, rather than trade unions, political parties, or other organized civil-society groups—although these often joined the protests and called on the government to restore subsidies (Seddon 1986; Walton and Seddon 1994). In Tunisia, violent demonstrations originating in the impoverished southwest and south of the country spread to the rest of the country within a couple of weeks (Seddon 1986: 1). In Algeria, protests began in major cities and spread throughout the provinces (Tlemcani 1990). These protests were not only a reaction to immediate price rises but also to deteriorating economic conditions and increasing social inequalities. For example, riots began in the poorest region of Tunisia with the highest unemployment rate (Seddon 1986: 9). In addition, they represented "protests against . . . corruption, nepotism, authoritarianism and regime incompetence" (Sadiki 1997: 139). Rioters targeted buildings associated with the ruling regime, such as ruling-party headquarters and the national parliament (p. 139). In Algeria, protesters chanted, "We don't want butter or pepper, we want a leader we can respect" (Roberts 1992: 435; Sadiki 1997).

Initially this popular unrest was met with repression. The armed forces were employed to quell protests. Security forces opened fire on crowds and at least 60 people were killed in Tunisia and 159 in Algeria, and many more wounded (Seddon 1986: 1; Tlemcani 1990: 14). Emergency law and curfews were declared. The protests were blamed on "foreign agitators" or politically motivated organizations, such as the communists and Islamists. Hundreds of activists, as well as ordinary protesters, were arrested in the days following the riots (Seddon 1986: 2ff; Tlemcani 1990: 14). Yet, the uprisings had the effect of forcing the governments to rescind the price increases and restore food subsidies. Within a few weeks, calm had been restored to the streets and the moral economy had been restored to state-society relations.

The protests dramatically signaled open and widespread dissatisfaction with the prevailing political, economic, and social conditions in Algeria and Tunisia. In Egypt, the regime managed to avoid a repeat of the widespread popular protests and rioting of 1977, partly as a result of the continual renewal of the emergency law since Sadat's assassination in 1981. Yet, worker militancy increased in the latter half of the 1980s in response to austerity measures (Shafei 1995). In particular, the iron and steel workers' sit-in of 1989 triggered a solidarity campaign among civil-society activists. Syria and Iraq did not witness open opposition to the regime. In Syria, peasants and workers continued to represent an important part of the populist coalition supporting the regime and, therefore, were protected from severe austerity measures, such as a reduction in subsidies on food and other basic items (Hinnebusch 2001: 112, 131–133; Longuenesse 1985). Meanwhile, the Islamist movement, as a focus for regime opposition, had been crushed during the Hama revolt of 1982 (Hinnebusch 2001: 101). In Iraq, the ongoing war with Iran played an important role in diffusing discontent by encouraging Iraqis to rally around the regime in order to defeat Iran (Khafaji 1988). Simultaneously, the policies of Saddam Hussein managed to weaken working-class organizations, culminating with a ban on public-sector trade unions in 1987 (Lawson 1992: 136–137).

In addition to austerity measures, the 1980s also witnessed moves toward greater political openness—thereby continuing a trend that had accompanied the *infitah* policies. Political liberalization was most dramatic in Algeria and Tunisia, where discontent with austerity measures had been widespread. In Algeria, the 1988 riots and the following public outcry against the incidence of torture and ill-treatment of protesters at the hands of the police gave further impetus to these reforms (Waltz 1995: 186). On 24 October 1988, President Chadli Benjedid announced free representation in elections and the creation of the post of prime minister. These reforms were endorsed by a popular referendum, paving the way for amendments to the constitution in February 1989 (Salah Tahi

1992: 399). The new constitution provided freedom of association and assembly (including the formation of associations of "political character"), freedom of expression, judicial independence, and the right to strike (Salah Tahi 1992: 399; Waltz 1995: 186). A new electoral law paved the way for local elections to take place in 1990. In addition, the regime abolished the state security court at Médéa, which had been used to try those accused of political crimes, released political detainees, and even appeared to cease the practice of torture (Waltz 1995: 186–187). These reforms stimulated new activism and paved the way for associational life to flourish (p. 187).

In Tunisia, political reforms followed the ouster of the former and ailing president, Bourguiba, by Zine El Abidine Ben Ali in 1987. Soon after the coup, he introduced limits on incommunicado pretrial detention, moved to abolish the post of general prosecutor and the state security court, and released hundreds of political prisoners (Halliday 1990: 25; Waltz 1995: 175). He promised political openness and respect for human rights. Four leaders of the LTDH (Tunisian Human Rights League) were given ministerial appointments in the new government (Waltz 1995: 175–176). He opened a dialogue with the opposition forces, including the Islamists (previously persecuted under Bourguiba) and proposed a national pact (*mithaq*) to discuss issues of national identity, the political system, economic development, and foreign policy. This was signed by six recognized political parties as well as representatives of several civil-society organizations, potentially preparing for "a more elaborate corporatist formula with a growing pluralist potential" (Ayubi 1995: 418–419). Multiparty parliamentary elections were held in April 1989.

In the case of Egypt, political liberalization also accompanied the coming to power in 1981 of a new president—Hosni Mubarak. He reliberalized the political sphere, releasing those imprisoned in the last month of Sadat's life and opening up a dialogue with them. Even the Muslim Brotherhood was tolerated (although not legalized) and members were allowed to stand for elections in 1984 on the Wafd Party list. Muslim Brotherhood members and sympathizers were also allowed to stand in elections for the boards of the various professional syndicates, and managed to win the majority of seats in the doctors' syndicate. In general, professional syndicates became an arena of relatively free speech and assembly (Kienle 2001: 38ff). Another arena in which civil society and the political opposition could make their voices heard was through the supreme constitutional court. Throughout the 1980s, the rulings of this court challenged the domination of the regime over political and civil life (Mustafa 2003). A constitutional challenge to the elections on the basis that they had excluded independent candidates resulted in the dissolution of the national assembly, an amendment to the electoral law, and the holding of elections in 1987. A similar fate befell that assembly, leading to another amendment that removed all restrictions on independent candidates and early elections in 1990 (Baaklini, Denoeux, and Springborg 1999: 230).

Even in Syria and Iraq, there were signs of political decompression. In Syria, parliamentary elections took place in May 1990. Although not multiparty elections, one-third of the seats were reserved for independent candidates who were freely elected (Perthes 1992: 15–16). Criticism of ministers was allowed in the state-run press, state control over personal travel was relaxed, and religious and some political prisoners were released (Hinnebush 2001: 108). In Iraq, moves toward greater political openness followed the end of the war with Iran (Farouk-Sluglett and Sluglett 1990: 20–21). In 1988, Saddam Hussein announced a general pardon to political prisoners and promised a multiparty system (Karsh and Rautsi 1991: 197). A special committee was established to draft a working paper on a new constitution (p. 197). Non-Ba'thists were allowed to stand for elections to the National Assembly in April 1989 and half the elected candidates were described as "independent." There were also signs of greater room for freedom of expression. A "Freedom Wall" was established at the University of Baghdad for students to air their grievances and the state media began to print criticisms of certain government ministers (Karsh and Rautsi 1991: 198; Tripp 2000: 250).

Political reforms were introduced not as an end in themselves but rather as a means to maintain regimes' hegemony in the face of economic downturn. Increased opportunities for political participation and expression helped to spread the responsibility for the necessary economic reforms to constituencies beyond the regime and its traditional coalition of workers and peasants, who stood to lose the most as a result of economic liberalization (Kramer 1992: 24). Neoliberal economic reforms necessitated cuts in state expenditure, thereby threatening the welfare gains made by these groups in the postindependence period. Therefore, these traditional allies of the regime represented the central opponents of economic liberalization. The Syrian elections of 1990 co-opted into parliament various independent businessmen and others outside the traditional "progressive front," thereby expanding the parliament beyond the traditional support base of the Ba'th Party (Perthes 1992). Similarly, the relaxation of bureaucratic controls, economic liberalization, and promises of multiparty democracy represented efforts by the Iraqi regime to build up new constituencies among the middle classes and the military and to deflect criticisms of the economic situation away from the political leadership (Farouk-Sluglett and Sluglett 1990: 22–23; Tripp 2000: 250). In Egypt, ruling-party endorsement of candidates in elections enabled the regime to increase the number of businesspersons into the national assembly (Thabit 1996: 123). With regard to the political reforms pursued by the Ben Ali regime, Emma Murphy argues, "[These] can be interpreted as an effort to relieve the political pressures on the state, to revive confidence in the inclusiveness of the political system and to revitalize the institutional basis of government" (1999: 223).

Political liberalization or decompression appeared to respond to the growth in civil-society demands for greater regime accountability and more freedom of dissent. This occurred at a time when regimes were no longer able to afford to maintain those levels of expenditure necessary to meet the terms of the moral economy. Political liberalization represented a means of compensating citizens for austerity measures. In effect, people were offered political and civil rights in return for the withdrawal of socioeconomic rights.

The holding of elections, the lifting of restrictions on associations, and the relaxation of censorship provided new avenues of dissent and official channels for government opponents to "let off steam," rather than challenge regime authority. By channeling this dissent through state-controlled structures (such as parliaments and the state-owned press), regimes hoped to co-opt and tame it. Nowhere did elections result in a handover of power from one government to another, except for Algeria, where electoral victory for the Islamists resulted in a military coup. Electoral systems were designed to favor the ruling party (Baaklini, Denoeux, and Springborg 1999: 229; Salah Tahi 1992: 401).[1] For example, in Tunisia, not a single opposition candidate won a seat in the 1989 elections, despite the Islamists (running as independents) winning 17 percent of the vote (Halliday 1990). Parliaments continued to be subordinated to the executive and to lack powers to hold it accountable (Tlemcani 1990: 15; Baaklini, Denoeux, and Springborg 1999: 228–229). As Volker Perthes argues with regard to Syria, "parliamentary reform can be understood as a corporatist strategy" (1992: 18).

In other words, the political liberalization of the 1980s aimed to transform some of the structures of corporatism—principally, the one-party system—in order to co-opt the political opposition and, thereby, to neutralize it. This transformation was not aimed at relinquishing the power of the ruling regime but maintaining it. However, by the early 1990s, it became clear that these early liberalization measures did not signal a gradual move toward democratization. Indeed, a focus on the holding of multiparty elections detracted the attention of observers away from measures undertaken to strengthen executive control, rather than to reduce it. As civil-society activity continued to grow beyond corporatist arrangements—including Islamist groups, human rights and women's rights organizations, wildcat labor strikes, and privately owned satellite channels—it became clear to regimes that it was impossible to co-opt all civil-society activity. Indeed, the experience of Algeria, where the Front Islamique du Salut (FIS) was poised to win the parliamentary elections at the end of 1991, perhaps signaled to regimes across the region that political liberalization could threaten regimes' hegemony.

Simultaneously, austerity measures to stabilize the economy gave way to structural adjustment measures that sought to dismantle the public sector and liberalize trade, among other objectives, in order to address the structural problems facing these economies (Pfeifer 1999). Following a number of false starts during the late 1980s, the Egyptian government finally embarked upon an IMF/World Bank–sponsored economic liberalization program in 1991. Far-reaching debt forgiveness by Western creditors, in return for Egypt's participation in the 1991 Gulf War, helped to soften the blow of accepting a structural adjustment program for the Egyptian government (Richards and Waterbury 1996: 227). In the same year, a law was passed to enable the restructuring of public enterprises, for example, by granting public enterprises autonomy from the state bureaucracy and putting them on an equal footing with private-sector companies (Ayubi 1995: 349). A gradual program of privatization was implemented throughout the 1990s. As a result of restructuring and privatization, workers have experienced threats to their income, increased job insecurity, and even, in some cases, job losses (Pratt 1998).

In Tunisia, the government adopted a structural adjustment program in 1986 and privatization began in 1987. Simultaneously, legislation was enacted to restructure public enterprises. The first public-sector companies to be privatized were hotels and commercial establishments. Following this, privatization was implemented for the larger industrial and transportation companies (Belev 2000: 21). Meanwhile, the ouster of Chadli Benjedid and the outbreak of civil war in Algeria in 1992 interrupted economic liberalization plans. However, following a drop in oil prices in 1994, the government was obliged to accept another IMF structural adjustment program. As part of this program, public-sector enterprises were restructured, leading to their eventual privatization or liquidation (Henry and Springborg 2001: 118). As a result, many workers lost their jobs, pushing up unemployment (p. 119).

Syria and Iraq (before the fall of the Ba'th) are exceptions to the regional trend toward economic liberalization. Syria has both refused to entertain an IMF-style structural adjustment program or to introduce restructuring of the public sector. The reasons for this may be twofold. On the one hand, the regime has not wanted to antagonize the trade union leadership, which is part of the ruling coalition and represents a significant regime constituency (Lawson 1992: 140). On the other hand, privatization could boost the economic prominence of the Sunni/commercial bourgeoisie, from whose ranks came the militant Islamist opposition to the regime (Ayubi 1995: 362). Instead, the regime has chosen to reduce restrictions on the private sector and to encourage private investment, echoing the *infitah* policies of the 1970s. Like these policies, such measures have not succeeded in addressing economic stagnation (Hinnebusch 2001: 135). In Iraq, during the war with Iran, the regime embarked upon privatization of agricultural enterprises and a number of factories for food processing, construction materials, and textiles, among others. However, the state continued to dominate the economy through its control over oil revenues and its investment in larger industries, such as iron and steel, engineering, and petrochemicals (Aziz Chaudhry 1991: 15). The regime hoped that Arab and foreign countries would reschedule the severe debts amassed by Iraq during the war. When this was not the case, the regime invaded Kuwait in the summer of 1990 (Ayubi 1995: 367). The imposition of sanctions actually constituted an opportunity for the regime to maintain its authority. The regime was able to blame the severe economic deterioration on the UN sanctions, supported by the United States and United Kingdom. Meanwhile, it could manipulate the food-rationing system to strengthen patron-client networks, which helped to underpin the regime's authority (Tripp 2000: 269).

While austerity measures initially coincided with political openings, the introduction of structural adjustment programs and/or ongoing economic deterioration ushered in a period of political "deliberalization," as Eberhard Kienle refers to Egypt in the 1990s (2001). Economic liberalization measures, deemed necessary to address deep structural problems within the economy, threatened an important basis of regime authority. In the postindependence period, the public sector served as a significant resource for the regime's distribution of welfare benefits to citizens and maintenance of corporatist structures, such as the trade unions. Deprived of the material means to meet the terms of the postindependence moral economy and to maintain the official structures that would enable regimes to co-opt civil-society activism, regimes reversed the political liberalization process as a means of maintaining their authority. This not only took the form of resorting to previous ways of containing civil-society activism. In addition, new measures were introduced in the form of new laws, increased use of extrajudicial security measures, and reorganization of security services.

## The Reorganization of Authoritarianism

Optimism about the political reform measures taken in the 1980s was reflected in a Human Rights Watch (HRW) observation: "It would be hard to say that 1990 had been a bad year for human rights in the Middle East and North Africa. Indeed, there were a number of positive developments."[2] However, by 1993, HRW claimed, "After a period of several years in which acknowledgment of human rights as an issue with which local rulers had to contend, whatever their political system, appeared to be gaining greater acceptance, in 1993 this trend went into reverse."[3] The reversal in the trend toward a greater respect for human rights suggested a similar reversal in the political liberalization process initiated in many Arab countries. It was not only that the 1990s seemed to usher in a continuation of the authoritarian politics of previous decades; in addition, new measures were introduced to clamp down on a more assertive civil society.

### Measures Against Civil-Society Actors
Islamist groups were the first to experience regime measures to contain civil-society activism. From the end of the 1980s onward, regimes began to clamp down on Islamist activism.[4] In Tunisia, the regime refused to recognize al-Nahda in 1988, and again in 1989, despite the fact that al-Nahda leaders signed the national pact. Following this, the regime embarked upon a systematic harassment of the group, leading to their virtual disappearance from Tunisia in the 1990s (Garon 2003: 31–33). In Egypt, the success of the Muslim Brotherhood in parliamentary and professional syndicate elections, together with the targeted assassinations of state officials and foreign tourists by al-Jama'a al-Islamiyya and al-Jihad, led the regime to initiate a huge crackdown on all Islamist groups (nonviolent and violent) from the early 1990s (Abdalla 1993). The expected victory of the FIS in the 1992 elections triggered a military coup bringing the multiparty experiment to a halt and imposing a ban on the Islamist party. This repression helped to fuel violent opposition to the regime. The banning of the FIS paved the way for the emergence of the Groupe islamique armé (GIA), which waged a bloody war

against the regime, targeting civilians and foreigners along the way. In Egypt, the widespread crackdown on all Islamists did little to stem the violence waged by al-Jama'a al-Islamiya and al-Jihad throughout the 1990s.

In their attack on Islamists, regimes resorted to increased use of emergency measures, such as indefinite detention, during which individuals faced a greater likelihood of being tortured.[5] In addition, extrajudicial measures against suspected Islamists were used. In Algeria, more than a thousand men and women were forcibly "disappeared" by government forces.[6] Egyptian security forces engaged in "hostage-taking" of family members of suspected Islamists in order to force fugitives to surrender to authorities. Elderly parents, young siblings, male and female, were intimidated. Female family members were often threatened with rape in order to pressure fugitives into giving themselves up for the sake of protecting their "family's honor."[7]

It was not only those suspected of engaging in violence who were targeted by the authorities. Exceptional and even extralegal measures were also used against nonviolent Islamist groups. Members of al-Nahda were tried before a military court based on disputed evidence.[8] In Egypt, Muslim Brothers were put on trial before military courts in 1995 and 2000, accused of membership in an illegal organization. These arrests occurred prior to parliamentary elections in which some of those detained had intended to stand as candidates.[9]

Meanwhile, regimes harassed lawyers representing jailed Islamists and journalists and human rights activists who reported on regime measures utilized against Islamists. In Tunisia, the government dismissed claims by the Tunisian League for Human Rights that Islamists had been denied basic human rights in detention and, in early 1992, called in the league's president for questioning (Waltz 1995: 183). In Egypt, journalists from the newspaper *al-Sha'b,* mouthpiece of the Islamist-leaning Labor Party, were detained by state security prosecutors in 1993, and interrogated about their writings on al-Jama'a al-Islamiyya.[10] Abdel Harith Madani, lawyer and legal adviser to members of al-Jama'a al-Islamiya, died in police custody in April 1994, the day after being detained. Authorities resisted calls for an independent autopsy to ascertain the cause of death, leading many to suspect that he died due to torture.[11] Meanwhile, human rights organizations were attacked by the government for reporting abuses committed in the government's war against the Islamists and "tarnishing Egypt's reputation abroad."[12] In 1996, the Algerian authorities attempted to ban an opposition weekly devoted to human rights on the grounds that it constituted an apology for terrorism. In 1997, human rights lawyer Rachid Mesli was sentenced to three years in prison after an unfair trial on charges of aiding "terrorist" groups.[13]

What began as a systematic attempt to repress the Islamist movement, rapidly led to the regimes' introduction of new measures to restrain civil-society activity, often using the threat of Islamist violence as a justification. Throughout the 1990s, a number of laws and legal amendments were introduced in Egypt that aimed at reducing the margins of freedom for civil society (Kienle 2001). The first casualty was the professional syndicates, where Muslim Brotherhood members had made substantial gains in elections to syndicate boards. In 1993, the government rushed through a law stipulating that elections were only valid where a minimum of half of a syndicate's membership voted. If a quorum of one-third was not achieved by the third attempt, the syndicate fell into administrative control by the judiciary. The law clearly aimed at preventing Islamist candidates being elected by well-organized minorities (Mustafa 1995: 114). Although the law did not result in any syndicates falling under judicial control, it clearly represented a threat to the independence of the syndicates and was vigorously opposed by many of their members. Next, the government turned its attention to the trade unions. In 1995, the government amended the trade union law to permit retired workers and those appointed to managerial positions to continue to serve on trade union boards. As a result, following the 1996 trade union elections, there was no turnover in the membership of the board of the General Federation and only a 40 percent change in the members of the boards of the national unions, thereby preventing the election of trade unionists opposing the government's privatization program ('Abbas, Barakat, and Rif'at 1997: 4; *Al-Wafd* 1996). In 1999, the government attempted to amend the law on civic associations in order to close legal loopholes that were enabling nongovernmental organizations (NGOs), particularly human rights organizations, to operate beyond the control of the Ministry of Social Affairs. The new law criminalized groups that carried out the activities of an association without permission from the authorities. By subjecting all NGOs to the associations law, this placed restrictions on activities and sources of funding of the various types of human rights organizations that had emerged from the 1980s onward.[14]

In Tunisia, the regime also attempted to control civil-society activity by amending the associations law in 1992. The Tunisian League for Human Rights (LDHT) became classified as a "general association," thereby forbidding board members of associations from occupying leadership positions in political parties and creating a forcible right for individuals to join associations. The former provision had the effect of disrupting the LDHT's leadership, which was made up of a balance of different political trends that had agreed to cooperate for the aim of promoting human rights. The second provision opened up the league to infiltration by proregime individuals. As a result, the league suspended activities in 1992 and then resumed with a new (less critical) board in 1993, following a judicial ruling in its favor.[15] In 2000, following the election of a new, outspoken leader, the authorities closed the league's offices and a court annulled the elections—thereby obliging the league to organize new elections.[16] As of 2004, the LDHT remained in legal limbo, while appealing the court decision, and in a financially precarious position, as the regime had prevented it from receiving European Union funding. Another human rights organization, the National Council for Liberties in Tunisia (CNLT), founded in 1998, was also refused permission to operate.

In addition to the introduction of new legislation, the Ben 'Ali regime opted for the systematic harassment of activists—ranging from administrative measures against organizations to imprisonment of individuals, in addition to the use of extralegal tactics.[17] The Tunisian human rights community, as a source of open dissent against the regime's authoritarian tactics, constituted a particular target of regime intimidation. Harassment of human rights activists coincided with the LDHT's criticism of regime abuses against al-Nahda members at the beginning of the 1990s. In 1992, the government used the state-controlled media through which to launch a propaganda war against the league, accusing its leadership of being agents of foreign powers and of excluding other Tunisians from joining the organization.[18]

In addition to targeting human rights organizations, the Tunisian regime conducted a systematic campaign to intimidate individual human rights activists, lawyers, journalists, members of political parties, and anyone else who engaged in activities that challenged the regime's political monopoly. Tactics of intimidation have included cutting telephone lines, interception of mail and faxes, police surveillance, threats against and harassment of individuals and their family members, passport confiscation, and dismissal from their jobs.[19] In addition, several individuals have been arrested. Moncef Marzouki, former president of the LDHT and member of the CNLT, was first arrested in 1994 for the "propagation of false news" (that is, publication of human rights abuses) and served four months. On his release, he was subject to continual harassment by the authorities. In 1999, he was arrested again on charges of belonging to an illegal group (that is, the CNLT) and in 2000 was handed down a one-year suspended sentence. In 1996, human rights activist Khemaïs Chammari was imprisoned for five years for defending Mohamed Muada, president of a legal opposition party, who was facing trumped-up charges of treason.[20] He was released in 1998, just as former LDHT vice-president Khemaïs Ksila was imprisoned for three years.[21] The types of intimidation employed against peaceful civil-society activists is not unique to Tunisia—and can be observed in varying degrees in other Arab countries. However, in light of Tunisia's earlier moves toward political liberalization, its relatively successful economy, and its reputation as a "moderate" country, the level of regime abuses against civil and political freedoms is alarming and has been the subject of attention by the international human rights community, particularly since 2001.

In Algeria, the civil war that raged throughout the 1990s represented a huge obstacle to sustained civil-society activism. Members of various civil-society groups were threatened with violence and even became deliberate targets of violence. This intimidation was not only perpetrated by the Islamists but also by forces associated with the state. A number of individuals associated with previously outspoken civil-society groups were assassinated. The victims included the president of the Algerian League for Human Rights (Youcef Fethallah), several leaders of the Berber Cultural Movement (Mahfoud Boucebci, Tahar Djaout, and Lounes Matoub), and a prominent feminist (Nabila Djahnine). Despite the widespread terror, many brave individuals participated in efforts to bring an end to the war and to call for justice on behalf of the victims of violence.[22]

## Measures Against the Press

The media and journalists represented another target of regimes from the 1990s onward. Whereas the relaxation of controls on press reporting was a hallmark of the liberalization period, new attempts to control the flow of information in the public sphere became frequent in the 1990s. The appearance of independent newspapers, satellite television, and Internet sites on Arab issues all presented new challenges to regimes. In 1998, the Freedoms Committee of the Arab Journalists Union, meeting for two days in Beirut in July, noted "the deteriorating conditions in some Arab countries regarding freedom of expression as well as political and legislative restrictions imposed on the press." The committee cited, in particular, "tightening sanctions on journalists, including jail sentences, increased financial penalties, and mounting manifestations of intellectual terrorism by various forces and trends."[23]

New regulations were introduced to control press freedom by limiting the conditions under which a new newspaper could be established
and by criminalizing offenses such as defamation and the publication of
"falsehoods." In Egypt, a 1995 law regulating the press resulted in the
interrogation of almost a hundred journalists, editors, and directors of
publications, of which thirty-three were prosecuted within the first year
(Kienle 2001: 98ff). The severity of the law resulted in widespread
opposition from among journalists and led to an amendment in 1996.
Despite a reduction in some of the harshest penalties and the number of
offenses constituting crimes, several journalists received prison sentences for their criticism of regime officials.

In Algeria, throughout most of the 1990s, the civil war provided a
pretext for repressing freedom of the press. The press was pressured to
rely almost exclusively on official dispatches to cover news about the
internal security situation.[24] Newspapers were suspended and journalists
imprisoned for reporting independently on the violence and alleged
abuses by security services. In addition, dozens of journalists became
targets of assassination in the struggle between the regime and the
Islamists. Following the end of the war, new obstacles to freedom of
expression were introduced with the 2001 amendment to the penal code.
This has led to the arrest and imprisonment of several outspoken journalists on charges of defamation. The government has also used the
state printing press to control newspapers—by selectively calling in
debts from private newspapers, thereby threatening them with closure
for financial reasons.[25] Despite attempts across the Arab region to control the freedom of expression of the domestic media, increasing numbers of people have access to alternative news sources—predominantly,
satellite television news channels such al-Jazeera. Internet usage is still
relatively low—nevertheless, certain websites are blocked by the Tunisian
and Syrian governments.

## The Manipulation of Parliamentary Elections

The 1990s demonstrated the limits of parliamentary elections in Arab
countries. Rather than providing an avenue for democratic participation,
elections have served as a means to legitimize incumbent regimes and co-
opt the political opposition (Pripstein Posusney 1998). A variety of legal
and extralegal tactics have been used by regimes to hold onto sizable
majorities within their parliaments. The design of the electoral system
(usually by a government committee, in consultation with a ruling party–
dominated parliament) has, unsurprisingly, favored the regime party, helping them to win the overwhelming majority of seats in parliament in all

elections held in Arab countries (Pripstein Posusney 1998). Apart from legal arrangements, ruling-party candidates have benefited from their association with the regime, which controls substantial state resources. State-owned media dedicates relatively little time to opposition candidates, while reporting extensively on the activities of the regime (which is from the ruling party). Ruling-party candidates are situated within patronage networks that give them access to state-owned resources for their campaigns (such as using public-sector vehicles to transport propaganda material) (Singerman 1995: 225; Kienle 2001: 55–56). Finally, the stuffing of ballot boxes, the doctoring of electoral registers to allow the dead to vote, the forging of the final results, the use of thugs to intimidate opposition candidates and their supporters, and other electoral irregularities all contribute to the overwhelming success of the regime party (CHRLA 1995; EOHR 1996; Kienle 2001: 51ff). The lack of separation between the ruling party, the regime, and the state makes it virtually impossible for elections to lead to a peaceful change in power.

Regime efforts to contain the growth of an assertive civil society, which emerged during the 1970s and 1980s, led to the introduction of new measures. Until the 1970s, authoritarian rule relied heavily upon the existence of a state-controlled economy as a means of co-opting and channeling dissent within the confines of corporatist structures. The implementation of economic reforms associated with structural adjustment threatened the material basis of corporatist structures. Regimes have increasingly utilized coercive mechanisms, including new legislation, intimidation, and violence, in an attempt to strengthen corporatist structures such as parliaments, trade unions, and professional syndicates, and eliminate all opposition forces beyond these structures. In the process, they have reversed the political liberalization/decompression process initiated during the 1980s.

Yet, as I argued in Chapter 1, it is both costly and difficult to maintain regime authority based on coercion alone. The construction of consent is also necessary to the functioning of authoritarianism. During the early postindependence period, consent was rooted in the widespread support for the goals of national modernization. As discussed in Chapter 3, these goals were expressed in terms of populist-nationalism, including strident anti-imperialism and an end to traditional structures of authority. While national modernization was seen as essential to nation-state building, it also enabled the construction of an authoritarian system, while radical nationalism helped to disguise the social and political inequalities engendered, thereby normalizing authoritarianism. The

belief in national modernization was, for the most part, upheld throughout the 1970s, even as political dissent was expressed by civil-society
activists.

The restructuring of the postindependence political economy and
the strengthening of corporatist structures during the 1990s was also
accompanied by a restructuring of the ideological basis for regime
hegemony. The transition from a state-dominated toward a liberalized
economy not only brought into question the material basis of authoritarian rule but also its ideological basis, leading, in particular to contestations over the nature of national identity and culture. As the margins of
political criticism narrowed, "culture" came to constitute a sphere in which
civil-society actors, for the most part, were able to express opposition
and criticism. This was aided by increased access to mass communication technologies, such as audio and video cassettes—particularly used
by political Islamists (Eickelman and Piscatori 2004: 125ff). Meanwhile, regimes have attempted, with varying degrees of success, to
manipulate public culture as a means of normalizing the new social and
political hierarchies resulting from economic liberalization and political
deliberalization, as well as co-opting new constituencies of support. In
most cases, this has served to intensify the contestation among civil-
society actors and between civil-society actors and the regime over public culture, with various implications for regimes and the authoritarian
systems that they head.

## Public Culture and the Reconfiguring of Consent

The major protagonists in the contestations over public culture have not
only been political Islamists on one side and regimes on the other. "Secularists" within civil society have also been part of the struggle, as well
as non-Muslim minorities such as the Copts in Egypt. In addition, culture clashes have also pitted different institutions of the state against
one another. Here, we examine three case studies of contestation over
culture and identity. While the sphere of culture has operated as a vehi-
cle for opposition to regimes, simultaneously regime manipulation of
culture has also contributed to reproducing consent for authoritarian
rule by disguising the new political and social hierarchies engendered
by economic liberalization.

### Religion and Public Culture in Egypt

In the 1980s, the Egyptian regime attempted to undermine appeal for
the Islamists by introducing doses of Islam into public life (education,

TV, and radio programs) (Ismail 2003). Simultaneously, the state-dominated national religious institution, Al-Azhar,[26] expanded its influence. While this center of Islamic learning had previously always been invited to give *fatwas* on state laws (generally to legitimize them), it began to show some independence in its pronouncements and a greater assertiveness, demonstrating its desire to assert its autonomy from the government. Simultaneously, the emergence of a radical Islamist movement directly challenged Al-Azhar's moral and religious authority, with certain Islamists claiming that Al-Azhar did not have a monopoly over the interpretation of Islam (Ayubi 1991: 67). From the 1980s onward, Al-Azhar sheikhs benefited from the government's desire to suppress the Islamists. They were increasingly represented on legislative committees, to ensure the compatibility of state policies with *shari'a* (Islamic law) (Zaki 1995: 124–125). A key turning point occurred in 1994, when Al-Azhar sought an administrative court opinion regarding the extent of its legal authority to censor material for publication and broadcast. The court ruled that Al-Azhar could express an opinion on all matters relating to Islam (p. 125). Although this role was not codified, it gave moral weight to Al-Azhar's efforts to impose its interpretations of religion on society by insisting that all institutions with a role in research, publishing, and media, including the Ministry of Culture, "submit their products to it as the only body qualified to deliver authorizations" (Kodmani 2005: 17). In 1992, at the Cairo Book Fair—probably the most important annual event for intellectual life in Egypt—Al-Azhar was responsible for seizing copies of books deemed in violation of Islamic principles from bookstands, in breach of the law (Kienle 2001: 110).[27]

While Al-Azhar has managed to increase its authority in public life, this did not have the effect of reducing support for the Islamists or in reducing their militancy. In 1992, Egyptian human rights activist and known defender of secular values, Farag Foda, was assassinated, and in 1994 there was an attempted murder on Nobel laureate novelist the late Naguib Mahfouz. In 1996, after several years of appeals and counter-appeals, Nasr Hamid Abu Zayd, author of *A Critique of Religious Discourse,* was ordered by a court ruling to divorce his wife, on the grounds that a Muslim woman is forbidden wedlock with an apostate—forcing the couple into exile (Bakr, Colla, and Abu Zayd 1993). These events illustrated the extent to which the domain of public culture had become the object of contestation between various religious trends and secularists.

As Al-Azhar expanded its powers, the Ministry of Culture engaged in a renewal of Nasserist cultural institutions.[28] The Supreme Council for Culture was resurrected, and high-profile cultural figures were appointed to managerial positions within the ministry.[29] The ministry established a series of cheap reprints of works by contemporary Arab writers from countries other than Egypt, titled *Afaq al-Kitabah* ("Horizons of Writing") and edited by the Egyptian novelist Ibrahim Aslan. There was also a sister series devoted to the work of Egyptian writers, *Aswat Adabiyyah* ("Literary Voices"), edited by the eminent Egyptian novelist and short-story writer Mohammed Al Bisati.[30] The incorporation of high-profile cultural figures, all of whom were secular, into the state cultural organizations gave the appearance of the state fighting back against the Islamization of public culture, in response to demands by secular intellectuals for the government to assert its authority against Al-Azhar's influence on cultural life.

The Ministry of Culture became the object of attacks by those seeking to uphold Islamic morals. The most violent struggle occurred in 2000, when *al-Sha'b* (newspaper of the Islamist-oriented Labor Party) denounced the ministry's publication of Syrian novelist Haydar Haydar's *A Banquet for Seaweed.* The newspaper deemed the novel to be blasphemous and called on Muslims to defend their religion against this cultural onslaught. In response, hundreds of students at Al-Azhar university protested against the publication of the novel and clashed with state riot police. Following this, the minister of culture, Farouk Hosni, withdrew the "blasphemous" novel from the market and appointed a committee of "experts" to investigate the charges against it. The experts acquitted the novel and its author, but the minister, under pressure from parliament, forwarded the novel to the head of Al-Azhar, Sheikh Muhammad Tantawi. He concluded that the novel should have been referred to Al-Azhar in the first place and that it contained "words and sentences that despise and insult all holy beliefs, including God himself, Prophet Mohammad, Doomsday and other religious values."[31] The State Security Department called in the editor and managing editor of *Afaq al-Kitabah*—the series that had published *A Banquet for Seaweed*—and formally charged them with reprinting a book that "ridicules religion, threatens social peace and incites strife."[32] More than 350 secular artists, journalists, and other supporters submitted a request to the prosecutor-general to be included as defendants in the case as "accessories" to the publication of the novel. Commenting on the conflicts that had arisen over the novel, the minister of culture commented, "Personally, had I found the novel to be offensive . . . , as a Muslim who wants to protect his religion, I would have stopped its publication."[33] However, he also argued that freedom of creativity and expression were "constrained by the value system prevailing in the social context in which this freedom is exercised" and that those employed by the ministry "are constrained by certain red lines, the most important of which is that the text does not include indecent language and does not deride religion."[34] Finally, the government's Committee for Parties' Affairs suspended the Labor Party and closed its newspaper, *al-Sha'b,* after orchestrating a conflict within the party over the leadership contest.[35] It was understood that the party was being punished for inciting the protests against the novel and, implicitly, challenging the authority of the government in an election year.

Yet, this did not bring an end to the "culture clashes." Soon after the *Banquet for Seaweed* debacle, a Muslim Brother member of parliament, Gamal Hishmet, called the minister of culture to account for the ministry's publication of three novels that he considered "pornographic." This time, the episode played out differently. Farouk Hosni claimed "the ministry does not publish porn" and that, following the *Banquet for Seaweed* debacle, employees of the General Organization of Cultural Palaces had been instructed "not to let controversial material reach the print works."[36] Mohammed Al Bisati, the editor of *Aswat Adabiyyah,* the series responsible for the publication of the three novels, Girgis Shukri, his managing editor, and Ali Abu Shadi, head of the General Organization of Cultural Palaces, were all sacked and the book was banned.[37] For Abu Shadi, the dismissals represented a clear defeat for secular intellectuals: "The government has surrendered to the Islamists and my dismissal will strengthen the enemies of culture."[38] On the other hand, for Heshmat, this represented only the first victory in a longer battle, commenting that "the three novels were not the first offence . . . [we want] a real change in the policy of the Ministry of Culture."[39] In response to the dismissals, six editors of ministry publications resigned, while a significant number of intellectuals threatened to boycott the Cairo Book Fair.[40] As one observer noted, there was at least "one paradox" to the drama.

> The writers staging the boycott have themselves frequently been associated with the ministry. This is partly explained by the fact that the General Organization of Cultural Palaces . . . is Nasserist in origin and remains for many not only a historical triumph of the left but an instance of culture for the people. Regardless of their faults, and of the forms or names under which they operate, the cultural palaces have, until, it seems, very recently, constituted the connection between intellectuals and the ministry.[41]

The defeat of the leftist/Nasserist camp of intellectuals in this instance not only weakened their link with the state. It also demonstrated that they were no longer able to claim to speak for the people, in the name of the "popular" cultural palaces. This mantle had passed to the Muslim Brotherhood, whose campaign against secular cultural productions was waged in the name of protecting the morals and values of "the people."

The challenges to the Ministry of Culture represent one in a series of struggles over the conceptualization of public culture in the 1990s (Ismail 2003: 58ff). In "allowing" the Islamists to gradually appropriate public culture, the regime has, to some extent, been able to co-opt the Islamist challenge (Ismail 2003: 80–81), as the banning of the three novels would indicate. Simultaneously, the dismissal of secular intellectuals from state organizations illustrates the regime's distancing from the leftist/secular populism associated with Nasserism and its appropriation of the Islamist populism of the Muslim Brotherhood. However, this conflict between different "cultural trends" does not only concern members of civil society. In the contestations over public culture, Al-Azhar has clearly asserted its authority over the realm of cultural production within society, as well as over certain institutions within the state—namely the Ministry of Culture. The Muslim Brotherhood's challenge to the regime in the sphere of culture has enabled one part of the state, Al-Azhar, to expand its authority at the expense of another part of the state and, in the process, has absorbed some of the Islamist challenge to the regime. Consequently, the contestation over culture has enabled the regime to reproduce its authority by adjusting the "cultural" discourse promoted.

## The Use of Islam and Tribalism in Iraq

State-sponsored culture in Iraq, until the end of the 1970s, promoted a vision of Iraqi national culture as secular and inclusive of all sectors of society (Davis 2005: 183). However, this changed in the 1980s. The war with Iran, the deteriorating economic situation, and the appearance of corruption in government created an impetus for a shift in the discourses of public culture. The secular, national identity of the 1970s was replaced by the increasing use of Islamic symbolism to legitimize Saddam Hussein's leadership, as well as to defend Saddam's religious credentials in the face of Iranian criticism during the war (Karsh and Rautsi 1991: 151). Saddam argued that Islam and Arab nationalism were indivisible and that it was the Arabs who "carried and defended the banner of Islam until it reached the furthest corners of the earth, including the land on which Bani Sadr now stands" (cit. in Karsh and Rautsi 1991: 152).

In particular, a public discourse emerged that compared the Iran-Iraq war to the historic battle of al-Qadisiyya and Saddam to the Arab commander Sa'd Ibn Abi Waqqas.[42] Posters and murals in public represented

Saddam as Waqqas. Iraqi television programs reenacted the battle of Qadisiyya (Davis 2005: 188). Saddam commissioned a huge victory arch in the form of Saddam's hands holding the "sword of Qadisiyya" (Khalil 1991b: 10–11). There was also increased reference to Shi'ite religious symbols. During the war with Iran, long-range missiles aimed at Tehran were called 'Ali and Husayn (the two most revered figures in Shi'ism after the Prophet Muhammad) (Graham-Brown 1999: 201). At the inauguration of the "sword of Qadisiyya," Saddam rode a white horse under the arch, symbolizing the horse that Husayn rode when he was martyred on the plains of Kerbala in A.D. 680 (Khalil 1991b: 11). In addition, state funds were lavished on Shi'ite religious sites, even as the regime continued to crack down on oppositional Shi'ite clerics. Known among the Shi'a as the "carrot and stick" approach, this policy aimed at increasing his legitimacy among this community and absorbing any opposition (Davis 2005: 191).

From 1992 onward, with the imposition of sanctions, the Iraqi economy continued its decline and, alongside it, the secular, modernizing discourse that had accompanied the rapid expansion of the state and economy from the 1970s onward. Instead, state-sponsored Islam continued to be promoted as a moral counterweight to the disintegration of Iraqi society. A number of laws were introduced in the 1990s to demonstrate the regime's religious credentials. In 1995, the regime closed nightclubs and banned the public sale of alcohol (Davis 2005: 232). "Islamic" punishments, such as the amputation of hands or feet for theft, were introduced in 1994, including the death penalty for organizing prostitution (Graham-Brown 1999: 187). These measures were justified as a necessary way to deal with the apparent increase in crime under sanctions.[43] The impact of religiously inspired laws was particularly dramatic in relation to women's rights. Whereas, in the 1970s, women (their education and employment) had been symbols of Iraq's modernization, during the 1990s women were reconstructed as symbols of the country's moral purity. This shift in regime discourse appeared to reflect the growing religious conservatism among the population in response to the breakdown in social values experienced under sanctions (Ali 2005: 745). Measures against women's rights included a law stipulating that women under forty-five must be accompanied by a male relative when traveling abroad (*mahram*), the legalization of "honor killings," and a campaign against prostitution, which led to the public beheading of dozens of men and women accused of being prostitutes or of procuring prostitutes.[44] These "Islamic" measures were presented as part of "our inherited Iraqi and family traditions, which distinguish us as Iraqis from the rest of the Arab countries" (cit. in Baram 1997: 14).

Another way in which the regime attempted to cultivate traditional values, while simultaneously expanding its own support base, was through the encouragement of "tribalism." This represented a reversal of Ba'th policies toward this social group. An original tenet of Ba'th ideology had been the rejection of tribalism as a "remnant of colonialism" and as "the epitome of backwardness and social reaction" (Baram 1997: 1). Policies of land reform implemented by the Ba'th largely succeeded in dismantling the power of tribal sheikhs (p. 3). Nevertheless, tribal sheikhs continued to exist and were often incorporated into local administration, while tribal identities were also considered in recruitment to the security services (pp. 4–6).

From 1991 onward, the regime began to publicly promote the role of tribes and tribal identities. Iraqis were encouraged to reestablish their tribal roots. The virtues of rural life and agriculture, in juxtaposition to deteriorating urban life, were promoted (Graham-Brown 1999: 197). Simultaneously, the regime sought to co-opt tribal leaders as a means of delivering the political loyalty of their communities (p. 195). Following the *intifada* of 1991, the regime needed the support of tribal sheikhs in order to prevent further armed challenges to its rule. To mobilize this support, the regime promoted the role of tribal sheikhs in tax collecting, local security, army recruitment, and administration (Baram 1997: 12; Graham-Brown 1999: 197). The president began to meet often with tribal chiefs in the presidential palace, where they would be requested "to bring with them their rifles and banner and to dance their tribal war dance (*al-hosa*) in his presence" (Baram 1997: 11). In return, tribal sheikhs offered their allegiance to Saddam Hussein. For example, in the Shi'ite south, in a meeting between the president and 586 tribal chiefs and clergy, the latter pledged, in the name of God, "our readiness to sacrifice . . . til martyrdom" (cit. in Baram 1997: 12).

The "re-tribalization" of Iraq was aided by the dire socioeconomic situation under sanctions. Reliance on kin constituted a survival strategy, and affiliation with social groups, such as tribes, provided protection for individuals and possibly greater access to resources. Moreover, tribalism provided a framework of imagined community in a context in which society was disintegrating under the stresses caused by sanctions. Consequently, urban dwellers several generations removed from the countryside began to "rediscover" their "tribal" affiliations and identities (Tripp 2000: 266).

From 1992 onward, as Iraqi society disintegrated under sanctions, state-sponsored Islam and tribalism thrived as avenues for individual survival, thereby reducing (although not eliminating) political pressure on the regime. As the secular, modernizing state began to crumble, so did the regime's (at least rhetorical) commitment to the notion of the national subject and universal citizenship. The promotion of the tribe, conservative Sunni religious groups, and "tradition" over the secular, urban middle classes symbolized the abandoning of the Ba'th's national modernization project and the exclusion of those who had been among the principal beneficiaries of it. The discourses of re-Islamization and retribalization naturalized the restructuring of social relations within Iraq in response to changing socioeconomic conditions. These shifts in power were underpinned by changing gender relations that emphasized more conservative roles and identities for women. That Saddam was still in power more than ten years following the imposition of sanctions is testimony to his political astuteness. His legacy survives in postinvasion Iraq, where tribal and religious leaders have largely displaced secular political parties, such as the Iraqi Communist Party, in shaping the post-Saddam polity, and women's rights are endangered (Ali and Pratt 2006).

## Contests over National Identity in Algeria

The legacy of French colonial rule, including its systematic attempts to eliminate local culture and language and its "divide and rule" strategy between Arabs and Berbers, rendered the issue of building a consensus about the nature of Algerian culture "at least as formidable as the political and economic tasks independent Algeria faced" (Ruedy 2005: 224). As discussed in Chapter 2, a consensus was articulated in terms of Arab and Muslim identities and this was consolidated through "Arabization" and the nationalization of Islam. However, this consensus depended on the repression of Berber culture and language within Algerian identity. During the anticolonial struggle in 1949, many Berber militants left or were expelled from the Front de Libération Nationale (FLN), while in postindependence Algeria, Berber was not officially recognized (Layachi 2005: 201–202).

While some Berber activists, with the assistance of Berber emigrants living predominantly in France, attempted to keep the language and culture alive in the face of state repression, it was not until the 1980s that a sustained movement for Berber cultural rights emerged. In 1980, the governor of Tizi-Ouzou (formerly "Greater Kabylia" and the home to a predominantly Berber population) banned a lecture on ancient Berber poetry because of the government's Arabization policy. This triggered a wave of student riots, which spread throughout Algeria and even to France (home to a substantial Algerian-Berber population) (Silverstein 1996: 12). The angry demonstrations, known as the "Kabyle spring," demanded recognition of Berber identity and culture and gave birth to the Berber Cultural Movement. The demands for official recognition of Berber identity were also tied up with growing disenchantment with the central authorities, who were considered to be repressive, corrupt, and ineffective in addressing the growing socioeconomic crisis within the country (which is discussed in the first part of this chapter). Throughout the 1980s, Berber activists, many of whom were part of a growing human rights activism, were arrested by the regime (Waltz 1995: 140–141).

Following the legalization of independent political entities in 1989, Berber activism was also channeled through political parties—the FFS (Front des Forces Socialistes—led by Hocine Ait Ahmed, a fighter in the war of independence) and the RCD (the Rassemblement pour la Culture et la Démocratie). Both parties stood against the regime's Arabization policy. The RCD was fiercely anti-Islamist, advocating the concept of a five-part Algerian identity as Arab, Berber, Muslim, African, and Mediterranean (Salah Tahi 1992). It supported the cancellation of the elections and the banning of the FIS, aligning itself with the regime in the fight against the radical religious movement (Layachi 2005: 206). The FFS was more conciliatory toward the Islamists and focused its opposition on ending the role of the military in politics and greater democratization of the state (ICG 2003: 12). In the first round of the 1991 national elections, the FFS and the RCD gained the most votes in Kabylia. Outside of Kabylia, the parties failed to garner many votes among Berber constituencies, and the parties have continued to remain essentially Kabyle-based parties.

During the 1990s, Berber activists attempted to maintain pressure on the regime, despite the fact that Berber political parties were divided in their strategy. The Berber protests were particularly targeted at the state's Arabization policies, which were seen as a direct threat to Berber identity. While Arabization had always been a long-standing policy of the postindependence regime (and central to its nationalist-populist identity), certain factors compelled the regime to deepen this process. By the 1990s, it was clear that the Arabization policy was "widen[ing] the social cleavages it was designed to bridge and exacerbat[ing] the tensions tearing at a still very fragmented society" (Ruedy 2005: 228). Those of the rural or recently urbanized strata tended to choose the Arabic track (where all school subjects are taught in Arabic), while those opting for the bilingual track tended to come from Berber or middle-class families. In the Arabic track, textbooks and training for teachers were generally inferior to those of the bilingual track (p. 228). As a result, young people from poorer backgrounds suffered discrimination in the job market and were more likely to be unemployed (Mezhoud 1993: 149). It was this sector (or at least the men of this sector) that formed a major part of those mobilized by Islamist groups. These had shown their strength in the 1991 elections and, by 1993, had become embroiled in an insurgency against the regime. In order to attempt to appease a significant section of the potential recruiting ground for the Islamists, the government stepped up its Arabization campaign. Two laws passed in the 1990s aimed to displace the French language from state institutions and firmly establish Arabic as the national language of Algeria: one law voted on 27 December 1990, which advocated the Arabization of all administrative offices and schools by 5 July 1992, and higher education establishments by 5 July 2000; and another voted on 17 December 1996 calling for nationwide Arabization to take effect from 5 July 1998.[45] The second law mandated that all governmental and nongovernmental organizations, institutions, and authorities would be obliged to substitute Arabic for French in all their official proceedings.[46]

Not only were Berber protests concerned with the regime's Arabization policies, but also with Islamic fundamentalism (Silverstein 1998: 4). The Islamists supported the complete Arabization of Algeria as a necessary part of the Islamization of the country. In addition, the Islamists represented a threat to the largely secular Berber movement. The FIS conceptualization of public culture excluded all manifestations of the secular and anything deemed "unauthentic" to Algerian culture. In neighborhoods where the FIS had a strong presence, men were encouraged to monitor the behavior of female relatives and neighbors to enforce modesty, while alcohol consumption and satellite dishes were banned (Ismail 2003: 131–133). During the election campaigns in March 1991, the FIS announced its opposition to the public performance of music, including *rai* (the Algerian "pop" music made internationally famous by people like Cheb Khaled). FIS hostility to *rai* as "un-Islamic" reflects the cultural music's symbolism as "a cultural border zone of syncretism and creative interminglings of French and Arab" (Gross, McMurray, and Swedenburg 1992: 16) and, therefore, diametrically opposed to FIS attempts to promote an "authentic" Algerian identity. Growing feelings of intimidation, compounded by the assassination of the singer Cheb Hasni in 1994 and the producer Rachid Baba-Ahmed in 1995, led many *rai* singers to immigrate to Paris and Marseilles (Silverstein 1996: 12). The targeting of *rai* artists, as well as other secular intellectuals and artists, represented a bloody escalation in the war to Islamize public culture. Another arena of this struggle was the education system, as a major institution in the diffusion of national identity and culture. In its war against the state, the Groupe islamique armé (the armed wing associated with the FIS) targeted schools, burning them down and killing schoolgirls for the continuation of mixed-sex classes and refusal to wear headscarves.

In light of the opposition to the FIS among Berber quarters, it is unsurprising that Berber intellectuals and artists were also targets for Islamist violence—illustrated by the assassination of writer Tahar Djaout and kidnapping, then assassination, of singer/songwriter Lounès Matoub in 1998 (Silverstein 1996: 13). The assassination of Matoub, who had been an outspoken critic of the Arabization law, occurred just five days before the imposition of Arabization in July 1998 (Silverstein 1998: 3). His death led to widespread and angry demonstrations by Berbers, who held the regime policy responsible for his death. The timing of his assassination appeared to symbolize the danger that the regime's Arabization campaign could provide a justification for anti-Berber violence.

During the 1990s, Berber activists were able to force some concessions from the government. In response to protests in 1994 by Berber students, a presidential commission to examine the demands of the protestors was established, representing the first official recognition of such ethnic claims (Silverstein 1996: 13). Following this, the 1996 constitution recognized "Amazighité" (Berber culture and identity) as an element of Algerian national identity and a High Amazigh Commission was established as an advisory board, organizing workshops and conferences and publishing a review in the Berber language (Silverstein 1998: 4). In addition, literature in Berber became widely available in shops throughout Algeria, Berber place names were restored, and the Kabyle airport was renamed Abane Ramdane, after the Kabyle leader of the FLN in 1956–1957 (ICG 2003: 12).

Yet these measures failed to address the long-standing feelings of cultural exclusion, exacerbated by rising youth unemployment (Ruedy 2005: 280). Since 2001, the Berbers' conflict with the state has become more sustained (Layachi 2005: 195). Triggered by an incident of police repression, Kabyle erupted into rioting in spring 2001, resulting in over a hundred dead and many more injured. The demands of the protesters were not only for official recognition of the Berber language and culture, but also for democratic and economic rights (p. 225). After an initial period of repression of the Berber movement, President Bouteflika made several concessions. Notably, in March 2002 he asserted that twenty-four gendarmes had been imprisoned for "homicide and abusive use of firearms" against the uprising and that the constitution would be amended without a referendum to include Tamazight as a national language (Ruedy 2005: 281). Nevertheless, these concessions were not considered sufficient by the leaders of the movement and a boycott of the elections was called in May 2002, supported by the FFS and the RCD (p. 281). In 2003, the government opened talks with the movement leaders. However, these broke down after just one week (Layachi 2005: 221). As one observer argues, "Without formal representation in the political system, and without a clear, coherent, and unified strategy for attaining its objectives, the protest movement risks being completely taken over by its radical ethnicist faction, which would push to the fore the particularism of the Berberophones of Kabylie and of the region itself. In other words, autonomy or independence will become its only demand" (p. 219).

Simultaneously, the regime has (at the time of writing) failed to totally quell violent Islamist groups, despite the extension of political amnesties in 1999. The adoption of a charter of national reconciliation in 2005, which granted an amnesty to all those who committed acts of violence during the war, aimed at finally bringing an end to Islamist-related violence. Yet the Charter of Peace and National Reconciliation aims to end violence by extending impunity to the perpetrators of abuses during the civil war, while also refusing to acknowledge the state's own role in the violence[47]—thereby failing to address a significant source of resentment against the regime and calling into question its commitment to liberalization of the political system.

The Islamist violence and Berber uprisings do not represent security problems alone. They demonstrate the degree to which the question of Algerian identity is intrinsically linked with the nature of the ruling regime and of the polity. The dominance of the military in politics, the absence of a rule of law, and the weakness of democratic representation, both centrally and regionally, are all contributing factors in the continuation of the crisis. While antiregime protests/violence are expressed in terms of culture clashes, they cannot be solved by cultural means alone. Indeed, the regime's Arabization campaign has failed to appease the Islamists, while provoking opposition from among the Berbers. Simultaneously, regime attempts to recognize Berber culture do not go far enough. In other words, the regime has so far failed to restructure national identity in order to maintain its hegemony and has relied on the military to maintain stability. National reconciliation and the establishment of an inclusive national identity are dependent upon the ability of civil-society actors to debate and interact, free of the fear of violence with impunity.

## Conclusion

The 1980s appeared to herald a shift toward greater political openness, in tandem with economic reforms. The political liberalization experiments represented strategies for regime maintenance in the face of a civil society growing in complexity and assertiveness, as well as a means of defusing discontent with regard to austerity measures. However, political liberalization did not succeed in co-opting new civil-society actors, while the introduction of structural adjustment programs threatened regimes' ability to use state economic resources to absorb contentious politics. Indeed, the Islamists were successful in using multiparty elections to mobilize political opposition to regimes. In response to the growing challenge of Islamist political activism, as well as political violence, regimes reversed the political liberalization process and sought to repress not only the Islamists but all civil-society actors beyond regime control. In the case of Egypt, this was predominantly achieved by tightening corporatist structures (the professional syndicates, trade unions, and civic associations), as well as increasing regime control over parliament. In Tunisia, Syria, and Iraq, independent civil-society activity was repressed through the systematic harassment, intimidation, imprisonment, and even assassination of activists, as well as tight controls over the media. In Algeria, the extreme violence provided a justification for the regime to reassert its control over society and to maintain the role of the military in politics.

Unable to co-opt civil-society actors through institutional or economic means, regimes resorted to the repression of civil-society participation in the political arena. To a large degree, this shifted struggles between the regime and its citizens to the sphere of public culture. Simultaneously, regimes attempted to reconfigure public culture in order to contain civil-society activism and to reassert their hegemony in the face of adverse conditions. In other words, cultural struggles did not displace politics but rather constituted the pursuit of politics through other avenues. The struggle over public culture in the 1980s represented a struggle over the ideological dimension of hegemony. The appropriation of public culture is central to any political project. However, without recourse to material means to construct hegemony, the ideological element grew in importance to become central to political struggles, often with violent implications.

While cultural battles appeared to signal the autonomy of civil-society actors from the regime within this sphere, this did not strengthen the prospects for democratization. Partly, this was because authoritarian regimes used culture to co-opt new constituencies in ways that undermined universal citizenship and political and civil rights. This was certainly the case in Egypt, in response to demands by the Muslim Brotherhood, and Iraq, with the retribalization and Islamization of national identity. Moreover, the emergence of more conservative official discourses helped to shape social relations in ways that served to reproduce authoritarianism (as a political system). Again, Iraq is particularly illustrative of this point. In addition, regimes also presided over civil societies that were extremely polarized by cultural issues, as demonstrated by the Algerian case. In some cases, this enabled the regime to "play off" the demands of one group against another and, consequently, to ensure its survival. In particular, the Algerian regime was able to count on the support of the Berber RCD to quell the Islamist insurgency.

In other words, regimes attempted to neutralize different actors through a strategy combining co-optation through cultural measures, "divide and rule," and the exercise of political repression, with varying degrees of success. High levels of repression in Tunisia and Syria eliminated the Islamist challenge to both the regime and to public culture and preempted the culture clashes experienced in other countries. Simultaneously, both regimes also stifled all independent civil-society activity. In Egypt, tactics of co-optation and repression contributed to preventing widespread antiregime mobilization, while also allowing some freedom for civil-society activism. In Algeria, the state's exclusion of Berber identity, coupled with the resort to a military solution against the Islamists, helped to transform "culture clashes" into direct political, and often violent, opposition. The Iraqi regime, faced with the dire circumstances of sanctions, utilized a combination of repression and a reconfiguration of public culture to maintain its power until its overthrow in 2003. In the wake of the fall of the Ba'th regime, contestations over culture have come to the fore and threaten to fragment the polity. Indeed, a major sticking point in the negotiation of the permanent constitution in 2005 was the role of Islam in public life.

This chapter has demonstrated the degree to which regimes were forced to reconfigure authoritarian rule in response to changing socioeconomic conditions from the 1970s onward. The failure of the national modernization project, as illustrated by ongoing economic recession, provoked dissent, much of which was expressed in attempts to reconfigure public culture. Cultural discourses also represented a means of challenging existing formulations of national identity as a central pillar underpinning authoritarian regimes. In all cases, regimes used coercion to repress dissent. They also attempted, with varying degrees of success, to reproduce consent for their rule through ideological means. Contestations over the nature of public culture represented an opportunity toward this end. While not successful in eliminating civil-society activism independent of the regime, manipulation of culture has constituted an important mechanism for regimes seeking to buttress their legitimacy. The next chapter examines how debates within civil society are central to understanding the potential for unseating authoritarian regimes and promoting a transition to democracy.

## Notes

1. Christopher Alexander, "Authoritarianism and Civil Society in Tunisia," *Middle East Report Online*, no. 205, http://www.merip.org/mer/mer205/alex.htm, accessed 15 June 2005.

2. Human Rights Watch (HRW), "Overview: 1990," http://www.hrw .org/reports/1990/WR90/MIDEAST.BOU.htm#P10_0, accessed 30 June 2005.

3. HRW, "Overview: 1993," http://www.hrw.org/reports/1994/WR94/ Middle.htm#P0_0, accessed 30 June 2005.

4. In Syria and Iraq, the repression of Islamists predates this period. The Syrian regime eliminated the Muslim Brotherhood during the Hama uprising in 1982. The Iraqi regime targeted Shi'a Islamists from the 1970s onward as part of its general intolerance of dissent (Tripp 2000).

5. For example, see HRW, "Algeria: Human Rights Developments," 1994, http://www.hrw.org/reports/1994/WR94/Middle-01.htm, accessed 14 July 2005; HRW, "Trials of Civilians Violate International Law," July 1993, http://www .hrw.org/reports/1993/egypt/, accessed 14 July 2005.

6. HRW, "State-Sponsored 'Disappearances' in Algeria," February 1998, http://www.hrw.org/reports98/algeria2/, accessed 14 July 2005.

7. HRW, "Egypt: Hostage-Taking and Intimidation by Security Forces," January 1995, http://www.hrw.org/reports/1995/Egypt.htm, accessed 14 July 2005.

8. HRW, "Military Courts That Sentenced Islamist Leaders Violated Basic Fair-Trial Norms," October 1992, http://hrw.org/reports/pdfs/t/tunisia/tunisia .92o/tunisia920full.pdf, accessed 14 July 2005.

9. HRW, "No Justice for Civilians in Egypt's Military Court," November 1999, http://hrw.org/english/docs/1999/11/11/egypt1951.htm, accessed 14 July 2005.

10. HRW, "Overview: 1993."

11. HRW, "Egypt: Human Rights Developments, 1995," http://www.hrw .org/reports/1995/WR95/MIDEAST-02.htm, accessed 14 July 05.

12. HRW, "Overview: 1995," http://www.hrw.org/reports/1996/WR96/ MIDEAST.htm#P6_0, accessed 30 June 2005.

13. HRW, "Overview: 1996," http://www.hrw.org/reports/1997/WR97/ME .htm, accessed 14 July 2005; HRW, "Overview: 1997," http://www.hrw.org/ worldreport/Mideast.htm#TopOfPage, accessed 30 June 2005.

14. The 1999 law was overturned by the constitutional court in 2000 for procedural reasons. Almost the same law was successfully passed in May 2002. For details of the law and the campaign against it, see Pratt (2004a).

15. Human Rights First, "Human Rights Defenders in Tunisia," http:// www.humanrightsfirst.org/middle_east/tunisia/hrd_tunisia.htm, (n.d.), accessed 14 July 2005.

16. Amnesty International, "Tunisia: Fear for Safety: Human Rights Defenders," 15 December 2000, http://web.amnesty.org/library/index/ENGMDE 300292000?open&of=ENG-TUN, accessed 14 July 2005; http://www.omct.org/ pdf/observatory/2005/obs_annual_report_2004_eng.pdf, pp. 411ff, accessed 14 July 2005.

17. Christopher Alexander, "Authoritarianism and Civil Society in Tunisia"; Human Rights First, "Human Rights Defenders in Tunisia."

18. Human Rights First, "Human Rights Defenders in Tunisia"; CNLT, "Rapport sur l'état des libertés en Tunisie," 15 March 2000, p. 33, http://www .cnlt98.org, accessed 14 July 2005.

19. Human Rights First, "Human Rights Defenders in Tunisia"; CNLT, "Rapport sur l'état des libertés en Tunisie."

20. HRW, 'Tunisia: Human Rights Developments, 1996," http://www.hrw .org/reports/1997/WR97/ME-09.htm, accessed 14 July 2005.

21. CNLT, "Rapport sur l'état des libertés en Tunisie," p. 33; Human Rights First, "Human Rights Defenders in Tunisia."

22. For example, International Women's Human Rights Law Clinic and Women Living Under Muslim Laws, "Shadow Report on Algeria to the Committee on the Elimination of Discrimination Against Women," n.d., http://www .nodo50.org/mujeresred/argelia-shadowreport.html, accessed 29 October 2005.

23. HRW, "Overview: 1998," http://www.hrw.org/worldreport99/mideast/ index.html, accessed 31 October 2005.

24. HRW, "Overview: 1993."

25. Committee to Protect Journalists (CPJ), "Attacks on the Press: Middle East and North Africa, 1994," http://www.cpj.org/attacks04/mideast04/algeria .html, accessed 15 July 2005.

26. The Egyptian government finances and appoints the heads of all three main Islamic institutions: Al-Azhar, Dar al-Ifta, and the Ministry of Religious Endowments. However, "this power structure does not result in the subordination of the religious establishment to the political authority. The reality of the relationship is a complex combination of interdependence, competition, and muted struggle" (Kodmani 2005: 5).

27. Egyptian Organization for Human Rights, "Defending Freedom of Thought and Creation: Al-Azhar Judicial Seizure Deals a Hammer Blow to Freedom of Thought" (Cairo: October 2004), http://www.eohr.org/press/2004/ pr1024.htm, accessed 6 July 2005.

28. Samia Mehrez, "Take Them out of the Ball Game: Egypt's Cultural Players in Crisis," *Middle East Report Online,* http://www.merip.org/mer/mer 219/219_mehrez.html, accessed 6 July 2005.

29. Ibid.

30. Sabry Hafez, "The Novel, Politics, and Islam," *New Left Review,* September-October 2000, http://www.newleftreview.com/NLR23908.shtml#_edn14, accessed 6 July 2005.

31. Khaled Dawoud, "Banquet Serves up Indigestion," *Al-Ahram Weekly Online,* 25–31 May 2000, http://weekly.ahram.org.eg/2000/483/eg13.htm, accessed 15 May 2006.

32. Ibid.

33. Omayma Abdel-Latif, "In the Way of Truth," *Al-Ahram Weekly Online,* 25–31 May 2000, http://weekly.ahram.org.eg/2000/483/eg12.htm, accessed 15 May 2006.

34. Ibid.

35. Mehrez, 'Take Them out of the Ball Game."

36. Yousef Rakha, "Floating Bureaus," *Al-Ahram Weekly Online,* 18–24 January 2001, http://weekly.ahram.org.eg/2001/517/cu1.htm, accessed 15 May 2006.

37. Ibid.

38. Mohamed Sid Ahmed, "The Intelligentsia and Politics," *Al-AhramWeekly Online,* 18–24 January 2001, http://weekly.ahram.org.eg/2001/517/op3.htm, accessed 15 May 2006.

39. Hossam Bahgat, "Cultural House of Cards," *Cairo Times,* 18–24 January 2001; hosted at: http://www.amcoptic.com/fatawy_islamiah/cultural_house_of_cards_the_fal.htm, accessed 15 May 2006.

40. Rakha, "Floating Bureaus."

41. Ibid.

42. At the battle of al-Qadisiyya, A.D. 637, a numerically inferior Arab army defeated the Persian Empire and forced it to embrace Islam. Sa'd Ibn Abi Waqqas was one of the oldest companions of the Prophet.

43. Amnesty International, "Iraq: State Cruelty: Branding, Amputation, and the Death Penalty," 1 April 1996, http://web.amnesty.org/library/Index/ENGMDE 140031996?open&of=ENG-IRQ, accessed 10 July 2005; Human Rights Watch, "Iraq's Brutal Decrees," June 1995, http://www.hrw.org/reports/1995/IRAQ955 .htm, accessed 10 July 2005.

44. Amnesty International, "Iraq: Fear of Further Extra-Judicial Executions," 3 November 2000, http://web.amnesty.org/library/Index/ENGMDE140152000 ?open&of=ENG-IRQ, accessed 10 July 2005.

45. The fifth of July is the anniversary of Algerian independence.

46. Amira Howeidy, "No Peace Without Tamazight," *Al-Ahram Weekly Online,* 2–8 July 1998, http://weekly.ahram.org.eg/1998/384/re5.htm, accessed 6 July 2005.

47. HRW, "Impunity in the Name of Reconciliation," background report, September 2005, http://hrw.org/backgrounder/mena/algeria0905/index.htm, accessed 31 October 2005.

# 5

## The Politics of Democratization

AS PREVIOUS CHAPTERS ILLUSTRATED, MOST Arab countries possessed an assertive and diverse civil society by the 1990s, thereby challenging the arguments of some scholars that civil society is alien to the Arab-Muslim world. From the 1970s onward, civil-society actors emerged to challenge the postindependence hegemony—as a result of corruption, lack of democracy, and deteriorating socioeconomic conditions. In search of avenues for political expression, they formed human rights groups, Islamist movements, and community associations (Ibrahim 1995: 39). They benefited from even limited political liberalization measures, such as elections, relaxed controls on the press, and the rhetoric of democracy and human rights, in order to claim new spaces in which civil society could operate. They were given a boost by the demonstration effects of Eastern European civil societies not only challenging their one-party regimes but actually overturning those regimes (Norton 1995: 4).

The emergence of civil-society actors beyond corporatist structures was heralded by observers as part of the process of democratization. Students of politics of authoritarian regimes were optimistic that the growing activism of civil society was the key to ushering in democratization and consolidating democracy (O'Donnell and Schmitter 1986; Ibrahim 1995; Diamond 1999). The liberal conception of civil society, rooted in the writings of Tocqueville and Montesquieu, portrays civil-society organizations as a counterbalance to the government, thereby preventing state monopoly of power and encouraging transparency and accountability (Diamond 1999: 239–242). In this way, civil society acts to protect the individual's civil and political rights from state encroachment and facilitates her/his participation in public affairs, as well as contributing to pluralism (Ibrahim 1995; Diamond 1999: 242ff). Moreover, civil society constitutes a sphere of mobilization for the normative and social dimensions of democracy. Through participation in civic organizations, citizens learn the values of civility and tolerance, which are prerequisites for the consolidation of democracy (Ibrahim 1995). Moreover, it is civil-society organizations, including social movements, that have been at the forefront of advocating civil liberties, human rights, women's rights, poverty eradication, and environmental protection at both national and international levels (Fisher 1998; Keck and Sikkink 1998; Falk 1999; O'Brian et al. 2000).

Since the initial euphoria surrounding the potential of civil society, there have been many critiques of the concept and its application. The empirical "facts" do not necessarily demonstrate the argument that a strong civil society necessarily leads to democratization (Allen 1997; Stewart 1997; Carothers 2002; Abdel Rahman 2002; Hawthorne 2004). To begin with, not all civil-society organizations have an interest in promoting democratization. A large number of the organizations that are counted as being part of civil society are service-providing NGOs, who are generally indifferent to whether they operate under authoritarian or democratic conditions. Indeed, as authoritarian regimes have been forced to reduce welfare expenditures, they have increasingly relied on service-provision NGOs to meet the welfare needs of their citizens. Neoliberal economic reforms have also boosted the voices of certain sectors of civil society over others—namely, businesspersons' organizations over trade unions. These are courted by regimes in order to create a constituency for economic reforms and to encourage private-sector growth (Hawthorne 2004; Abdel Rahman 2002). Yet, due to the nature of the historical evolution of the bourgeoisie in the Arab world, businesspersons do not necessarily push for democratic reforms (Bellin 2002).

The most significant sector of civil society in the Arab world, in terms of numbers, are the Islamists, whose commitment to liberal values of tolerance and freedom has been questioned—although there exists a "moderate" trend that is committed to standard procedures of democracy, such as multiparty elections (Hamzawy 2005). On the other hand, those promoting liberal values, such as human rights and women's rights, constitute a minority within Arab societies and are often perceived as a "Westernized" elite (Hawthorne 2004). Finally, rather than leading to democratization, the growth of an assertive civil society since the 1980s has coincided with the introduction of further measures to restrict freedoms and clamp down on political opposition (as the previous chapter examines).

There also has been substantial criticism of the concept of civil society as being part of a neoliberal discourse (for example, Leftwich 1994; Allen 1997; Hewitt de Alcántara 1998). The rise in interest in the concept of civil society corresponds to the retreat of the state due to the implementation of neoliberal economic measures. Nonstate actors are not only appreciated for the welfare services they provide but are encouraged to do so through the availability of international donor funding, in order to mitigate the effects of structural adjustment programs. In this way, the civil-society discourse is perceived as the latest mechanism of the West (IFIs, Western governments) for weakening the Arab state. The proliferation of NGOs formed from the 1980s onward have been accused by some Arab civil-society activists as tools of "Western" government interests at the expense of local interests (for example, Sha'rawi 1994; Fergany 1994; Masri 1998 and 1999). If not a ploy to weaken the state, then the civil-society discourse represents a diversion from strengthening political movements or parties seeking the political and socioeconomic transformation of Arab societies (Langohr 2004 and 2005). Young, talented activists, instead of getting involved in politics, are attracted into relatively well-paid jobs in the NGO sector, in which political concerns are eschewed for "technical" solutions to the problems besetting "developing country" societies. Moreover, because they are supported through international funding, NGOs develop stronger links with the international community, rather than their own communities, and are not forced to build domestic constituencies for social and political transformation (Stewart 1997; MERIP Report, 2000; Langohr 2004 and 2005).

Despite opposition to the concept of civil society and its association with democratization, the term is adopted by Arab activists themselves to describe the appearance of actors beyond state corporatist institutions (Bellin 1994). For example, the Beirut-based Centre for Arab Unity Studies organized a symposium on *al-mujtama' al-madani fi-l-'alam al-'arabi* ("Civil Society in the Arab World") in 1992. Simultaneously, the Ibn Khaldoun Centre for Development Studies, in Cairo, began issuing its monthly newsletter entitled *Civil Society* (Sayyid 1995a: 133–134). The use of the term by a variety of actors (Islamists, human rights organizations, and Arab intellectuals) reflects their desires to challenge despotism and to engage in political life (Bellin 1994).

Yet the meaning of the term is contested by the different actors that utilize it. There exist two different conceptions of civil society—the formal/associative and the informal/affective. The first conception defines civil society as the collection of civic associations between state and family, for example, professional associations, political parties, human rights groups, and community development associations. According to Egyptian sociologist and prodemocracy activist Saad Eddin Ibrahim, different conceptions of civil society "revolve around maximizing volitional organized collective participation in the public space between individuals and the state" (Ibrahim 1995: 27–28). The second definition rejects the former definition on the grounds that it is rooted in Western historical experience and can only lead to the conclusion that civil society is weak in the Arab world because civic associations have been infiltrated or curtailed by the authoritarian state. Burhan Ghalyun, a former Marxist turned Islamist from Syria, argues that "traditional" groupings, such as the mosque, religious orders, and primordial solidarities, constitute the strongest section of civil society because they are autonomous from state authority and are rooted in the people (Ghalyun 1992). The argument that civil society in the Arab world includes informal organizations (based on family, kin, tribe, and other affective solidarities) has also been propounded by Western academics such as Diane Singerman. Based on ethnographic fieldwork, she notes that informal networks in Cairene popular neighborhoods operate through a "familial ethos" based on cooperation and trust, thereby constructing the normative dimensions of civil society (Singerman, n.d.). The notion of building networks through a "familial ethos" is not dissimilar from Robert Putnam's notion of social capital as the basis of democracy (1993 and 2000).

This is not merely an ontological debate. As argued in Chapter 1, civil society represents the terrain upon which are waged the ideological battles that shape the social relations giving rise to the state (Gramsci 1971: 235). Contestations between different actors over the definition of civil society reflect ideological contestations over the nature of the polity, including the concept of citizenship and democracy. Associative civil society is perceived as the basis for a democratic polity based on a liberal conception of rights. Meanwhile, affective civil society represents a more organic or communal conception of the polity, in which a democracy would enable the group, rather than the individual, to be the bearer of rights (in my mind, to the detriment of the individual). In attempting to implement their different visions of civil society, actors are forced to make decisions about the type of civil organizations to form; their relations with the regime, the state, and other civil-society actors; types of activities undertaken; and strategies pursued. These decisions may appear to be tactical but they attempt to advance a particular notion of civil society. Consequently, they often result in conflict between different actors, thereby making or breaking alliances and triggering splits within established organizations.

In this way, the outcome of contestation shapes civil society and, in turn, shapes the ideological underpinnings of the polity, including the potential for democratization. In other words, democratization is not the outcome of a growth in the number of civil-society actors or the existence of a civil society independent of the regime. Rather, democratization depends upon the ideological debates between civil-society actors and, in particular, the ability or desire of civil-society actors to put forward a vision that challenges authoritarianism, thereby paving the way for democracy. This chapter examines some of the major decisions facing civil-society actors as they have grown in strength. These decisions reflect the outcome of debates within civil society that have, in turn, shaped civil society. Simultaneously, these debates reflect different visions of a future polity and, in this sense, they represent projects that may or may not challenge the political status quo. These debates are presented here under different themes.

## In Search of Autonomy: The Dilemma of Human Rights Groups

The issue of the form of the relationship between civil-society actors in the Arab world to the state/regime has been particularly significant for the identity of evolving forms of civil-society actors from the 1980s onward because, in many cases, these actors have sought autonomy from the state corporatist institutions that dominated political and civil life in the postindependence period. For ideological as well as practical reasons, civil-society actors came to reject state corporatist institutions as inefficient, corrupt, and antidemocratic. The creation of organizations beyond state corporatism represented an attempt to construct an alternative public sphere, free of the pernicious influences of the regime. Yet, in practice, this autonomy has not been easy to protect, due to certain pressures generated by regime actions toward civil society. Consequently, actors have been forced to make decisions about whether to operate illegally, whether to cooperate with members of the regime, and whether to work with/within corporatist institutions. In the process of making such decisions, actors have established structures that shape the future of civil society.

Human rights groups are emblematic of the new civil-society actors because their establishment has represented a conscious attempt to work beyond regime-dominated structures in order to hold regimes account-able for human rights abuses. The earliest independent human rights organization was the Tunisian League for Human Rights (LTDH), founded in 1977. The fact that the organization has a longer history than other human rights groups in the region makes it a useful case study for a num-ber of key issues that have faced one organization or another in its time. Yet, its formation in the 1970s, before the onset of limited political liber-alization, differentiates it from other human rights organizations in the region and renders its trajectory unique in many respects.

Despite the authoritarianism of then President Bourguiba, the LTDH was given official permission to form in 1977. Its aims were, ini-tially, restorative rather than contentious in that the founders "sought not to overthrow a system, but to reform and redirect it" (Waltz 1995: 134–135). The founders were individuals who had been part of the regime but, on being expelled from the ruling party, they desired to pressure the Tunisian government to open up the political system and accommodate the voices of those excluded (pp. 134, 157). In order to receive official recognition, the new organization was obliged to include seven members of the then-regime party (PSD—Parti Socialiste Destourien) on its board. Yet, the founders were able to select those individuals from the PSD who were like-minded. Consequently, the LTDH was able to take an inde-pendent stance on human rights issues within Tunisia, including monitor-ing abuses in prison and making public statements on press freedoms (pp. 136ff). It objected to the monopoly of the regime/party over politi-cal life and promoted political pluralism (p. 154). The standing of the league's board protected it from harassment by the authorities.

In 1987, a coup replaced the aging Bourguiba with Zine El Abidine Ben Ali. There was a transformation in political discourse and the new president began to speak of political liberalization, including respect for human rights. As part of this political shift, the regime invited four of the LTDH's members to join the government, including its then presi-dent, Mohamed Charfi. Other members of Tunisian civil society were also courted by Ben Ali, with a promise that civil liberties would im-prove inside Tunisia once Ben Ali had managed to remove the old guard from the ruling regime (Garon 2003: 29). A national pact was signed by a range of civil-society actors, including the trade unions, student and women's groups, and even the Islamist Mouvement de la Tendance Islamique (which later became al-Nahda). In this context, it was possible to view regime overtures toward human rights activists as evidence that the regime was adopting the demands of the movement. Yet, the loss of the league's head and some of its founders contributed to destabililizing the organization and left it confused about its relationship to the regime (Garon 2003: 35; Waltz 1995: 139).

Relations between the LTDH and the regime began to deteriorate in light of criticisms of regime abuse of Islamists after 1990. The government-controlled media began to criticize the LTDH for being exclusionary and the tool of foreign powers. In a bid to suppress what had become practically a lone voice defending the civil liberties of the Islamists, the government introduced a new law of association in 1992. The law mandated that membership in associations should be open to all and that there should be no overlap between the leadership of a civic association and that of a political party—in order to prevent associations from operating as "thinly disguised political parties" (Waltz 1995: 184). This criticism of associations had some resonance given that political parties felt that real political liberalization was blocked by the continuing monopoly of power by the ruling party, which was renamed the Rassemblement Constitutionnel Démocratique (RCD) in 1988.

The associations law presented the LTDH with a dilemma. If it met the requirements of the law, it would open itself up to regime infiltration and would also lose a significant number from its leadership. On the other hand, failure to comply would entail dissolution (Garon 2003: 36). Initially, it chose dissolution. However, it later succumbed to the law and elected a new leadership. Yet the organization never fully recovered from the change in law and an independent voice supporting human rights was effectively muted.[1]

The tactic of strangling independent civil society through infiltration by RCD members has also been used with regard to other organizations (Bellin 1995: 140). In addition, the regime has established its own NGOs, such as Avocats sans Frontières (Lawyers Without Borders) and Association des Mères (The Mothers' Association) in order to "crowd out" independent civil-society organizations.[2] Finally, the regime has employed systematic harassment of civil-society activists, such as Nejib Hosni, Moncef Marzouki, Siham Bensidrine, and Radhia Nasraoui.[3]

The experience of the LTDH and other "neutralized" civil-society organizations led some long-standing human rights activists to establish the National Council for Liberties in Tunisia (CNLT) in 1998 (Garon 2003: 182). The CNLT was created with a board independent from political parties, including the ruling party. In the words of one founder, the CNLT refused to become a "political platform," which, in light of the events besetting the LTDH, could be interpreted as a refusal to become hostage to a political contest between the regime and the opposition.[4] Official recognition of the council was denied, despite the political independence of the organization, demonstrating that the regime is hostile to the concept of autonomous civil society. The CNLT has been forced to work illegally, while its members have been subject to constant harassment and threats of imprisonment. Nevertheless, it has managed to issue press releases and reports highlighting the government's continued abuse of human rights in Tunisia, predominantly by way of the Internet.[5] Moreover, many CNLT figures have appeared on Arab satellite channels, such as al-Jazeera and al-Arabiya, to publicize human rights abuses by the Tunisian regime.

Other organizations, such as the Comité de Soutien aux Prisonniers and the Rassemblement pour une Alternative au Développement, which have not been officially recognized, have also turned to "civil disobedience" as a tactic for promoting autonomous civil society in the face of extreme government abuses of civil liberties.[6] Inadvertently, the regime has helped to create a new movement within civil society by denying these organizations legal recognition. Despite attracting systematic harassment by the authorities, some activists have come to embrace illegality as a new means for advancing civil-society autonomy. Indeed, there is evidence that even those within regime-dominated organizations such as the judiciary and the Tunisian Journalists' Association have become more vociferous in their complaints against the regime (Garon 2003: 183–184). By refusing to work within the regime-dominated system, this small but vocal group of dissidents challenges not only the legitimacy of the system, but also the legitimacy of the postindependence consensus that historically viewed the regime/state as the representative of national interests.

The experience of independent civil-society organizations in Egypt differs substantially from that of Tunisia in that, initially, they, for the most part, circumvented the associations law in order to maintain their autonomy, but since the introduction of new legislation in 1999, they have been forced to comply and subject themselves to the authority of the Ministry of Social Affairs. The relative absence of systematic harassment in the style of the Tunisian regime enabled the emergence of a core of vocal human rights groups. This does not mean that Egyptian civil society evolved without constraints in the 1990s. The regime has continued to limit freedom of assembly through the emergency law in place since 1981, in addition to controlling much of the domestic media. This has meant that human rights groups have found it difficult to reach out to a broad constituency. However, the greatest obstacle has been the ambivalence of many civil-society activists toward human rights work.

In Egypt, the first human rights group established was the Egyptian Organization for Human Rights (EOHR), in 1985, under the umbrella of the Arab Organization for Human Rights. As one of the first civil-society formations that brought together a range of actors of various political and ideological outlooks, the evolution of the EOHR played a significant role in shaping many actors' perceptions of civil society's role and its relation to the regime/state. Moreover, the process of establishing the organization helped to define a new paradigm for civil-society activity in Egypt. Whereas the original founders saw the organization as a continuation of leftist/nationalist political activism of the postindependence period, by the end of the 1980s the organization had evolved as an expression of a break from this type of activism.

The original founders sought to register the EOHR as a civic association, which would have placed the organization under the supervision of the Ministry of Social Affairs. This would have obliged the EOHR to comply with a host of bureaucratic regulations concerning its internal governance, scope of activities, and fund-raising abilities (Salem 1991). The law created a corporatist framework for associational work, in that all associations were obliged to be part of a national federation, controlled by the ministry (Pratt 2004a). At that time, there were no associations operating beyond this law. The Arab Women's Solidarity Association, founded by outspoken government critic and feminist activist Nawal El Saadawi, had managed to operate under the ministry's supervision since 1982, thereby making EOHR members hopeful that the government would also accept the formation of a new human rights organization.[7]

However, the application for registration as an association was rejected by the authorities, sparking a debate within the organization. The majority of the board felt that a human rights organization could not operate illegally and, therefore, the EOHR must freeze its activities until it could achieve official recognition. On the other hand, a minority of board members argued that the EOHR should continue to operate under the rubric of "under establishment," while appealing the ministry's decision through the courts. Moreover, the law was clearly contrary to the UN Covenant on Civil and Political Rights, which guaranteed freedom of association, and which was ratified by the Egyptian government. The majority of the membership supported the latter position and, after three years of existing on paper, the organization finally became active in 1988 with a new board and secretariat. Meanwhile, those that had opposed working without official permission resigned from the organization.

By refusing to abide by the administrative decision of the Ministry of Social Affairs and recognizing the power of international covenants over Egyptian law, the EOHR members chose to operate beyond the corporatist system. This gave the organization an autonomy not previously enjoyed by Egyptian civic associations in the post-1952 period and represented the beginnings of a new organizational paradigm, albeit one that was created initially by default rather than by express design. This autonomy would become a defining feature of newly emerging civil-society organizations in the 1990s.

Many of the organizations founded after 1987 and advocating human rights, including the rights of women, children, workers, and peasants, did not seek official registration but were formed as "civil companies"—that is, nonprofit companies under commercial law—in order to avoid interference by the Ministry of Social Affairs (Pratt 2004b: 242ff). The experience of the EOHR was salutary. In addition, many of those involved in establishing new civil-society organizations, such as the Cairo Institute for Human Rights Studies, Centre for Human Rights Legal Aid, Nadim Centre for the Rehabilitation of Victims of Torture, and the Centre for Trade Union and Worker Services, had previously experienced state harassment and intimidation due to their activism in the student movement, political parties, and the trade unions. In a few cases, individuals had been subjected to torture. These past incidents made them reject any possibilities of working within state institutions to achieve their objectives (p. 244). The "civil company" format not only enabled organizations to avoid interference by the authorities but also to control their "membership," thereby protecting them from regime infiltration. By keeping the organization small, this also helped to mitigate against internal rifts. However, some felt that by refusing to form membership associations, in line with the law, new civil-society organizations failed to create transparent and internally accountable organizations. Moreover, they isolated themselves from officially registered associations because their antiregime stance invited harassment by the authorities, thereby making it dangerous to associate with them.

For the most part, the civil company tactic worked and enabled the diversification of new civil-society organizations in the 1990s. However, by the end of the 1990s, the regime sought to mute these independent voices by closing the legal loophole that enabled civil-society organizations to form as civil companies. In 1999, the new legislation on associations was passed, sparking a debate among "civil company" organizations over whether to operate illegally or to register officially (Pratt 2004a). On the one hand, a group of eight human rights organizations issued a statement that they would not abide by the new law and would seek to establish a human rights office abroad in order to protect their ability to highlight human rights abuses in Egypt (Egyptian human rights NGOs 1999). A second group of five human rights organizations issued a statement in which they accused organizations of being unpatriotic for threatening to establish an office abroad and refusing to comply with the new law.[8] This split the successful coalition that had campaigned against the law (which had also included officially registered associations, and was supported by a significant number of other members of civil society), as well as causing a split within one of the member organizations of this coalition (Pratt 2004a: 329–330).

Subsequently, the 1999 law was overturned by the constitutional court for procedural reasons and a new law on associations was drafted and passed in May 2002. The broad coalition formed against the 1999 law was not resurrected and domestic opposition to the 2002 law was less prominent. Civil company organizations, which had spearheaded the original campaign, were placed in a similar dilemma to that of the Tunisian League for Human Rights in 1992—that is, to register and compromise the organization's autonomy from the regime, or to not register and be threatened with prosecution and/or the elimination of the organization.

After 1999, the regime capitalized on rifts within the civil-society coalition to clamp down on civil-society activists. In 2000, the head of the Ibn Khaldoun Centre and long-established civil-society activist, Saad Eddin Ibrahim, was arrested and charged with accepting international funding without government permission, in addition to "tarnishing Egypt's reputation abroad." His trial, which resulted in his receiving a prison sentence of seven years in 2002, sent shock waves throughout civil society and a message that the regime could clamp down on independent voices—even when they belonged to a high-profile and well-connected individual such as Ibrahim. On the other hand, the regime extended an "olive branch" by co-opting some independent civil-society voices onto the National Women's Council, established in 2000, and the National Council for Human Rights (NCHR), established in 2004.[9] The participation of individuals who once rejected regime supervision over civil society in regime-created bodies has divided civil society yet again on the question of how it should define its relationship to the regime. On the one hand, some viewed the creation of a national council as the outcome of civil society's demands for greater regime accountability concerning human rights abuses and an opportunity to impact government policy. For others, the council represented "window-dressing" for the regime, rather than a serious attempt to improve its human rights record.[10]

The first NCHR report, issued in April 2005, was highly critical of the government, thereby disproving expectations that its official status would oblige it to be lenient toward the regime. It highlighted the systematic abuse of detainees by police and called for the repeal of the emergency law ahead of the autumn elections. The report's independent stance has earned it credibility internationally—from the likes of Human Rights Watch and the US State Department.[11] On the other hand, despite government refusal of the report's findings, the fact that the NCHR is a state body provides legitimacy to the regime's claims to incremental reform.[12]

Meanwhile, the Kifaya ("Enough") movement that grew from the Egyptian antiwar demonstrations in 2003 (see Chapter 6 for further details) has adopted civil disobedience in the form of street protests as a tactic in calling for democratic reforms. Under the emergency law, public demonstrations without official permission are illegal. While street politics are not new to Egypt, the call for public protests as a strategy in pushing for democratic reforms is novel and has attracted significant media coverage from Arab satellite news channels, as well as the Egyptian independent and opposition press. In this case, civil disobedience has been instrumental in building a proreform movement that has grown to include previously politically quiet social groups such as the Egyptian Judges' Club.

Civil disobedience as a strategy for civil-society activism represents a challenge to the regime and its domination of civil society through corporatist structures. Working beyond corporatist structures is one way in which civil society may challenge the postindependence hegemony underpinning authoritarian rule. However, hegemony not only depends upon the existence of the right institutions but also upon a widespread belief in the moral-ideological dimensions of the project. One of the most obvious moral-ideological divisions within civil societies in the Arab world revolves around the issue of religion and its place in public life.

## Islamists and Secularists Within Civil Society

Islamists are part of the prodemocracy Kifaya coalition in Egypt. Their incorporation into the proreform movement marks a new point in the evolution of the nonviolent Islamist group, the Muslim Brotherhood, in addition to representing a change in attitude among non-Islamist civil-society activists. In Egypt, the Muslim Brotherhood cannot be considered a new civil-society actor, having been founded in 1928. However, its transformation since the 1980s shares many of the characteristics of nonviolent Islamist groups in other Arab countries, such as the Tunisian al-Nahda, established at the beginning of the 1980s.

The Muslim Brotherhood was banned in Egypt in 1954 and, since then, has operated illegally. Under Nasser, the Brotherhood was persecuted and imprisoned. However, under Sadat there was a rapprochement between the authorities and the Brotherhood, due to Sadat's strategy of using the Islamists to defeat the leftists. Under Mubarak, Brotherhood members have been periodically rounded up and detained, and even put on trial before emergency courts. Despite this level of harassment and lack of official recognition, the Brotherhood has taken a compromising attitude to the ruling regime and avoided confrontation as far as possible. Based on the writings of its founder, Hassan al-Banna, the philosophy of the organization has been to Islamize society from the bottom upward. Within that context, it operated within the existing political system (Sullivan and Abed-Kotob 1999: 52ff).

During the 1980s onward, the Muslim Brotherhood fielded candidates in the elections by forging alliances with recognized opposition political parties (the Wafd in 1984 and the Labor and Liberal Parties in 1987). During the 1990s, after the amendment to the electoral law, the Muslim Brotherhood fielded candidates as independents. While Hassan al-Banna opposed the concept of political parties, claiming that the work of *da'wa* (proselytization of Islam) was larger than the function of a political party, the Muslim Brotherhood has used parliamentary elections as an opportunity for *da'wa,* rather than as a means to take power directly (Sullivan and Abed-Kotob 1999: 58). In addition, the Brotherhood has been successful in elections for professional syndicates, student associations, and university faculty clubs (pp. 54–55). Meanwhile, Islamists have channeled energies into establishing associations to provide health, education, and other services for the poor. In sum, the Muslim Brotherhood strategy has focused on attempts to appropriate corporatist structures as a means of dominating civil society.

The formation of the Wasat ("Center") Party in 1996 represented a shift in thinking among some of the Brotherhood's younger cadres, led by Abu 'Ila Madi Abu 'Ila, former deputy secretary-general of the Engineers' Syndicate. The government's clampdown on Islamist activity within the syndicates, including the Engineers' Syndicate, together with continuing arrests of Muslim Brotherhood members, led some to rethink the Muslim Brotherhood's traditional strategy of not seeking political power as a means of avoiding confrontation with the state (Abu 'Ila, Habib, and al-Gawhary 1996). Simultaneously, the new party represented an attempt to reformulate traditional Islamist thinking to incorporate concepts of human rights, pluralism, and democracy (Rosefsky Wickam 2004: 207).

The shift from a fundamentalist interpretation of Islam toward a moderate one among certain nonviolent Islamists is rooted in a body of writings that emerged from the 1970s onward, disputing the claim that Islam represents both religion and state (*din wa dawla*) and arguing that the concept of an Islamic state or *khilifah* is a human improvisation, based on the writings of early Muslim jurists, not on the Quran, *hadith* or *sunna* (Ayubi 1991: 202ff). These writings, calling for *ijtihad,* or independent reasoning, paved the way for the emergence of a nonfundamentalist trend among Islamists.

Within the context of this evolution in Islamist thinking, the Wasat Party platform differs from historical Muslim Brotherhood thinking by making the people (or *umma*), rather than *shari'a,* the source of authority (Abu 'Ila, Habib, and al-Gawhary 1996). While the Wasat still seeks to establish a political system based on Islamic law, its critical reassessment of the source of authority enables it to accept political and social pluralism (Rosefsky Wickham 2004: 207). The Wasat also supports equal rights for all citizens, including women and non-Muslims. Rachid al-Ghannouchi, founder of al-Nahda, has also made similar arguments in favor of the compatibility of Islam and democracy (Ismail 1995: 102).

In some respects, the moderates have been politically marginalized. The Wasat Party was denied recognition by the authorities and its members were expelled from the Muslim Brotherhood in 1996. In Tunisia, al-Nahda was practically eliminated and its leadership forced into exile in Europe. Even in countries that permit Islamist parties, such as Jordan and Morocco, Islamists face restrictions on their activities. An exception to this trend is Algeria, where Islamist parties have adopted moderate positions in order to end the violence and be brought into the political process (ICG 2004b).

Rejection of the Wasat members has not precluded an acceptance of Wasat thinking. Recognizing the need to rejuvenate the group and its fortunes, the Muslim Brotherhood announced a political reform plan in March 2004 that went beyond the previously raised slogan, "Islam is the solution." The plan included calls for an end to the emergency law, a check on presidential powers, releasing political prisoners, and rotation of political power through free and fair elections. In addition, the Brotherhood's supreme guide stated that "[Coptic Christians] must be on equal footing with Muslims in terms of having equal rights," and that "women must be authorized to occupy all kinds of top posts."[13]

The adoption of political reform demands has facilitated the Muslim Brotherhood's alliance with some political forces, including leftist activists, in the National Coalition for Reform (NCR), whose goal is the introduction of a real multiparty democracy.[14] This is in contradistinction to the 1980s, when the Brotherhood refused to cooperate with the leftist Tagammu' Party on the basis that the party contained "atheists" (Kramer 1995: 121). The NCR is part of a wider movement for political reform, grouped under the Kifaya movement umbrella, which includes individuals from across the political spectrum and from a range of civil-society organizations. The participation of the Muslim Brotherhood alongside other actors for political reform is new and contradicts the Brotherhood's previous strategy of not directly antagonizing the regime.

However, civil-society actors remain divided over whether to cooperate with the Brotherhood. Similarly, in other countries where Islamists represent a substantial element within civil society, not all non-Islamist activists have welcomed the Islamist trend. Since the 1980s in Tunisia and Algeria, civil-society groups have wavered over the question of whether to side with Islamists against authoritarian regimes (Garon 2003). Three different positions may be discernible: refusal, cooperation, and defense. Many secular civil-society actors have refused to cooperate with Islamists, fearing that to do so would boost the Islamists at the expense of civil liberties in the long run. In line with writers such as Farag Foda and Fu'ad Zakariya, certain actors believe that calls for an Islamic state are fundamentally incompatible with individual freedoms, which can only be guaranteed within a secular system (Flores 1988; Ayubi 1991: 206ff; Ismail 1995: 101–102).

In Egypt, one of the most consistent opponents of cooperation with the Muslim Brotherhood is former head of the leftist Tagammu' Party, Rifaat Said. He views the Muslim Brotherhood's adoption of demands for political reform as opportunistic.[15] Within the Kifaya movement, there are some that have not joined the NCR since they believe that it is the Brotherhood that will ultimately benefit from a more democratic system.[16] In Tunisia and Algeria, fearing that Islamists would come to power by the ballot box, many elements of secular civil society tacitly supported the authoritarian measures against al-Nahda and the FIS (Garon 2003). The Syrian regime was able to capitalize on the fear of the Islamists coming to power, especially in light of Syria's multireligious and multiethnic makeup, to justify the massive clampdown on the Syrian Muslim Brotherhood (Hinnebusch 1990: 227, 233).

Even where Islamists have stated a commitment to democracy, there are plenty of examples that demonstrate that this does not, by any means, signal a commitment to liberalism. For Islamists, Islam remains the ultimate frame of reference for individual rights. Freedoms of expression, thought, and creativity are only permitted to the extent that these do not, in any way, contradict Islam or what they perceive to be the fundamental tenets of Islam. As the last chapter demonstrates, the realm of intellectual thought and literature has been an object of contestation for Islamists. At the trial of the killers of writer Farag Foda, Sheikh Mohammed El-Ghazali, close to the Muslim Brotherhood, testified that Fuda was an apostate and that it was the duty of Muslims to carry out the death sentence (al-Sayyid 1995b: 277). Throughout the 1990s, Islamists intervened in the realm of culture through the courts. Egyptian Islamic studies professor Nasr Hamid Abu Zayd, and feminist Nawal El Saadawi, were both accused of apostasy on the basis of opinions that concern Islam and tried in separate court cases brought by Islamists.[17] Both cases sought to divorce the individuals from their partners on the basis that their views placed them outside the community of Muslims and, therefore, they could not remain married to Muslims (Bakr, Colla, and Abu Zayd 1993).[18]

In particular, many women's rights activists are concerned about cooperation with Islamist groups because they believe that an Islamic state represents one of the greatest obstacles to women in gaining equal rights. Moderate Islamists usually claim that they support equal citizenship rights for men and women—such as the right to vote and to stand for public office. However, this glosses over the thorny issue of women's role within the family, and the wider issue of state regulation of sexuality. Even Islamist women activists agree that women's primary role is within the family and that modesty is a Muslim's duty (Sadiki 2004: 284ff). The question of a woman's right to marry whomever she chooses became one of the major sticking points (along with the right to change one's religion) in the formulation of a charter for the Tunisian League for Human Rights in 1985, dividing the organization internally. Islamists, together with social conservatives, within the LTDH opposed the notion that Muslim women may marry other than a Muslim man, on the grounds that this was contrary to Islam (Dwyer 1991: 171ff). Moreover, during the electoral campaign of 1989, al-Nahda attacked Tunisia's relatively liberal family code, which prohibits polygamy and grants women relatively liberal rights with regard to divorce (Brand 1998: 194).

Some fear that in attempting to find common ground, some members of civil society are willing to overlook the illiberal position of Islamist groups toward women's rights and religious freedom. The tension between building a broad movement through alliances with moderate Islamists versus building a movement that excludes illiberal positions is apparent in the Kifaya movement. As a loose coalition of individuals, no one point of view predominates. The glue that keeps these individuals together is their commitment to political reform. Some see this arrangement as an advantage in that it enables secular-oriented activists to benefit from the large constituency of the Muslim Brotherhood. Meanwhile, the Brotherhood can hope to gain greater support when the government periodically clamps down on its members. Moreover, in the wake of a string of bomb blasts in Egypt since October 2004, some activists view an alliance with moderate Islamists as a means to isolate the extremist elements who resort to violence to express their political demands. On the other hand, one activist believes that, by failing to address issues concerning the relationship between religion and democracy, the reform movement is failing to confront the thinking that gives rise to violent Islamist groups.[19]

The willingness of some civil-society actors to enter into alliance with moderate Islamists is a reflection of the diversity of views that exist within the "secular camp." As Nadje Al-Ali argues, "The increased interest in Islamist movements . . . does not generally take into account that, far from presenting a singular category, secular tendencies display a range of positions, political affiliations and attitudes toward religion" (2000: 129). Some activists who identify with secularism may possess conservative views with regard to issues such as freedom of expression and issues pertaining to sexuality. Even if Islam does not provide a political framework for many, it does provide a cultural framework for some, in which certain rights demands can be excluded on the basis that they are un-Islamic or alien to local values.

The starkest example of how the issue of "culture" may divide secular civil society is that of the "Queen Boat Case" in Egypt in May 2001. The case refers to the arrest and prosecution of more than fifty men for alleged homosexuality, following a raid by security services on a Nile boat disco. The event generated substantial domestic debate—overwhelmingly in condemnation of the men as "perverts," endangering Egyptian national security (Pratt, forthcoming). The Egyptian human rights community was split over their response to the case. A small group of organizations spoke in defense of the men's rights to a fair trial and to lead their private lives without state interference.[20] In addition, lawyers from these groups represented the men in court. On the other hand, a significant number of organizations rejected not only the idea of the right to express diverse sexual orientations but also refused to represent the Queen Boat defendants on the grounds that homosexuality is not part of Egyptian culture and sexual orientation is not a human right but a Western cultural practice.[21]

While matters of sexuality have been approached through a cultural/religious framework, issues pertaining to civil and political rights

have been approached through a universal framework (thereby reproducing the dichotomy of a national identity that is "modern" on the outside but "traditional" on the "inside"). Human rights groups have, for
the most part, been the most consistent in this respect with regard to the
treatment of Islamists, even though Islamists oppose their reference to
universal norms. In Egypt, human rights groups have consistently been
vocal in opposing state abuses of violent Islamists—such as extrajudicial killings, torture, unfair trials—as well as the harassment and arrest
of Muslim Brotherhood members. This has led the government to accuse
human rights groups of supporting terrorists. Equally, they have opposed
killings by Islamist groups, as well as defending the freedom of expression of secular intellectuals accused of apostasy by Islamists (EOHR
1990, onward). In Tunisia, the LTDH's public condemnation of the regime's repression of al-Nahda members contributed toward the regime's
clampdown on the human rights group itself, thereby muzzling its critical
voice (Waltz 1995: 139, 163). In Algeria, the Algerian League for the
Defence of Human Rights (LADDH), led by Abdennour Ali Yayia, sys-
tematically highlighted abuses by the regime against the Islamists (p.
168). Meanwhile, the president of the Algerian League for Human Rights
(LADH), Youcef Fethallah, condemned political killings by both Islamists
and the government (p. 231). The killing of Fethallah in 1994 and Abdel-
Hafid Megdou, a LADDH activist, in 1995 not only demonstrated the
extreme danger in which human rights activists worked during this period
but the degree to which the universalism of human rights was seen as an
enemy of not only the Islamists but also the (secular) government.

On the surface, the role of religion in public life appears to divide
civil-society actors between Islamists and secularists. Yet this division
is not the most apt. The Islamists' adoption of concepts of democracy
has led them to join with secularists in prodemocracy coalitions. In
other circumstances, both (secular) state and (Islamist) nonstate actors
have vilified human rights activists for their defense of universal norms.
In other words, the label "Islamist" or "secular" does not indicate a per-
son's approach to democracy. Yet, alliances between secular and Islamist activists may be to the detriment of democratization. These alliances
demonstrate that there are those within the secular camp that share
Islamists' notions of essentialized Arab-Muslim culture and, therefore,
are willing to sacrifice certain individual rights that are seen as contrary
to this "culture." In reproducing such notions of culture, certain secularists and Islamists are contributing to maintaining an ideological dimension of authoritarianism.

## Redefining the State Modernization Project:
## The Dilemma of Women and Workers

When the regime denies rights and perpetuates abuses, it is often easier to achieve a consensus within civil society that opposes such antidemocratic practices. However, it is less clear what position to take in relation to those regime measures that have promoted the rights of certain groups. As discussed in the previous chapter, workers and women constitute two groups that have particularly benefited from state-led modernization projects in the postindependence era. On the other hand, the regime's monopoly over questions pertaining to workers' and women's rights has been an obstacle in the emergence of independent groups protecting the rights of these groups. Until the 1980s, workers' interests were represented in regime-dominated trade unions (such as the General Federation of Egyptian Trade Unions (GFETU) and the Union Générale Tunisienne du Travail (UGTT)), while women's rights were represented through state feminism, in addition to regime-dominated women's unions (such as Union Nationale de la Femme Tunisienne and the national women's unions in Syria and Iraq). The reduction in state expenditure due to economic recession impacted upon state provision of rights for these groups. In response, new civil-society organizations, such as the Centre for Trade Union and Worker Services and the New Woman Centre in Egypt, emerged in the 1980s with the objective of protecting these groups' rights.

While there exists a near consensus within civil society with regard to the rights of workers, there does not exist a consensus over how to organize to protect these rights. In Egypt, labor activists, trade unionists, and leftists are debating the future of trade unionism. On the one hand, there are those who believe that the unified federation must be abolished and replaced by a pluralistic trade union system. They believe that a plurality of independent unions would be better equipped to defend workers' interests in the face of economic liberalization. On the other hand, there are those who insist that trade union pluralism could open the way for divisive tactics by employers and the government. In their opinion, it is far better to call for the democratization of the current unified trade union system in order to rid it of government interference (Darwish, Shukr, and Mahmud 1997). In between these two positions, the Centre for Worker and Trade Union Services is arguing for independent trade unionism, whatever form this may take. The priority is to rid workers of the executive-controlled federation, which stands as a huge obstacle to independent workers' activism (CTUWS, n.d.: 4). Whether pluralistic or unified, any future trade union must be able to accommodate the interests and concerns of Egypt's increasingly differentiated labor force (Pratt 2000/2001).

Moreover, it is difficult for trade unionists to contemplate relinquishing the corporatist structures that have, historically, given them access to policymaking circles. The UGTT, like the GFETU, has played a key role in the postindependence history of Tunisia. Its power has derived from its ability to deliver organized popular support for the regime (Bellin 2002: 136). Even though the regime has successively clamped down on workers' protests and has also intervened in UGTT internal affairs, the trade union has benefited from its relationship with the state (p. 137ff). During the 1990s, when structural economic factors should have dampened wage increases, the UGTT was surprisingly successful in negotiating wage levels (Alexander 1996). Consequently, avoiding confrontation with the regime is a priority of trade union officials and has led them to distance themselves from demands for democracy (Bellin 2002: 148).

Meanwhile, rank-and-file workers have demonstrated their disillusionment with corporatist arrangements by organizing wildcat strikes and protests. In Egypt and Tunisia, workers have registered their opposition to measures imposed due to economic reforms, such as job losses, early retirement, and loss of bonuses and/or workplace benefits. In Egypt, between January 1998 and December 1999, 287 workers' protests, including 90 strikes, were recorded, compared to 37 between 1988 and 1989 (Pratt 2000/2001). In Tunisia, the number of strikes and lock-ins, a large number of which have been illegal, have remained high since the 1980s, with 380 recorded in 2001 alone.[22]

These actions reflect workers' disillusionment with the regime and the trade union bureaucracy. However, they do not necessarily seek to oppose the postindependence moral economy, within which workers sacrifice their independence for the sake of contributing to national development. Coming in direct response to cuts in working conditions, the protests are restorative rather than reformist. Moreover, because they are organized independently of a national union, they are necessarily localized. The challenge for those who seek to guarantee workers' rights is to bring workers' protests within an independent national movement (that does not replicate the problems of the nationalist movement). Moreover, there is a need to envision a political economy in which respect for the rights of working people is guaranteed, without denying the civil and political rights of citizens.

The legacy of state feminism has contributed to shaping perspectives of what constitutes a legitimate demand for women in Arab countries. As part of the state-led modernization project, Algeria, Egypt, Tunisia, Iraq, and Syria promulgated constitutions that guaranteed women's equal rights to vote, to hold public office, and to leave the house to work and seek education. Many women's groups, including women's sections of political parties, have focused their activism on protecting the legacy of the state-led modernization project in the face of structural adjustment programs. Their goals include eradicating illiteracy, protecting equal rights for women in the workplace, advancing women's political participation, and promoting women's economic position through income-generation projects (NWRC 1996).

On the other hand, personal status laws in Arab countries, which deal with rights in marriage, divorce, inheritance, and child custody, have been slower to evolve and have stood as a contradiction to promoting women's public participation. Women are treated legally foremost as mothers and wives who are dependent upon men. To different degrees, personal status codes are influenced by *shari'a*. Despite Tunisia's reputation as the most progressive personal status code in the region, its women are still legally obliged to obey their husbands and the man is considered the head of the household (NWRC 1996: 91–92). The government has used the threat of Islamist resurgence to refuse to amend the code to grant women greater rights. Consequently, independent women activists have found themselves in a dilemma in defining their position in relation to the amendment of the personal status code. One woman activist described discussions that occurred in writing about the issue for a women's journal, *Nissa,* in the 1980s: "The Personal Status Code was then being attacked by the Islamists, but at the same time it was strongly defended by the government. There was no question, of course, of allying ourselves with the Islamists, but we didn't want to sound like a mouthpiece for the government either" (cit. in Dwyer 1991: 202).

Similarly, in Egypt, where women have enjoyed formal equality in the public sphere, there is no consensus among activists around defining priorities. On the one hand, one could argue that differences in priorities between groups creates an effective division of labor. On the other, different priorities reflect different understandings of the causes of women's oppression within society and therefore generate discussions between different activists. As noted above, many women activists have tended to focus on the struggle for women's equality within the public sphere (political and economic participation and education), rooted in understandings of women's oppression in terms of modernization or dependency paradigms (Al-Ali 2000: 152ff).

In the 1980s, some groups began to emerge that challenged the predominant paradigms for explaining women's oppression. The Arab Women's Solidarity Association (AWSA), founded in 1982 and closed by the authorities in 1991, and the New Woman Research and Study Centre (NWRC), founded in 1990, constituted the first attempts to organize women around an understanding of oppression that encompassed women's experiences within the private sphere (Dwyer 1991: 184ff; NWRC 1996: 35–39). AWSA founder Nawal El Saadawi was one of the first writers to discuss publicly issues of female genital mutilation, sexual abuse, and prostitution in her 1977 book, *Al-wajh al-ari l-il-mar'a al-'arabiya* ("The Hidden Face of Eve"). NWRC was one of the first organizations to address the issue of violence against women in the home.

These issues have not been embraced by all activists—even those who seek to ameliorate the position of women. Some activists view issues pertaining to sexuality as reflecting a Western feminist agenda and not reflective of the interests of "ordinary" Arab women (Al-Ali 2000: 170). Within the discourse of nationalism, marriage and divorce laws, female sexuality, and family relationships are issues to be kept away from politics and public discussion, especially in front of Western representatives at international conferences, even if Arab activists disagree with some of the practices that happen within the private sphere. These are perceived as necessary measures in order to protect national culture—"the foundation of the nation"—from Western cultural invasion (Hetata 1997).

In both Tunisia and Egypt, by discussing issues pertaining to the private sphere, activists are challenging the state-led modernization project that has either monopolized the issue of women's position within the family (as in Tunisia) or that has excluded the private sphere as relevant for action ameliorating women's situation (as in Egypt). This creates dilemmas for women activists, in that gender concerns are already marginalized within civil society. By going against the grain, women activists may not only be further marginalized, but also encounter hostility (Al-Ali 2000: 170). Consequently, there are significant pressures on women activists to "moderate" their positions, for example, by cooperating with the state or by not discussing certain taboo issues (Dwyer 1991: 201ff).

For both workers and women, there exist a number of difficulties in formulating an alternative to the regime-led national modernization project of the postindependence period. On the one hand, this project has afforded these groups certain measures of protection that are now threatened by economic liberalization. On the other, it has operated to subordinate the interests of these groups to the objectives of modernization, thereby denying autonomy to these groups and marginalizing certain aspects of their rights. Attempts to restore the economic and legal benefits of the national modernization project without challenging the institutional or ideological components of this project serve to protect the social and political relations that underpin authoritarianism (as a system).

## Conceptualizing National Identity: The Issue of "Minorities"

As previously discussed, the construction of a national identity in Algeria, Egypt, Iraq, Syria, and Tunisia has been central to the national modernization project and state-building processes in the postindependence period. National identification has entailed the erasure of national difference in order to construct unity within the nation-state. While all Arab countries are multiethnic and multireligious, Iraq and Syria represent the most heterogeneous countries of the region. It is probably for this reason that these countries proved to be fertile territories for the development of Arab nationalism and communism as nominally secular ideologies (thereby uniting citizens of different religions). Simultaneously, these countries, particularly Iraq, have experienced the greatest hostility to Arab nationalism as an ideology that promotes an exclusively Sunni Arab identity to the detriment of non-Sunni Arab communities.

One feature of new civil-society actors is their attempts to redefine the nation to include previously marginalized voices—on the bases of class, gender, region, religion, or ethnicity (Halliday 2000: 31). In so doing, these actors destabilize historical constructions of national identity. This opens up the potential for more pluralistic conceptions of the nation that may also be more democratic. Simultaneously, the challenge to national identity represented by the claims of communal groups pose new problems concerning the management of difference within a unified state.

In Iraq, fears about state disintegration helped to defuse opposition to Saddam Hussein's regime, and civil-society actors were (and continue to be) divided over the question of the identity of the Iraqi state. During the war against Iran (1980–1988), Saddam was able to neutralize the various opposition forces (Shi'a and Kurdish groups, pro-Syrian Ba'thists, and the Iraqi Communist Party), while galvanizing regime-dominated civil-society groups in defense of Iraq. Saddam reformulated Ba'thist ideology from its pan-Arabist origins to become a new synthesis of Arabism, Islamism, and Iraqi patriotism, thereby appealing to Kurds and Shi'a, as well as to Sunnis. None of the opposition groups were able to overcome the popular appeal of Iraqi patriotism to construct a position that would mobilize people to oppose Saddam (Abd al-Jabbar 1992). Despite the destruction and disillusionment wrought by the first Gulf War on Iraqi society, by 1988 the opposition was in crisis and considering a policy of reconciliation with Saddam. Devoid of any alternative political leadership, the popular uprisings after the second Gulf War were easily quashed by Saddam (Abd al-Jabbar 1992). Moreover, the potential dominance of Shi'ite Islamism played a factor in preventing the emergence of wide-scale support for the uprisings among Sunnis and secular-minded Shi'a (Abd al-Jabbar 1992; Davis 2005: 230).

Following the uprisings, the development of independent civil-society actors faced huge obstacles. The imposition of sanctions increased even further Iraqi citizens' dependency upon the state. Moreover, aware of the depth of opposition to his rule, Saddam increased his ruthless persecution of potential centers of opposition. Consequently, organized groups inside Iraq were forced underground and/or abroad. These groups included the Iraqi opposition in exile: the Iraqi National Congress (INC), led by the secular-oriented Shi'ite Ahmed Chalabi; the Iraqi Communist Party; the Supreme Council for the Islamic Revolution in Iraq (SCIRI); the Da'wa Party; and the Iraqi National Accord, which consisted of ex-Ba'thists, disgruntled military officers, and former members of the security services, led by Iyad Allawi (Davis 2005: 257–258). In addition, by the 1990s there were huge numbers of Iraqi exiles living in Europe and North America, who had left in successive waves since the Ba'th had come to power in 1968. Some of these individuals established nonpartisan organizations, such as the Iraq Foundation and the Iraqi Forum for Democracy, based in the United States, and Act Together (Iraqi and non-Iraqi women), based in the United Kingdom. Such organizations have played a role in promoting discussion of the concepts of human rights, women's rights, civil society, antisectarianism, and democracy among expatriate Iraqi groups. In their experiences of repression, opposition groups found much shared ground around the principles of human rights and democracy (pp. 268–270). However, while a consensus emerged in support of democracy, for some, democracy was considered a means to an end (of ridding Iraq of Saddam with international support), rather than a commitment to the principle of universal human rights.

Following 1991, the Kurdish region managed to escape rule from Baghdad and to establish its own elected assembly. As a result, greater spaces for civil-society activism were created. These included the establishment of women's organizations, human rights groups, and community development associations, as well as the growth in importance of a radical Islamist party (Ansar al-Islam). Nevertheless, the region remained dominated by the two Kurdish nationalist parties (the PUK and the KDP), which, following a bloody war between the two groups (1992–1996), created a de facto separation of the region. The continued significance of nationalist resistance, including the existence of Kurdish fighters (the *peshmerga*), has militarized society with negative consequences for human rights and women's rights. The latter remain subordinated to the aims and objectives of the Kurdish leadership, while there has been an increase in "honor killings" in the autonomous region since 1991 (Mojab 2004).

Following the fall of the regime, the application of principles of democracy and human rights has been complicated by the realities of deciding how to govern the Iraqi polity. The fall of Saddam created the opportunity for the establishment of a democratic system. However, it also led to contestations over state resources and the establishment of institutions that are rooted in competition between the leaders of different communal groups for political power. This politicization of sectarian identities poses the problem of how to accommodate the interests of the three major communal groupings emerging out of Ba'thist Iraq without entrenching sectarianism and compromising the integrity of the Iraqi nation-state.

Communal identities are rooted in the historical development of the Iraqi state. Despite the rhetoric of one nation, decades of Ba'th rule have created a state where networks of family, clan, and tribe have played an increasingly important role, particularly under sanctions (Tripp 2000; Zubaida 2003). As state resources shrank, individuals looked to kin, clan, and tribe for socioeconomic survival, thereby bolstering communal identities based on religion, tribe, and ethnicity. Moreover, the former regime's mass persecution of groups on the basis of their communal identity (Shi'a, Kurds) rigidified sectarian differences. These networks and identities have not disappeared in post-Saddam Iraq and play a major role in shaping the Iraqi polity—at the expense of human rights and democracy.

In the past, differences over the future nature of the Iraqi polity were relegated to the priority of ridding the country of Saddam Hussein. In the post-Saddam period, these differences became major sticking points between political representatives in the drafting of a new constitution in 2005 and have contributed to engendering conflict within Iraqi society. Issues such as federalism (including whether the multiethnic city of Kirkuk will be included in a Kurdish area, and the formula for the distribution of fiscal revenues), the role of Islam, the disbanding of Kurdish and Shi'a militias, and women's representation constituted some of the areas that proved difficult to resolve in the process of drafting a constitution. They reflect the difficulty of reconciling competing visions of Iraq, rooted in different interests and mobilized around different communal identities. The insistence of Iraq's government, pressured by the United States, to stick to the 15 August deadline, meant that the drafting committees were forced to paper over many of these differences through the adoption of vague language. Moreover, the short time frame left little time for widespread consultation within civil society (Brown 2005). In other words, these differences concerning the nature of the Iraqi polity will continue to haunt the country for the foreseeable future and to fuel violence against civilians.

The case of Iraq demonstrates how challenges to the postindependence national identity, which suppressed diversity, do not necessarily support a pluralization of the polity. Rather, suppressed communities mobilize around communal identities to claim resources and political power. This may be at the expense of ensuring universal citizenship, regardless of the identity ascribed to an individual. That is not to argue that, consequently, diversity must be suppressed. Rather, political claims that are made on the basis of identity fail to engender democratization and reproduce essentialized notions of the national "subject" that negate political pluralism and underpin authoritarianism.

## National Identity and the Issue of the West

The question of the relationship between national identity and civil society has also arisen in the context of considering the relationship of the state to the West. National identity construction in the postindependence period has occurred against the backdrop of colonial domination, in addition to continued Western domination of the region. Within this context, there has existed a widespread rejection of cultural influences that are deemed "Western." In this context, civil-society groups that are perceived as being too "Western" are discredited, not on the basis of their claims, but on the basis of their supposed cultural orientation.

In Egypt, human rights and women's rights groups have been at the center of debates about links to the West. To begin with, the concept of rights is often portrayed as alien to the Arab-Muslim culture, even by those who are sympathetic to them. In response, rights groups have been involved in debates over their "authenticity" and, linked to this, their legitimacy. This has taken the form of debates about the Islamic sources of human rights or women's rights. In addition, the women's movement has been involved in reconstructing feminist history in order to demonstrate the "native" roots of feminist movements (Ali 2000: 58). Meanwhile, human rights organizations have also been forced to defend the nature of their relationships with Western rights groups and also their method of working (CIHRS, EOHR, and GDD 1998).

One of the most public debates within civil society concerning its links with the West has taken place around the issue of foreign funding. This debate originates within the EOHR, where the issue of the receiving of funds from abroad was first raised in 1991 in response to an urgent need for money to finance an expansion in the organization's activities (El-Sayed Said 1994: 73). At that time, those in favor of accepting foreign funding tended to put forward a pragmatic argument that the organization could not continue to exist at the current level of funding, while the political, social, and economic situation prevented domestic fund-raising (p. 76). Yet this position entailed an important shift in thinking among certain EOHR members that the West could no longer be viewed as a monolithic enemy and that alliances with certain groups and individuals within the West could be beneficial for the promotion of human rights in Egypt. Opponents of foreign funding within the EOHR did not accept the idea that links with the West could be productive. Rather, many opponents of foreign funding argued that receiving foreign funding would lead the Egyptian human rights movement to be dependent upon the West at the expense of building a domestic democratic movement (for example, Sha'rawi 1994: 271; Fergany 1994: 29). After four months of discussion, the board took a majority decision to accept foreign funding on the condition that specific grants would not compromise the goals of the EOHR and that they came from nongovernmental sources (EOHR 1994: 18).

Although this debate was apparently resolved within the EOHR, the issue of foreign funding has continued to arise in relation to the establishment of other human rights and women's rights groups. Approaches to the issue range between outright rejection of foreign funding to acceptance of external grants on the basis of certain conditions. Some activists argue that there is a large degree of hypocrisy in these positions (Al-Ali 2000: 201). However, the different approaches by various activists to the issue demonstrate the significance of negotiating links with the West as part of the process of negotiating one's own identity. In most cases, activists resort to hybrid solutions, for example, by accepting grants from NGOs abroad on the condition that their country's foreign policies toward the Arab world are not perceived as harmful (see Pratt 2002, chap. 3, for more details).

Given that rights organizations challenge monolithic constructions of national identity by deconstructing the historical binary divide between the West and Egypt/Arab world, it is unsurprising that these organizations have attracted criticism, not only from the Egyptian government but from other activists within civil society. In 1998, an EOHR report about police brutality in a predominantly Coptic Christian village led to charges by some (including a former board member of the organization) that the EOHR had harmed Egypt's reputation abroad and compromised national security (Pratt 2005: 86).[23] The government has used the issue of foreign funding to persecute activists that raise the issue of human rights and democracy in international forums. In 1999, secretary-general of the EOHR Hafez Abu Seada was held for two weeks and questioned about the aforementioned report and its links with a British Parliament check for $25,000, and then charged (but never tried) in 2000 for receiving foreign funding without official permission. Pro-democracy activist Saad Eddin Ibrahim was put on trial before a state security court in 2001, then again in 2002, and found guilty of charges that his organization had received foreign funding without government approval and that he had "tarnished Egypt's reputation abroad."[24] In 2005, a campaign by the state-controlled press against Ayman Nur, one of the few candidates to stand against Hosni Mubarak in the presidential elections that year, portrayed him as an agent of the US government.[25] The government has drawn on widespread suspicion of the West to justify imposing controls over Egyptian NGOs' fund-raising. Unsurprisingly, the 1998–1999 NGO campaign against government attempts to increase control over associations downplayed the issue of foreign funding in order to mobilize domestic support for its cause (Pratt 2004).

The representation of the West as being in fundamental opposition to the Arab world has also operated in other contexts to weaken human rights organizations in other countries. Within the LTDH, there were sharp debates over whether to oppose the 1991 war against Iraq. Arab nationalists and Islamists opposed the war on the grounds that it was the West's war against the Arab world (Garon 2003: 35). Meanwhile, others, including the organization's president, sought to refocus the debate in terms of international law and human rights principles, rather than political affinities. The ensuing rifts within the organization spilled out onto the pages of the Tunisian press. The LTDH president was attacked by some members as well as other sections of civil society of having "sold out to the West" (Garon 2003: 35; Waltz 1995: 169–170).

## Conclusion

This chapter demonstrates that there exists a plurality of voices within civil societies in the Arab world. A number of debates occur within civil society over questions of activists' relationship to state structures, the nature of their demands, and the character of alliances, both domestically and externally. These debates reflect differences among civil-society actors on the basis of class, gender, religious, ethnic, and ideological orientations. In some cases, debates are framed in terms of the most effective strategy and priorities for achieving actors' aims of democratic reform—for example, in building alliances between secular and Islamist forces or calling for the establishment of independent trade unions. Most importantly, these debates reflect different visions of civil society and the polity.

The different views of civil-society actors demonstrate a variety of positions with regard to the hegemonic project constructed in the post-independence period. As discussed in previous chapters, this project has been constructed around support for the objective of national moderniza-tion and political sovereignty, based on essentialized notions of national identity and the construction of corporatist structures as a means of uni-fying the nation to achieve these objectives. The positions of civil-society actors range between accommodation of and resistance to this consensus. Accommodation of the postindependence consensus is reflected in posi-tions of cooperation with state institutions or working within state corpo-ratist structures, taking up demands that are "socially legitimate" with regard to women's rights, and rejection of "Western" cultural influences over authentic "Arab/Islamic" identity. Resistance to the postindepen-dence consensus is reflected in positions of rejecting state domination over civil-society organizations and accepting the validity of trans-national links in promoting human rights and democracy.

In general, the Islamist groups are the most accommodating of the postindependence consensus in that their discourse emphasizes notions of authentic Islamic identity, which they seek to propagate by working through corporatist institutions, where possible. This reflects a concep-tualization of civil society as "affective" and of the polity in organic or communalistic terms. Some secular civil-society actors have also endorsed such a view of the polity, for example by criticizing those NGOs that accept foreign funding and denying the existence of certain rights pertaining to sexuality as "alien" to national culture. At the other end of the spectrum, human rights and women's rights organizations are often the most resistant to the consensus, by rejecting state domination of civil society, promoting the rights of the individual above "national security," challenging patriarchal notions of the family, and seeking transnational alliances. This reflects an associative concept of civil society and a more liberal and/or cosmopolitan vision of the polity. However, regime intimidation and criticism by other members of civil society have made it difficult to consistently maintain this position. Many civil-society actors position themselves at different points on the spectrum between resistance and accommodation.

The concept of resistance to/accommodation of the postindependence hegemonic consensus is significant in understanding the potential for civil society to bring about democratization. It is not sufficient that civil-society actors accept concepts of human rights and democracy—indeed, almost all of them do. Nor is it sufficient for civil society to oppose the regime—which is also very common among activists. Rather, challenges to the ideological and material foundations upon which authoritarianism (as a system) is based pave the way for democratization. Currently, the strongest trend within civil society in most Arab countries—that of the Islamists—is the most accommodating of the hegemonic consensus. Their more recent support for liberal democracy indicates that an Islamist-dominated government could lead to the establishment of procedural elements of democratization, such as guarantees for civil and political rights. Indeed, as I have demonstrated here, minimum guarantees of such rights are necessary to protect civil society as a space within which projects for the future of the polity are conceptualized. However, in a context in which there still remains a consensus within civil society (both Islamist and secular) that supports notions of the polity in organic or communal terms, the long-term protection of such rights remains questionable. Within such a scenario, there would be little intellectual or political resistance to the erosion of civil and political rights (either on paper or in practice) on the grounds of "national interest" and protecting "authenticity" from the "Other" (whether the West or other ethnic/religious communities). Consequently, a change in regime that leads to a government dominated by those who share a view of the polity rooted in communal relations (whether Islamist or secular)—

even one that accepts the procedures of democracy—will likely represent a continuation of the political and social relations that underpin authoritarianism rather than a transition to democracy. This is not due to any inherent contradictions between Islam and democracy but rather to the logic of current Islamist projects for political reform.

Before democracy can be built, civil-society actors must be able to fully debate the questions that arise from the historical experience of the emergence of the nation-state in the Arab world. The current question among civil-society actors is no longer whether democracy is a desirable system, but rather what sort of polity can sustain democracy. The question of the fragility of the postindependence project of nation-state building often underlies concerns over how to promote civil-society demands without jeopardizing the future existence of the state or, on the other hand, lending credence to the regime that controls the state. These questions about a future polity are contained within the debates examined in this chapter and include: how to protect groups that are discriminated against socially without promoting the authority of an undemocratic regime; how to govern a multiethnic and multireligious nation without jeopardizing the integrity of the state (and its ability to safeguard rights) or repressing difference; and how to interact with the West without becoming subordinate to the West. Currently, civil-society actors remain divided over most of these issues. The potential for sustained democratization depends upon the creation of a new consensus within civil society that answers these questions in ways that challenge the material and ideological bases of authoritarianism. However, this will not happen overnight. In the short term, some procedural guarantees of liberal democracy may be sufficient to sustain civil-society activity but this, in and of itself, will not ensure a democratic transition.

## Notes

1. Lawyers Committee for Human Rights, "Background Paper: What Happened to the Human Rights Movements in Egypt, Tunisia, and Kuwait?" 28 November 2001, http://www.humanrightsfirst.org/middle_east/ME_background .pdf, accessed 1 August 2005, p. 5.

2. EMHRN, "The State of Liberties and Human Rights in Tunisia," November 1999, http://www.euromedrights.net/english/Download/tun-liga_eng.pdf, accessed 1 August 2005.

3. Lawyers Committee for Human Rights, "Background Paper," p. 5.

4. "Naisance du Conseil national pour les libertes en Tunisie," http://marika.demangeon.free.fr/textes/tunisie/tunisie9901.html, accessed 21 July 2005.

5. See CNLT website, http://welcome.to/cnlt, accessed 15 July 2005.

6. "Commemoration du VIe anniversaire du CNLT," 26 December 2004, http://www.geocities.com/for_dem_lib/Com261204.htm, accessed 1 August 2005.

7. However, the AWSA was closed by the authorities in 1991, following El Saadawi's open opposition to Egypt's participation in the Gulf War, demonstrating the vulnerability of associations under the law.

8. Legal Research and Resource Centre for Human Rights (LRRCHR), Centre for Egyptian Women's Legal Aid, Land Centre for Human Rights, Arab Program for Human Rights Activists, Centre for Social and Economic Rights (Adala), and Muhammad 'Abd al-Mun'im (member of the Centre for Human Rights Legal Aid) (1999)."As for Us, We Are Staying," Cairo, 4 June; online at: http://www.geocities.com/llrc.geo/NGO/staying.htm, accessed 18 February 2001.

9. Nicola Pratt, "Egypt Harasses Human Rights Activists," *Middle East Report Online,* 17 August 2000, http://iticwebarchives.ssrc.org/Middle%20East%20Research%20and%20Information%20Project/www.merip.org/mero/mero081700.html, accessed 2 August 2005; Amira Huweidy, "Asserting the Priceless Value of Rights," *Al-Ahram Weekly Online,* 22–28 January 2004, http://weekly.ahram.org.eg/2004/674/eg3.htm, accessed 2 August 2005.

10. Amira Huweidy, "Rights at a Crossroads," *Al-Ahram Weekly Online,* 18–24 May 2000, http://weekly.ahram.org.eg/2000/482/eg6.htm, accessed 2 August 2005; Huweidy, "Asserting the Priceless Value of Rights."

11. Gihan Shahine, "NCHR Speaks out, Finally," *Al-Ahram Weekly Online,* 21–27 April 2005, http://weekly.ahram.org.eg/2005/739/eg5.htm, accessed 3 August 2005.

12. Joshua A. Stacher, "Egypt's National Council for Human Rights," *Middle East Report Online,* no. 235, http://www.merip.org/mer/mer235/stacher.html#_edn11, accessed 3 August 2005.

13. Gamal Essam El-Din, "Brotherhood Steps into the Fray," *Al-Ahram Weekly Online,* 11–17 March 2004, http://weekly.ahram.org.eg/2004/681/eg3.htm, accessed 27 July 2005.

14. Omayma Abdel-Latif, "Tactical Considerations," *Al-Ahram Weekly Online,* 21–27 July 2005, http://weekly.ahram.org.eg/2005/752/fo6.htm, accessed 4 August 2005.

15. Gamal Essam El-Din, "Brotherhood Steps into the Fray."

16. Omayma Abdel-Latif, "Strategic Engagement," *Al-Ahram Weekly Online,* 30 June–6 July 2005, http://weekly.ahram.org.eg/2005/749/eg5.htm, accessed 22 July 2005.

17. Although El Saadawi claims that quotes from an interview she gave were misrepresented.

18. For more details, see, Khaled Dawoud, "Case of Incitement," *Al-Ahram Weekly Online,* 12–18 July 2001, http://weekly.ahram.org.eg/2001/542/eg7.htm, accessed 4 August 2005.

19. Fatemah Farag, "What Lies Beneath," *Al-Ahram Weekly Online,* 5–11 May 2005, http://weekly.ahram.org.eg/2005/741/eg10.htm, accessed 22 July 2005.

20. These groups included the Hisham Mubarak Law Centre, the Nadim Centre for the Rehabilitation of Victims of Torture, and the Egyptian Initiative for Personal Rights.

21. *Rose al-Youssef,* "Special Report: How Could Anyone Believe Them After This Ridiculous Statement? They're Defending Egyptian Perverts Under the Pretext of 'Human Rights'!" 15 July 2001, hosted on the website, GayEgypt .Com: http://gayegypt.com/amrep08andro.html, accessed 6 December 2004.

22. LABORSTA Internet, http://laborsta.ilo.org/, accessed 5 August 2005.

23. The issue of Egypt's Coptic Christian community is historically sensitive. Colonial powers used the question of ethnic and religious minorities in the Arab region to "divide and rule." The Egyptian anticolonial movement rejected the notion of Copts constituting a religious minority in order to unite Egyptians against British rule. Today, the existence of religious discrimination or sectarianism is almost universally denied within Egypt, despite the fact that Copts do not enjoy equal rights with regard to freedom of worship. See also Karim al-Gawhary, "Copts in the 'Egyptian Fabric,'" *Middle East Report,* no. 200 (July-Sept. 1996), pp. 21–22.

24. Mona al-Ghobashy, "Antinomies of the Saad Eddin Ibrahim Case," *Middle East Report Online,* 15 August 2002, http://www.merip.org/mero/mero 081502.html; Nicola Pratt, "Egypt Harasses Human Rights Activists," *Middle East Report Online,* 17 August 2000, http://www.merip.org/mero/mero081700 .html, both accessed 10 August 2005.

25. Warren P. Strobel, "Egyptian Opposition Politician Accuses Government of Smear Tactics," *Knight Ridder Newspapers,* 20 April 2005, http://www.realcities.com/mld/krwashington/11443935.htm, accessed 10 August 2005.

# 6

## Transnational Links and Democratization

UNTIL NOW, THIS BOOK HAS examined the process of democratization as one that involves actors within the borders of the nation-state alone (whether state or nonstate actors). Yet, over the past few decades there has been an increasing interest in the impact of actors that are not confined to the nation-state, but that operate across nation-state borders. These "transnational" actors are predominantly nongovernmental actors, particularly civil-society actors, including NGOs, trade unions, and social movements.

The increasing interest in transnational actors reflects the dramatic growth in their numbers and their increasing importance in international politics in the postwar period. For example, the number of nongovernmental organizations (NGOs) with UN consultative status grew from zero in 1945 to almost 2,500 in 2002.[1] Likewise, other transnational actors (for example, transnational corporations, transborder crime networks, and migrants) have increased in number and frequency since World War II.

The growth in transnational actors has been aided by the transformations in technology experienced in the postwar period. For example, the Internet has facilitated global communication flows by making them cheaper and quicker. This has enabled individuals and groups in different countries to share information and mobilize across borders around common issues of concern, such as the war on Iraq. In addition, the evolution of "universal" norms in the postwar period around respect for human rights, environmental protection, and poverty reduction, among others, has created global "terms of reference" for citizen action across borders. Simultaneously, many contemporary problems, such as ecological degradation and the regulation of capital, cut across national borders, obliging social movements to target multilateral organizations and cooperate across borders in order to address issues that impact upon the rights and welfare of individuals.

The increasing importance of transnational actors is reflected in their influence on global public policy. For example, the International Campaign to Ban Landmines is credited with mobilizing international government support for the ratification of the Convention on the Prohibition of the Use, Stockpiling, Production, and Transfer of Anti-Personnel Mines and on Their Destruction in 1997 (Scott 2001). The Jubilee 2000 campaign has been instrumental in putting debt relief on the agenda of the World Bank, IMF, and G-7, as well as some national governments (Collins, Gariyo, and Burdon 2001).

In addition to influencing public policymaking, transnational civil-society actors play a role in transforming norms that shape policy agendas. Over the last few decades, transnational civil-society organizations have been at the forefront of campaigns to recognize gender-based violence as a human rights issue, the right to development as a human right, and the concept of corporate social responsibility, among others (Keck and Sikkink 1998; Falk 1999; Bunch et al. 2001). In this respect, transnational civil society may be seen to have a democratizing effect upon international affairs (Falk 1999; Keck and Sikkink 1998). Indeed, the mere act of "global citizen action" is claimed by many within the antiglobalization movement to be an inherently democratizing act, since it represents a counterbalance to the power of global corporations and markets that appear to override the powers of national governments and the interests of ordinary people. On the other hand, the increased influence of nongovernmental actors in global affairs raises fears among some observers about the loss of public accountability of decisionmakers (Jessop 1997; Matthews 1997).

Transnational links may represent a challenge to national governments, and particularly Arab governments that lack accountability. In such circumstances, multilateral forums and transnational movements may represent the only spaces in which citizens of Arab countries can make their voices heard. Transnational links may facilitate opportunities for civil societies to pressure their authoritarian governments. The "boomerang effect" signifies that where domestic civil-society actors make links with international actors such as foreign governments, international NGOs, and social movements, the latter may pressure authoritarian governments from outside to comply with international standards regarding human rights, women's rights, the environment, and other democratic norms (Keck and Sikkink 1998; Risse, Ropp, and Sikkink 1999). In a sense, governments are "shamed" within the international arena for their lack of democracy and therefore may feel obliged to implement the necessary reforms.

Moreover, international attention to events within a particular nation-state may protect local civil-society activists there from harassment or imprisonment by the authorities. This is certainly the underlying assumption of the letter-writing campaigns and urgent action appeals by human rights organizations such as Amnesty International and the Fédération Internationale des Droits de l'Homme, among others. Egyptian prodemocracy activist Hafez Abu Seada benefited from international pressure on the Egyptian regime to protect him from prosecution in 1999. However, in the majority of Arab countries, international pressure has been insufficient to protect civil-society activists, and many have served prison sentences or continue to languish in prison until today and/or to face continual harassment by the authorities. Another Egyptian prodemocracy activist, Saad Eddin Ibrahim, was obliged to spend several years in prison before being released by the Egyptian authorities. In other words, transnational links may help to create the necessary space for domestic civil society to mobilize for democratic reforms, but this is usually dependent on diplomatic intervention from a major Western country (as in the case of Abu Seada, where interventions by representatives of the UK/EU and the United States may be seen to be significant in this regard). However, the case of Ibrahim demonstrates that not even diplomatic pressure may be sufficient to protect activists. Indeed, it is possible that US pressure actually strengthened the resolve of the authorities to keep Ibrahim in prison.

Despite the fact that transnational links may not be sufficient for guaranteeing the construction of democratic spaces, they may still contribute to democratization at a normative level. The growth in transnational links facilitates intercultural exchanges and acts of solidarity that blur distinctions between nations and communities by breaking down the "us and them" attitude toward those located beyond the nation. This process enables new combinations of identities to be created, resulting in a "hybrid" culture that resists the notion that there exists one "authentic" national identity (Nederveen Pieterse 1995). In some cases, these new identities can become a resource for the creation of transnational social movements or a movement for "globalization from below" that seeks to democratize global and local politics (Keck and Sikkink

1998; Falk 1999). The blurring of boundaries between different national cultures also contributes to challenging the notion of internal national homogeneity that excludes those who do not conform to expectations about what is appropriate to national culture. Challenging essentialized notions of national identity and culture may empower previously suppressed or ignored social groups, based on class, gender, ethnicity, religion, sexuality, or other identities (Held and McGrew 2000).

The growth of the human rights movement in the Arab world has been aided by links with international human rights groups and concerned donor agencies, as we saw in Chapter 3. Moreover, human rights activists have often been engaged with articulating a "postnationalist" politics. On the other hand, the movements examined in this chapter have formed with objectives other than engendering democratic reforms. In the process, they have formed transnational links that could potentially be seen as a challenge to the nation-state and to the state-centric political ideologies that have predominated within the Arab world. Consequently, it is important to examine whether these transnational links provide the possibility of reshaping the nationalist consensus and breaking down the essentialized identities that are resistant to the construction of democratized relations of power.

## Transnationalism in the Arab World: From Empire to Colonialism

Although transnationalism refers to relations that cross nation-state borders, it is also possible to see transnationalism as a continuation of the historical flows and networks that precede the modern nation-state. Indeed, the Arab world has experienced intraregional and extraregional links since ancient times due to shared language and religion, the historical predominance of pastoralism, the region's strategic location in east-west and north-south trade routes, the location of holy sites and places of pilgrimage for all three of the monotheistic religions, as well as the cycle of wars and invasions. These factors have brought people of the Arab region, at various times, into contact with Turks, Persians, Indians, Mongols, Africans, Romans, Byzantines, Franks, and Europeans. Therefore, the Arab world has been the site of many exchanges and interactions between people of different religious, linguistic, and geographical origins, creating cosmopolitan milieux at various moments in Islamic history (Zubaida 1999). This is reflected in the languages, cuisine, leisure pursuits, and architecture of the Arab countries today.

In addition, the Arab region has been home to a diversity of religions and ethnicities other than Muslim/Arab: Kurds and Berbers (although predominantly Muslim) constitute significant ethnic "minorities" within the region. Christian and Jewish communities were found in all Arab cities, with the exception of those in the Arabian peninsula, and they were recognized as "protected subjects" (*dhimmi*). They were integrated into public life, although they were also subject to certain restrictions on the basis of their religion (Hourani 1991: 117). In most cases, non-Muslims were not considered to be equal with Muslims. Nevertheless, the *dhimmi* system granted a certain degree of religious and cultural autonomy that protected minorities (pp. 118–119).

The growing influence of Europe within the Ottoman Empire from the end of the eighteenth century led to an exposure to European thinking and technology. By the nineteenth century, there were sectors of the intelligentsia within Arab countries that admired Europe's economic and military achievements and wished to fully adopt them. Some, such as the Tunisian reformer Khayr al-Din (d. 1889) believed that Islam could be compatible with European reforms in administration and military organization. Others, such as Jamal al-Din al-Afghani (1839–1897) and Muhammad 'Abduh (1849–1905), still regarded Islam as superior but believed it to be in need of purification from tyranny and superstition to pave the way for reforms that would rival Europe (Hourani 1983: 304ff).

European encroachment spurred many reforms and processes within the Ottoman Empire that stimulated links between different communities across the Arab world. The lowering of communal barriers through legal reforms and various social transformations enabled greater participation of non-Muslim elites in public life (Zubaida 1999). The establishment of European-type schools in Cairo and of mission schools in Beirut created a new market for printed materials in Arabic. European ideas and technology were discussed in the flourishing Arabic press of the time (Hourani 1991: 303–304). The spread of new media in the Arabic language enabled a greater exchange of ideas across the region via periodicals, while the publishing houses of Cairo and Beirut produced textbooks for the region's ever-increasing number of students, as well as books of literature, popular science, and history (Hourani 1991: 338–339). These regional cultural and literary links provided a basis for the emergence of a pan-Arab movement.

Although European influence contributed to the creation of cosmopolitan milieux within the Arab world and the flourishing of intellectual, artistic, and business links across the region and with Europe, the majority of the population were excluded from these developments. The humiliating experience of European colonialism for many people within the Arab region created a hostility toward Europe and all it represented, as well as those native groups (such as Christians and Jews) that appeared to benefit from links to the Europeans. In the cosmopolitan cities of Alexandria and Cairo in the late nineteenth and early twentieth century, native Egyptians represented a reservoir of functionaries, prostitutes, and servants. They were subject to segregation in certain public places, and discrimination and contempt by the cosmopolitan elites. Anticolonial groups such as the Muslim Brotherhood in Egypt not only opposed European political domination but also aimed to rescue Muslim youth from the corrupting cultural domination of the Europeans (Zubaida 1999: 26).

Despite political hostility/suspicion within some quarters toward Europeans, there were attempts toward the creation of transnational movements based on universal solidarities of feminism and communism. The International Woman Suffrage Alliance (IWSA), established in Berlin in 1904, attempted to reach out to women beyond the West through a tour of the East during 1911 and 1912. The Egyptian Feminist Union (EFU) and the Jewish Women's Equal Rights Association from Palestine joined the International Alliance of Women for Suffrage and Equal Citizenship (as the IWSA became) in 1923. To some degree a transnational sisterhood was created (Badran 1995: 109).

Yet, despite the alliance's commitment to upholding equal rights for men and women, it was unwilling to engage with the issue of colonialism and the fact that neither men nor women in the colonies were entitled to vote. Moreover, Western feminists often regarded the women of the East as objects of sympathy, rather than equal members of an international movement (Badran 1995: 69ff, 108ff; Bulbeck 1998: 24). The national interests of different members of the alliance often overrode gender interests. By the 1930s, the tensions between the imperial feminism of the European and North American members versus the antiimperialist nationalism of the Middle Eastern members increasingly surfaced (Badran 1995: 108ff, 246ff). From the late 1930s, EFU efforts were concentrated more toward the establishment of the Arab Feminist Union (founded in 1945) (p. 110). Moreover, the tendency to see feminism as a Western "import" that only proliferated among the European-educated elite led some civil-society activists within the Arab world to regard the Arab feminist movement with suspicion, while conservatives saw it as a fifth column against Arab or Muslim interests (p. 20).

Another movement that was transnational in character due to its internationalist ideology was the communist movement. The Soviet

Union established a Commissariat for Muslim Affairs in 1918. It refused to recognize the mandate system in the Arab region and was the first country to establish full diplomatic relations with Hijaz (later Saudi Arabia) and to recognize an independent Yemen (Ismael 2005: 9). Early communist activities within the Arab world predated the Bolshevik Revolution and tended to be led by foreign residents, such as Greeks and Italians in Alexandria and Cairo, French in Algeria, and Jewish settlers in Palestine (Ismael and El-Sa'id 1990: 12ff; Kaufman 1997; Sivan 1976). Communist parties, recognized by the Comintern, were formed across the Arab world from the 1920s onward (Ismael 2005: 9).

The communists formed part of the anticolonial struggle, as well as engaging in the organization of labor activism (Batatu 1978; Beinin and Lockman 1987; Ismael 2005: 2). In the 1930s, they also played a role in fighting fascism and participated in the international peace movement (Botman 1988: 6ff). Therefore, not only were the communists part of an international movement, with links to communist parties in other countries around the world, but they were also part of national movements of resistance and opposition within their own countries. Although communist movements were never numerically significant—except for in Iraq—they enjoyed strong party organization and resilience in the face of government harassment (Ismael 2005: 1). Consequently, they often had an ideological impact beyond their numbers, in terms of their participation in strikes and demonstrations and their contribution to journalism and political and philosophical publications (Botman 1988).

The multinational and cosmopolitan origins of the communist movement became problematic following the partition of Palestine and the creation of Israel after 1948. Arab communist leadership followed the Soviet line and endorsed the UN partition plan (Ismael 2005: 20). Despite the fact that communists had been active against Zionism in the years before partition, their support for the State of Israel opened the way for criticisms that the communists were pro-Zionist and subservient to the Soviet Union, thereby making them very unpopular, causing dissent among the rank-and-file members, and ultimately leading to suppression (Botman 1988: 86ff). This did much to weaken the movement and to turn it away from its cosmopolitan origins toward more Arab nationalist tendencies (Beinin 1998: 153ff; Ismael and El-Sa'id 1990: 68ff; Ismael 2005: 34). The voluntary dissolution of the Egyptian communist parties in order to support the Arab socialism of Gamal Abdel-Nasser in 1964 illustrates an outcome of these processes (Botman 1988: 144ff).

This history of Islamic empires, from the Umayyads to the Ottomans, demonstrates that the Arab world is not inherently resistant to links with countries beyond the region. Nor have the various empires been incapable of accommodating diverse ethnicities and religions—even if this were not on the basis of equality (a concept that was not widespread at the time). Growing links with Europe from the sixteenth century onward provided opportunities for increased intellectual, artistic, and commercial links between individuals in the Arab world and in Europe. Some of these intellectual links provided the basis for the growth of social movements within the Arab world that were part of transnational movements.

However, these transnational movements faced difficulties on a number of levels, reflecting the political realities within the international and national arenas. To begin with, movements within the Arab world were peripheral to the center of these transnational movements, which originated in Europe. Consequently, the national interests of movements within the Arab world were subordinated to those deemed relevant by the international leadership. While the international communist movement was anti-imperialist, the Arab communist parties/groups were able to position themselves within the nationalist struggle against colonialism. However, after 1948, the Soviet recognition of Israel forced communists in the Arab world to make a choice between emphasizing their links to their nation-state or to an international communist movement. Many chose the former as a means of ensuring their survival. Meanwhile, the international feminist movement regarded issues of national liberation as irrelevant to women's emancipation, thereby refusing the validity of the experiences of women in countries colonized by Europe. As a result, women's movements within the Arab world gravitated toward consolidating a pan-Arab women's movement.

In both cases, international marginalization and national political realities obliged movements within the Arab world to forsake a transnational focus. Moreover, the cosmopolitan origins of the leadership of these movements created suspicions or opposition among certain sections of the societies in which they operated. While the West continued to dominate the Arab world, either through direct colonialism or through indirect political, economic, and military influence, movements with European links were seen as a potential threat to the nation.

Rather than being an asset, transnational links beyond the Arab world became a liability for social movements. For several decades during the heyday of Arab nationalism, the promotion of links between Arab countries was politically favored (in rhetoric, at least) in order to strengthen Arab unity. The transformation of the international political economy from the 1970s onward created conditions for new types of transnational movements to emerge. Below, I examine three examples of such movements.

## The Islamist Movement

The Islamists provide an example of a transnational movement that began predominantly between Arab countries and now incorporates individuals and groups from around the world. In the wake of the 11 September 2001 attack on the World Trade Center in New York, the security fears of Western countries have created a popular image of a global Islamist bloc in conflict with Western "civilization." As Fred Halliday argues, "At first sight, Islamist movements are *par excellence* ones that defy the state and are transnational in ideology and organization" (2005: 239). The call for the establishment of the *umma,* representing a pan-Islamic political community, is an important objective of political Islamist groups. Yet, rather than portraying a unified and coordinated transnational Islamist movement, it is more apt to represent it as a collection of informal links between different nationally based Islamist groups around the world (*The Economist* 2005: 62). The diffusion of Islamist groups from the Arab world and other Muslim countries to Europe and North America parallels the migration of Muslims to these countries in the postwar period. It must be recognized that the goal of establishing the *umma* does not negate the validity for Islamist groups of working within nation-state borders and making claims on national governments.

Different Islamist groups around the world pursue different activities and adhere to different interpretations of religious doctrine. The major trends within the Arab world may be categorized as Salafi—a conservative current within Islam—and these movements are inspired by or linked to the Muslim Brotherhood. Some trends have adopted violence through doctrinal innovations, such as *takfir* (denouncing a fellow Muslim as a heretic) or *jihad* (religious struggle). Groups may also combine elements of different trends and doctrines, as occurred in Algeria (Ismail 2003: 125–126; ICG 2004a: 11). The first Islamist group in the Arab world, the Muslim Brotherhood, emerged in Egypt in 1928, and branches were established in Syria, Jordan, and Palestine (in the latter case, the group became known as Hamas). The establishment of these groups is rooted in the context of anticolonial struggle. However, in the postindependence period, they have evolved as opposition movements to indigenous governments. Today, these groups continue to exist with varying degrees of success. In Egypt and Syria, the Muslim Brother-hood is illegal, although Egyptian Brethren have been elected to parliament as independents and also hold the majority of seats on the boards of many professional syndicates. In Palestine, Jordan, Yemen, and Morocco, affiliates of the Muslim Brotherhood have seats in national and/or local assemblies. The group's success in diffusing Islamic culture/values/teachings via civil society (professional syndicates, parliaments, and student unions, as well as through mosques) illustrates its bottom-up approach, in that it seeks to Islamize society before Islamizing the state.[2] The group states that it has branches in seventy countries.[3] However, Muslim Brotherhood groups outside Arab countries have been less influential.

In addition to the Muslim Brotherhood, there exist other Sunni Islamist movements, which may also be categorized as Salafi. The Salafi movement originated in the thinking of Jamal al-Din al Afghani and Muhammad 'Abdu, who sought to renew Islam in order to adopt Western science and European ideas (Hourani 1983). Throughout the twentieth century, it evolved and came to be aligned with the conservative Wahhabi thought of Saudi Arabia, largely due to the financing of Salafi groups by Saudi Arabia after the 1970s. This approach to Islamist activism stresses personal moral behavior and seeks to impose what is considered licit (*halal*) and to prevent that which is illicit (*haram*). Another characteristic of Salafi thought is its emphasis on Muslim identity, as opposed to national or subnational identities. In this sense, Salafi thought particularly lends itself to the migrant experience, in that it presents a moral code for personal behavior and the basis for an identity that is not tied to a particular locality (ICG 2004a: 12).

Hizb ut-Tahrir al-Islami—founded in Jerusalem in 1952—is an example of a Salafi movement that has grown in strength among Muslims outside the Arab world, in particular in Britain (Mandaville 2004: 116). This party seeks to create an Islamic society as the basis for reestablishing the Islamic caliphate as a unified state for all Muslims. In this way, it aims to restore the global power of the Islamic world against the nonbelievers.[4] The party welcomes all Muslims, regardless of race, nationality, or gender, and this is reflected in its website, which is in several European languages, as well as Arabic, Turkish, and Urdu.

Another movement that is strong outside the Arab world is the Jama'at al-Tabligh al-Islami, or Tablighi Jamaat (Society for Propagating the Message), which originated in India. It has branches in the Indian subcontinent, Southeast Asia, the Arab countries, Europe, North America, and Africa (King 1997: 130). It is an apolitical movement whose focus is reaffirming the basic principles of Islam within Muslim societies. The central philosophy of Tabligh is to encourage adherents to travel widely and spread the faith of Islam through missionary work (p. 140). Like the Salafi movement, it possesses a strong normative agenda (Mandaville 2004: 16). Yet, unlike other Islamist movements, it is fervently apolitical (p. 144). Its refusal to articulate its translocal character in political terms represents a hurdle to its wider diffusion (p. 145).

Despite the transnational dimensions of the activities and membership of the above organizations, it would be wrong to conclude that they represent a threat to the nation-state. The focus of activity of these groups has been the local state or, in the case of the Tablighi, its accommodation toward the local state. In Arab countries, it is more accurate to say that Islamist ideology has been utilized to buttress nationalist discourse, rather than to replace it (Piscatori 1986). The emergence of Islamist groups has been facilitated by the state. For example, Egyptian president Anwar al-Sadat encouraged the growth of Islamist groups, particularly on university campuses, as a counterweight to the leftist/ nationalist opposition forces in the 1970s. In addition, Saudi Arabia has used a part of its oil surpluses to fund Islamist groups as a means of increasing its importance in regional and international politics.

Rather than aspiring to build a transnational movement, the priority of Islamist groups has more often been closer to home. Islam has been used as an ideological basis from which to oppose corruption and despotism, rather than to build a pan-Islamic community. In Egypt, Algeria, and Tunisia, Islam has been the idiom of protest against largely secular regimes. In Lebanon, Palestine, and Afghanistan (1979 onward), Islamist groups have been at the forefront of resistance to foreign occupation (Milton-Edwards 2004: 62–87).

Similarly, manifestations of political Islamist activism in Europe and North America have represented responses to the rejection and exclusion experienced by Muslim migrants in these countries and not necessarily representative of a desire to destroy the nation-state. In Europe, second- or third-generation Muslims have reformulated the Islam practiced by their parents and imbued it with new meanings in order to construct an identity of protest against exclusion from the societies in which they live (Kepel 1997). Paul Gilroy writes that the Britons held in Guantanamo Bay as post-9/11 inmates "manifest the uncomfortable truth that British multiculturalism has failed."[5]

Another example where pan-Islamism has been used to buttress the nation-state, rather than to undermine it, is the Organization of the Islamic Conference (OIC)—an intergovernmental organization of the Muslim world founded in 1969, whose charter recognizes the sovereignty of its member states. Rather than perceiving the conference as an attempt to promote pan-Islamic solidarity, it has been more effective as an arena for different nation-states to promote their own foreign policy interests (Eickelman and Piscatori 2004: 141). One case where the OIC has acted as an Islamic bloc upon the international stage, in concert with the Vatican and some US-based Christian groups, is to oppose a variety of UN declarations concerning women's reproductive rights and the recognition of the rights of sexual "minorities."[6] OIC actions are motivated and coordinated by the idea of an authentic Islamic culture that must be protected from decadent Western values concerning sexuality. Yet, the building of alliances with conservative religious groups/states from other parts of the world, which differ doctrinally and politically from OIC member states, demonstrates that certain values are not authentic to particular cultures but that these may be shared across nations and so-called different cultures.[7] Organized opposition to discussion of sexuality in UN documents provides an example of transnational movement activity that not only crosses international borders but also the borders of different religious communities.

Despite the transnational character of Islamist activism, national concerns and contexts shape the objectives and activities of Islamist groups in different countries. Among Islamist groups, there exist different visions of future polities in their respective countries. These different visions are expressed as different interpretations of Islamic jurisprudence. The experience of migration has led to transformations in Islamic thinking. On the one hand, some Islamists in the West challenge dominant conceptions of Islam "to open up a discursive space in which Muslim subjectivities can enunciate asala [that is, conceptions of what constitutes 'pure Islam'] in the plural" (Mandaville 2004: 180). This paves the way for the emergence of a critical reform of Islam that is more accommodating of different opinions. On the other hand, the experience of migration has contributed to strengthening organizations such as Hizb ut-Tahrir that seek to establish a monolithic and authentic Islam that is not accommodating of pluralist conceptions of the religion. Meanwhile, within the Arab world, Islamists are rethinking the relationship between democracy and Islam in response to the national contexts within which they operate. These different processes demonstrate that transnational activities do not inherently engender a democratization of Islam, although they may provide new opportunities to do so. Equally, the national sociopolitical arena also plays an important role in shaping Islamist thinking. Therefore, it is more accurate to see national and transnational spaces as overlapping and producing different outcomes in relation to those who operate within them. In addition, as previous chapters have argued, it is important to note that a democratization or pluralization of Islam does not necessarily engender a process of democratization of the wider polity in which Islamists operate. Indeed, the necessary exclusivity of Islam as a basis for political action, identity, and organization is difficult to reconcile with the normative basis of democracy.

## Solidarity with the Palestinians

The eruption of the second Palestinian *intifada* in September 2000 created a new phase in building transnational solidarity with the Palestinians under Israeli occupation. Arab satellite news channels, such as al-Jazeera and LBC (Lebanese Broadcasting Corporation), have played a role in broadcasting images of the second *intifada* and, thereby, in galvanizing public opinion of Arabic-speakers in solidarity with the Palestinians. Similarly, the Internet has also provided alternative news coverage that is more critical of Israeli policies than mainstream English-language news media.

Within the Arab world, the vast majority of public opinion has been opposed to the State of Israel since its creation in 1948. At times, this opposition has translated into public expressions of solidarity with the Palestinians. Yet, solidarity *movements* within Arab countries have been largely weak or nonexistent. To a large degree, this is due to the lack of legal space in which such movements could emerge, together with the existence of the prevalent view that the solution to the Israeli occupation of Palestine was through military conquest by the Arab armies, rather than through solidarity with the Palestinian people. The exception is Lebanon, where a large population of Palestinian refugees, coupled with a relatively greater margin of freedom of assembly, has created the conditions for a sustained solidarity movement—predominantly of diaspora Palestinians.

Nevertheless, there have been key events that have led to an upsurge in expressions of support for the Palestinians in Arab countries beyond Lebanon. After 1982, when Israel invaded Lebanon, there were displays of solidarity with the Palestinians, as well as the Lebanese. In Egypt, a National Committee for Solidarity with the Palestinian and Lebanese People was formed and included the opposition political parties, professional syndicates, and trade unions. Its activities mainly consisted of holding conferences and collecting donations in support of those living under the Israeli siege in Lebanon. Some committee members met with Yasser Arafat and Palestinian forces in Lebanon to express support. In addition, cultural events were organized, at which actors, singers, and musicians expressed solidarity with the Palestinians. However, attempts at public demonstrations were thwarted by the police. The committee's activities more or less ended following the feuding between the Palestine Liberation Organization and its former allies and its forced departure from Lebanon in 1982 (El-Sayed 1989).

The outbreak of the first Palestinian *intifada* in 1987 was extensively reported within the national media and roused expressions and actions of solidarity from other Arab countries. The Egyptian National Committee in Support of the Palestinian Uprising was founded by the major opposition political parties and supported by a variety of professional syndicates, the trade union federation, the Egyptian Organization for Human Rights, media celebrities, and the ruling party. Like the 1982 initiative, the activities of the committee were limited to meetings, conferences, and collecting donations. Public demonstrations were not tolerated by the authorities, despite nominal support by the government for the initiative (El-Sayed 1989).

The outbreak of the second *intifada* was covered not only by national media but also by the Arab satellite news channels, which are widely watched throughout the region. Video footage of Israeli troops firing on Palestinian civilians and, in particular, the image of the young boy, Mohammed Dorra, killed while sheltering from Israeli bullets behind his father provoked widespread outrage. Indeed, this image became symbolic of Israeli injustice against the Palestinians and was reproduced and distributed widely: in newspapers and on TV, on stickers in solidarity with the Palestinians, and even on postage stamps in Jordan. The second *intifada* triggered perhaps the largest and most radical spontaneous demonstrations in the Arab world since the first Gulf War. These demonstrations were mainly led by students, rather than by political parties or other civil-society actors. In Egypt, thousands of students took to the streets on a daily basis chanting, "With our souls and with our blood, we sacrifice ourselves for Palestine."[8] The demonstrations were met with police repression. In Syria and Jordan, police used tear gas to keep protesters away from the US and Israeli embassies.[9]

An even greater wave of protests was experienced throughout the Arab world following the Israeli invasion of the West Bank on 29 March 2002.[10] Again, these were predominantly student-led. In addition to the demonstrations, a plethora of public activities took place and declarations were made by a variety of organizations and parties in support of the Palestinians and against Israeli violence. These included boycotts of Israeli and US goods, hanging Palestinian flags in windows, and sit-ins inside the professional syndicates.[11] In some cases, Arab governments have also sought to show their solidarity. For example, in Egypt, First Lady Suzanne Mubarak led a convoy of relief trucks to the Egyptian border with the Gaza Strip.[12] Moreover, the very public mass protests provided justifications for Arab governments to reengage with the Israeli-Palestinian negotiations—using the anger of the "Arab street" as a means to pressure the United States to pressure Israel.[13] Yet governments are also aware that street demonstrations represent the potential for movements to develop that are not only anti-Israeli but also critical of their own governments. For example, in Egypt, some protesters also chanted slogans against the Egyptian government for failing to stand up to Israel.

The experience of the Egyptian Popular Committee for Solidarity with the Palestinian Intifada (EPCSPI) demonstrates the limits of Arab governments' desires to allow anti-Israeli protests to occur in public. The Egyptian committee was formed soon after the outbreak of the second *intifada* by a collection of twenty NGOs. It did not perceive itself as a domestic opposition movement but as a solidarity movement with Palestine. It sought to obtain legitimacy by inviting the support of high-profile political figures, such as then minister of foreign affairs, Amr Moussa, and by focusing its activities on collecting donations to send convoys of food and medicines to the Occupied Territories.[14] The solidarity committee represents an alliance of individuals of diverse political and ideological backgrounds, some of whom are involved in political opposition activities. However, the committee has not made declarations in support of domestic political reform. Indeed, in order to accommodate different tendencies within the committee, it has been necessary to avoid making any declarations beyond the group's stated aims of expressing solidarity with the Palestinian *intifada* and calling for an end to Israeli occupation. Nevertheless, the state security forces have periodically harassed and arrested committee members and prevented demonstrators accompanying convoys (EPCSPI 2004).[15] This has included the prevention of demonstrations that include international participants.

On the other hand, civil society in Europe and North America has had virtually unlimited space in which to mobilize expressions of solidarity with the Palestinians. Yet the apparent geographical remoteness of the issue of Israel/Palestine, together with media coverage considered by some to not fully represent the issue, particularly as regards its impact on Palestinians, has made it more difficult to mobilize sustained support for the Palestinians against Israeli occupation. Nevertheless, public mobilizations against Israeli occupation in Europe and North America emerged on a broad scale in response to Palestinian civilians facing Israeli military might during the first *intifada*. For the first time, the Western media provided extensive news coverage relatively hostile to Israel's actions. Grass-roots organizations sprung up in solidarity with the Palestinians in Europe and North America (Niva 1990). In the United States, Jewish groups registered their concern about Israeli actions to both the US government and to Israelis. This led to the Israel/Palestine issue being made a greater foreign-policy priority for the United States and European Union, as well as the Arab governments.

The outbreak of the second *intifada* also gave impetus to expressions of solidarity with the Palestinians around the world. Activities have included demonstrations, petitions, boycotts of Israeli goods, sponsoring motions within trade unions to condemn Israeli occupation, and lobbying of parliamentarians. One action that has attracted a significant amount of attention and represents a new form of solidarity activity was the initiative of the International Solidarity Movement, established in 2001. The International Solidarity Movement (ISM) is a Palestinian-led movement of Palestinian and international activists who utilize non-violent direct action to support the Palestinian struggle for freedom and an end to Israeli occupation.[16] Inspired by Mahatma Gandhi and the US civil rights movement, the ISM mobilizes international volunteers to travel to the occupied territories to participate in Palestinian-led non-violent resistance, such as marches, the breaking of curfews, and challenging house demolitions.[17] International participation aims to provide protection to Palestinians, since Israeli soldiers are less likely to fire on internationals. Moreover, international participation provides direct solidarity with Palestinians, as well as attracting international media coverage, thereby breaking Palestinian isolation.[18] There is also a recurring theme in much of the literature by ISM volunteers that the movement provides opportunities to build links between Palestinians, Israelis, and internationals, which in itself promotes a culture of peace.[19]

Initially, the existence of internationals in Palestinian demonstrations deterred Israeli soldiers from using live ammunition. However, the killing of Rachel Corrie in March 2003 by an Israeli bulldozer and the failure of the US government to investigate the case challenged the assumption that Palestinians could be protected from the Israeli army by international volunteers.[20] The case of Tom Hurndall, a British photographer shot by the Israeli army in the Gaza Strip in April 2003, and who died as a result of his injuries in January 2004, also raises similar questions.

Opposition to Israeli occupation by Israelis themselves also exists, and was initially expressed through left-wing political parties such as MAPAM (the United Workers' Party) (MERIP Reports 1987). Following the 1982 invasion of Lebanon, a number of grass-roots peace groups emerged, such as Mothers Against Silence, Israeli Women Against the Occupation, and Yesh Gvul (army reservists refusing to serve in Lebanon), and there were public demonstrations protesting the war. The first *intifada* gave further impetus to the creation of civil-society initiatives such as Women in Black and Gush Shalom, as well as the continuation of groups such as Yesh Gvul (which, in this case, refused to serve in the Occupied Territories). In addition, ad hoc committees were created linking Israelis and Palestinians in political solidarity (Kaminer 1996). Following the signing of the Oslo Accords in 1993, many Israeli peace groups became inactive (Sharoni 1998). However, since autumn 2000, in response to Israeli government actions toward the Palestinians, some defunct groups have come back to life, as well as new groups having emerged to build an Israeli movement of solidarity with the Palestinians' opposition to the occupation.

One Israeli group that has received widespread media coverage—both inside and outside Israel—is the Refusenik movement of Israeli soldiers and reservists that refuse to serve in the Occupied Territories. The refuseniks view the occupation of Palestine and the human rights abuses perpetrated by the Israeli army as being counter to the security of the Israeli state and contrary to the values of Zionism.[21] As a consequence of this refusal, the individuals involved have been imprisoned and have faced harsh public criticism. They have been called traitors, while in some cases protesters in support of the refuseniks have been physically attacked by ordinary citizens. Yet there is frustration among the Israeli peace movement that, in the context of the second *intifada,* such actions have had limited impact upon Israeli politics. As one observer reports, "despite the growing number of refuseniks (surpassing the numbers reached during the Lebanon war and the first intifada) . . . there is no response by the [Israeli political] leadership, and hardly any debate in the general public."[22]

On the other hand, the existence of an Israeli peace movement challenges the notion that Israel is a homogenous society and demonstrates the fact that it contains a variety of opinions, some of which oppose its own government's actions toward the Palestinians. This notion is perhaps better recognized among Palestinians than those within the Arab countries and even those internationally, who are generally only presented with evidence of official government positions and army actions within the West Bank and Gaza. Nevertheless, some Israeli and Jewish left-wingers are critical of the mainstream Israeli movement, such as Peace Now, as ultimately Zionist and therefore unable to accommodate the universalist values that underpin peace. Yet, it is also argued that their location within the political mainstream gives the Peace Now movement its authority to present an agenda that is antioccupation and for Palestinian self-determination.

Groups opposing Israeli occupation and expressing solidarity with the Palestinians are an international phenomenon—encompassing Arab countries, Israel, and countries beyond the region. Expressions of solidarity on an international scale play a role in lending moral support to Palestinians under occupation. This support, whether direct or indirect, does not necessarily protect Palestinians from the violence and hardships experienced (as the ISM experience demonstrates) but, to different degrees, these groups mobilize public opinion and pressure their own governments to act to bring peace between Israel and the Palestinians and to support Palestinian self-determination. In the case of Israel, peace groups have also attempted to challenge prevalent national conceptions of Zionism as exclusive, militaristic, and masculinist, as a means of democratizing Israel and ensuring peace (Sharoni 1998). Yet, mainstream Israeli peace groups are openly Zionist and seek to restore values perceived as authentically Zionist to the Israeli polity, rather than to challenge Zionism.

In the Arab world, movements in solidarity with the Palestinians have been historically thwarted by the limited space for civil society. Moreover, unlike in Europe or North America, Arab governments have consistently voiced opposition to Israeli occupation, thereby somewhat preempting popular mobilization on this issue. Nevertheless, despite the convergence of agendas, governments have been reluctant to allow public demonstrations of support for the Palestinians, and activities of solidarity groups have been generally limited to collecting donations and organizing cultural events. Transnational support for solidarity movements within the Arab region has been largely nonexistent because the focus is the situation of the Palestinians, rather than their Arab supporters. Rather, it is domestic support that has helped to bolster the solidarity movement in the Arab countries. The impact of the Arab news satellite stations, such as al-Jazeera, has been the strongest factor in arousing huge public anti-Israeli opposition among ordinary people within Arab countries. Moreover, the consensus in favor of supporting Palestinian self-determination has enabled the building of coalitions of different actors—including Islamists, human rights activists, nationalists, and leftists. Public demonstrations and other spontaneous activities by different actors have contributed to widening the space in which activists can operate and, in this sense, they contribute to a process of democratization. Yet this space is fragile due to regimes' arbitrariness.

Acts of transnational solidarity have thus constructed new spaces in which civil-society actors may build coalitions that debate and oppose injustices. Yet these spaces are not necessarily sustained by transnational activity, as the case of Egypt demonstrates. National political processes are also significant in shaping the ability of activists to engage in solidarity activism. Moreover, as in the case of Islamist movements, the construction of new spaces does not necessarily engender democratization. It is also significant to examine the ideological assumptions that underpin groups and individuals that participate in the solidarity movement. We find an array of positions, including feminist groups in Israel attempting to oppose Zionism and its masculinist character, Israeli peace groups reformulating Zionism, anarchist groups engaging in nonviolent direct action as a universal political tactic, Christian church groups seeking to bring peace, and Egyptian Islamists and nationalists seeking to eject Israel from what they see as Muslim/Arab lands (Seitz 2003; Sharoni 1998). Transnational links may help to shift individuals' outlooks and views. For example, the establishment of networks between Palestinians under occupation, Israeli peace activists, and peace activists from beyond the Middle East may help to undermine the essentialized identities upon which a politics of conflict is based. On the other hand, the objective of supporting Palestinian national self-determination within a nationalist framework may also reproduce assumptions about "them" and "us," Israelis versus Palestinians, Jews versus Muslims/Arabs, etc. Within this logic, Palestinian solidarity activism may reproduce a political world view that prioritizes homogenous national blocs over the welfare and rights of individuals, regardless of their background. In this sense, solidarity activism may share an ideological framework with the postindependence consensus that underpins authoritarianism.

## The Antiglobalization/Antiwar Movement

The emergence of a significant transnational antiglobalization/antiwar movement incorporating countries in every continent of the world provides a strong example of solidarity with fellow humans irrespective of national borders. Until 2001, this movement had largely bypassed the Arab world. Until then, the focus of the antiglobalization movement was overwhelmingly resistance to corporate power and neoliberal economic institutions, such as the World Trade Organization (WTO). While neoliberal reforms were certainly an object of opposition for certain civil-society activists in several Arab countries (Egypt and Tunisia), state-dominated economies continued to resist liberalization in the majority of Arab countries. More significantly, regional issues dominated the agendas of Arab civil-society activists—namely, political reforms and the situations in Israel/Palestine and in Iraq.

The events of 9/11 and its aftermath (that is, the US bombing of Afghanistan and the wider "war on terror") created a context in which the "global" antiglobalization movement became interested in the Middle East and US foreign policy. This interest was sustained by Israel's reoccupation of the West Bank and Gaza after the outbreak of the second Palestinian *intifada* at the end of 2000. More significantly, it was the US bombing of Afghanistan and the threat of war against Iraq that gradually managed to galvanize a really transnational antiwar movement.

The first signs of interest from Arab activists in the antiglobalization movement became apparent in Beirut in November 2001, during a two-day meeting of the Arab Forum for Resisting Globalization. The forum was attended by almost five hundred people from around the Arab world, from NGOs, political parties, and trade unions, as well as some activists from Europe and the United States, including French farmer José Bové (famed for having wrecked a McDonald's restaurant).[23] At this meeting, antiglobalization resistance at the Doha WTO talks (November 2001) was discussed, as well as calls for linking the resistance to globalization with the resistance to war throughout the region, including Israeli occupation of Palestine and US aggression against Afghanistan (which was being bombed at the time).[24]

Motivated by the growth of the global movement against globalization and the marginalization of the region from that movement, the forum's goal was to provide a unified "Arab voice" criticizing globalization from the standpoint of Arab world grievances.[25] While European activists may have seen the meeting as the recent emergence of a Middle East antiglobalization movement,[26] in fact the grievances raised at the meeting—US hegemony, the occupation of Palestine, the (then) sanctions on Iraq, and the impact of neoliberal economic reforms[27]— were not new themes among certain civil-society activists in the Arab world. As one of the forum's organizers told a British activist, "People [in the Arab world] are conscious that there is a link between the anticapitalist struggle, the struggle in Palestine and the resistance to the war against Afghanistan. All of these things are different expressions of the same capitalist and imperialist system."[28] While the call for anti-imperialist and anticapitalist resistance echoed with more familiar objectives of Arab civil-society activists (that is, opposition to Western political, economic, and military influence in the region), the association of global capitalism with Western intervention in the region represented a new theme for many antiglobalization activists in Europe and North America.

The Beirut initiative failed to mobilize a strong Arab opposition to the WTO talks in Doha. Nevertheless, it helped to pave the way for further antiglobalization initiatives in the region. In June 2002, the Anti-Globalization Egyptian Group (AGEG) was founded with a similar membership to that of the Egyptian Popular Committee for Solidarity with Palestine.[29] The AGEG organized its first event to coincide with the visit of World Bank president James Wolfensohn to Cairo on 2 October 2002. Approximately five hundred activists, including some international antiglobalization figures such as world-systems economist Samir Amin and UK anticapitalist activist Jonathan Neale, gathered to discuss regional issues of unemployment, poverty, workers' rights, Israeli occupation, and the impending war on Iraq. These were linked to the same process of globalization that had ignited the anti-WTO protests in Seattle in 1999,[30] illustrating that the organizers sought to present the group as part of the "broader international movement against globalization," while simultaneously advancing an Egyptian agenda.[31]

The antiglobalization initiatives in Cairo and Beirut not only reflected an increasing interest on the part of Arab activists to participate in the transnational antiglobalization movement, but also built upon the general radicalization of Arab society in response to the second Palestinian *intifada*. For the first time in many years, cities throughout the Arab world witnessed mass protests on the streets, together with widespread support for boycotts of Israeli and US goods. Pop songs were released that lambasted Israel and/or expressed solidarity with the Palestinians.[32] The Egyptian Popular Committee for Solidarity with the Palestinian Intifada was established by activists and intelligentsia of different political strands.

Following these events, Cairo was also the location for the convening of the first international conference to launch the International Campaign Against US Aggression on Iraq in December 2002.[33] The conference was attended by over four hundred delegates from the Arab world as well as European and North American antiglobalization/antiwar activists and mirrored the convergence of the antiwar and antiglobalization movements internationally. The outcome of the meeting was the issuing of the Cairo Declaration, which reiterated the link between resistance against US hegemony to neoliberal globalization and the occupation of Palestine and Iraq:

> We, the participants, reaffirm our resolve to stand in solidarity with the people of Iraq and Palestine, recognising that war and aggression against them is but part of a US project of global domination and subjugation. Solidarity with Iraq and Palestine is integral to the internationalist struggle against neo-liberal globalization. The Cairo meeting is not an isolated event, but an extension of a protracted international struggle against imperialism, from Seattle and Genoa to Lisbon and Florence, to Cordoba and Cairo.[34]

Although the conference organizers presented the conference within the context of the transnational antiglobalization movement, the focus was generally on US foreign policy toward the Middle East and the impending US attack on Iraq. Among the items on the event's agenda were "US globalization," "empire, globalization, and struggle," "genocide and ethnic cleansing as a new world order," and "popular movements and imperialist discourse." One speaker, an Italian economist, stated that "[the US] poses the greatest danger to humanity." An Egyptian businessman, who also contributed to funding the conference, said that "we should stand up to this barbaric war which has been waged against our nations and peoples." Former Algerian president Ahmed Ben Bella gave a speech accusing the Bush administration of "waging a ninth crusade which will begin in Iraq then move to Tehran, Sudan, and then Saudi Arabia."[35] In the weeks following the conference, antiwar activists, academics, artists, and ministers of parliaments from across the globe added their signatures to the declaration.[36] A coordinating committee was established, headed by former Algerian president and independence fighter Ahmed Ben Bella, John Rees of the UK Stop the War Coalition, and Elias Rashmawi of the US peace movement ANSWER.

Since then, three more Cairo conferences have been held: in December 2003, March 2005, and March 2006. By December 2003, the name of the campaign had changed to the International Campaign Against US and Zionist Occupation—reflecting the postwar realities of Iraq and the continuing opposition to the policies of the Israeli government toward the Palestinians. While the antiwar movements in Europe and North America suffered a lull in support once it became clear that they had failed to stop the war, the Cairo conferences have been well attended by Arab and international activists—with approximately eight hundred attending the second conference and almost a thousand at the third.

The second conference attracted well-known speakers, such as former British MP Tony Benn and British MP George Galloway, former US attorney-general Ramsey Clark, and former humanitarian coordinator with the United Nations in Iraq, Denis Halliday. Participants from the Arab world represented a wide range of political orientations, including Arab nationalists, communists, and Islamists.[37] In addition to denouncing US aggression and global capitalism and proclaiming support for the Palestinian and Iraqi resistance, several speakers also stressed the significance of Cairo as a meeting point between North and South, East and West.[38] A major theme emerging from the event was the opportunity to build links between Arab, European, and North American activists.[39]

The third conference of the International Campaign Against US and Zionist Occupation met under the slogan, "With the Resistance in Palestine and Iraq and Against Globalization, Imperialism and Zionism." In comparison to previous years, the conference attracted increased participation from other countries of the South, including India, South Africa, Brazil, and other Arab countries.[40] Moreover, a greater number of Islamists (from Egypt, Iraq, and Palestine) were present than at previous conferences. There appeared to be a near unanimous support expressed for the Palestinian, Iraqi, and Lebanese resistance (the latter referring to Hizbollah's refusal to disarm). Simultaneously, the conference increased its focus on the agenda of domestic political change within Arab countries—particularly Egypt, as host to the conference. Indeed, Kifaya (the Egyptian coalition calling for political reforms in Egypt) was one of the conference organizers and a demonstration was organized at the end of the conference that included chants against the Egyptian regime, as well as the United States, United Kingdom, and Israel.[41] In addition to calling for the reform of Arab regimes, the conference also included a forum for discussing workers' and peasants' struggles in Egypt and beyond—such as the severe police harassment of peasants in the village of Sarandu in Egypt and the Egyptian asbestos workers' strike.[42]

Relatively strong international and domestic participation in the Cairo conferences of December 2003 and March 2005 built upon the high-profile mobilizations by antiwar activists throughout the Arab world, and particularly in Egypt. Despite warnings from Middle East experts and Arab rulers that a US strike against Iraq would lead to "a state of disorder and chaos . . . in the region,"[43] public demonstrations in the Arab world against the war did not gain momentum until after the United States began bombing Iraq on 20 March (Fisk 2003).[44] This stood in stark contrast to Europe and North America, where the biggest antiwar demonstrations were witnessed before the war began. In particular, during the weekend of 15–16 February 2003, millions of people marched in cities in Europe and North America. There were demonstrations of over a million in Barcelona, Rome, and London, while around half a million went onto the streets of Madrid and Berlin.[45] The lack of demonstrations in the Arab world led commentators to conclude that "faced with catastrophe, the Arabs are like mice" (Fisk 2003).

Despite their small numbers, demonstrators in Cairo managed to win international support and to put the Egyptian antiwar movement in the global limelight. When fifteen antiwar activists were arrested by the Egyptian authorities, the UK Stop the War Coalition released urgent action appeals and organized a demonstration in front of the Egyptian embassy in London.[46] It is perhaps due to the momentum of being part of a global movement, as well as mounting anger against US aggression, that gave confidence to antiwar protesters in Egypt to continue to go out onto the streets and stage protests in universities and mosques around the country, despite government attempts to suppress them. Simultaneously, because of international criticisms, the Egyptian government finally allowed a "contained" protest rally at the Cairo Stadium on 27 February (which was attended by 100,000 people).[47] In addition, thousands of people took to the streets across Arab cities: 300,000 marched to the US embassy in Yemen on 1 March; 3,000 demonstrated in Bahrain on 28 February; and a few hundred thousand demonstrated in Casablanca on 2 March.[48]

Once the United States attacked Iraq and images of the destruction were flashed across TV screens via Arab satellite news channels, demonstration numbers swelled, leading some commentators in the West to breathe a sigh of relief that, finally, the "Arab street marches in step with global street" (*Socialist Worker* 2003: 3). Across the Arab world, hundreds of thousands of people—antiwar activists, leftists, Islamists, nationalists, trade unionists, students, and schoolchildren—took to the streets to voice their anger against the US war on Iraq.[49] They were confronted by police blockades, water cannons, dogs, tear gas, and police beatings. In Egypt, police made a massive number of arrests of antiwar activists on the streets of Cairo and many reported abuse and/or torture while in detention.[50] There were violent clashes between police and university students in the town of Maan, Jordan, and similarly in Bahrain, outside the US embassy.[51] In addition to opposing the war on Iraq, demonstrators also called for the end of the Israeli occupation of Palestine and shouted slogans against their own governments.[52]

Yet, as one antiwar leader in Egypt commented, while "there is a 'growing potential for alliances' between Egyptian antiwar activists and the global antiwar movement . . . restrictions on the domestic front continue to shackle those working in the non-governmental domain."[53] Government measures to ban public gatherings, the regular harassment of civil-society activists, in addition to police brutality in dealing with antiwar protestors, all served to make it difficult for an Arab antiwar movement to grow beyond a limited number of very committed activists. While the existence of a global antiwar movement gave political weight and moral support to the efforts of Arab antiwar protesters, in addition to placing government harassment of antiwar activists in the international spotlight, this was not sufficient to widen the sphere of freedoms necessary to enable the organization of a large antiwar movement.

Moreover, there is little evidence that the creation of a transnational antiwar/antiglobalization movement has contributed to reshaping the ideologies of the actors involved—whether in Europe and North America or in the Arab world. Rather, it is the convergence of the already existing agendas of movements in the West with those of civil-society activists in the Arab world that has created the opportunity for transnational links. While it is impossible to essentialize the movement (Eschle 2005), the dominant voices within the antiwar/antiglobalization movement are anti–US foreign policy in the region; anti–Israeli policy toward the Palestinians; and anticorporate capitalism/neoliberal capitalism, with strong support for protecting the sovereignty of Arab states from outside intervention through violent means if necessary. These themes resonate with the long-standing nationalist, anti-imperialist, and anti-Zionist beliefs of many civil-society activists within the Arab world that, as I have argued, have contributed to the maintenance of authoritarianism. Consequently, the antiglobalization/antiwar movement may simply represent a coalescence of already existing political and ideological views, rather than a reshaping of these views in the context of new transnational links.

Nevertheless, transnational antiwar mobilization in the Arab world has been encouraged by the demonstration effect of large antiwar protests in Europe and North America. Moreover, antiwar activism has created an opportunity for new linkages and alliances to be created within Arab countries between leftists, nationalists, and Islamists; between political parties and NGOs; and between people who have a history of activism and those who were not previously engaged. In other words, while transnational movement activity has not expanded the legal space for civil society or necessarily protected activists from government harassment, it has created the conditions for solidarity between individuals of different political orientations and institutional affiliations. This, in turn, has given people a new confidence to call for the political reforms that would enable greater legal space for civil society. The antiwar movement has also given rise to a new form of civil-society activism. Rather than holding conferences within the confines of political-party headquarters or professional syndicate buildings, the predominant means of protest against authoritarianism has become "street politics."

Egypt provides a striking example of sustained public demonstrations. Those who participated in the antiwar demonstrations of 20 March 2003 in Cairo have been central to the formation of a movement for political reform called Kifaya (meaning "enough" in Arabic). The Kifaya movement represents a coalition of groups, political parties, NGOs, and independent individuals of different political orientation, experience, and ages. Their rallying call, "Enough," refers to a desire for an end to the decades of political domination by Hosni Mubarak and the ruling National Democratic Party, to the continued enforcement of the emergency law, to systematic torture in police stations, to the economic recession, and to the "inheritance" of the presidency by Hosni Mubarak's son, Gamal.[54] In December 2004, around five hundred protested outside the high court for the first public demonstration against Hosni Mubarak's decision to run for president for a sixth term.[55] Protests have been organized on a regular basis since then and have helped to mobilize calls for an end to the regime's grip on all areas of life, from usually quiet quarters, such as judges and academics, as well as journalists, artists, and trade unionists.[56] While the movement did not manage to remove Mubarak from the presidency nor to reduce the ruling party's control of the national assembly during the autumn 2005 elections, it has provided an important impetus for prodemocracy activism within Egypt.

## Conclusion

The cases above demonstrate that transnational activity does not necessarily contribute toward a process of democratization but may constitute an enabling factor. Transnational activity creates new spaces in which national civil-society actors may participate. The causes of Palestinian self-determination, opposition to neoliberal globalization, and opposition to war have succeeded in mobilizing a variety of individuals from different countries and different political and ideological outlooks. In turn, this has provided new opportunities for various activists to meet, discuss, and build alliances. The case of Egypt demonstrates how the participation of a range of actors—including Islamists, nationalists, and human rights activists—in these movements has helped to build new coalitions that not only address transnational concerns but also seek to engender domestic democratic reforms.

It is also possible to argue that transnational activism has contributed toward prodemocracy activities in other ways. While the transnational links of Egyptian antiwar/antiglobalization activists did not protect them from arrest, they have provided moral and political support. Activities such as the international Cairo conferences demonstrate to activists within the Arab region that there are people around the world who are concerned with what happens inside Arab countries. A similar view may be detected among Palestinians with regard to the International Solidarity Movement (Seitz 2003). In the case of Egypt, this transnational support has helped to give confidence to the emerging democratic reform movement, Kifaya. The creation of new spaces for civil-society actors represents an important aspect of challenging authoritarianism. In all cases, national governments continue to restrict the space available for public activism, even where the object of that activism (whether against the war or in support of Palestine) does not appear to be directly opposing their rule. They recognize that the appropriation of public space by activists, whatever their cause, challenges regimes' ability to direct civil society and to maintain authoritarian rule.

Regimes' continued restriction of public space illustrates the degree to which the national context within which activists operate is also significant. The cases examined above demonstrate that the ability of activist groups to operate depends upon the degree to which they mobilize national (rather than international) public opinion. Islamist groups, such as the Muslim Brotherhood in Egypt, continue to exist, despite government harassment, because of a significant degree of popular sympathy, rather than the existence of transnational networks of Islamists. Similarly, Palestinian solidarity activism is sustained largely through street demonstrations, organized boycotts, and other activities by groups and individuals within particular domestic milieus.

In all the cases above, the object of transnational activism resonates with a wider public in Arab countries. This is because these causes fit easily within the hegemonic consensus that has developed in the postindependence period. The politics of identity—whether Arab or Muslim—are easily collapsed into the dominant discourses of the transnational movements examined here. Islamist movements are clearly based on the identification of interests based on one's religion. Within the antiwar movement, victims of US foreign policy are identified as Arab and/or Muslim. Within the Palestine solidarity movement, victims of Israeli policies are identified as Palestinian. In all cases, transnational move-ment activity is mobilized on the basis of the victimization of Mus-lims/Arabs at the hands of the US and its allies, including Israel. This discourse echoes the anti-imperialist, nationalist discourses that have been prominent among many civil-society actors in the Arab world. Indeed, the more that the US and its allies, including Israel, emphasize their own national security interests, the more that individuals and groups in the Arab world resist these declared national interests by affirming their own security interests based on the nation-state or pan-Islamic/Arab collective. These discourses of collective security tend to conceptualize the world in terms of discrete and competing interests on the basis of differentiated identities—"Arab" or "Muslim" vs. "Western." As discussed in previous chapters, the discourse of collective security interests (usually, "national interests") has often been utilized to delegit-imize movements for democracy and human rights within the Arab world.

By bringing together individuals of different backgrounds and pro-viding spaces for interaction, transnational activism contains the poten-tial to challenge the dichotomization of interests based on particular identities. For example, the existence of Israeli peace groups within the Palestinian solidarity movement challenges a view of Israeli society as a monolithic bloc of interests unified behind its government's practices and policies. Similarly, the participation of Europeans and North Amer-icans at the Cairo conferences demonstrates to Arab activists that not all "Westerners" support their governments' policies toward the Arab world. However, the objective of maintaining a unified movement com-prising individuals with radically different political and ideological world views can lead to a situation in which different viewpoints are evaded in order to avoid rifts. Dominant representations of the Palestin-ian and antiwar causes operate to strengthen those groups within transnational movements who are ideologically wedded to a dichoto-mous view of the world—namely, Islamists, Arab nationalists, and even radical leftists (Marxists/socialists) in the West. The latter world views are further strengthened by the nature of US foreign policy and Israeli actions, which appear to confirm that Arabs and Muslims are victims whose dignity must be restored. In turn, this marginalizes those who seek to challenge, on ideological grounds, the assumptions of a world divided into "them" and "us"—such as feminists and human rights activists. Con-sequently, it is currently not possible to conclude that transnational activ-ity unequivocally supports democratization.

## Notes

1. Peter Willetts (2002), "Graph of the Numbers of NGOs in Consultative Status with the United Nations Economic and Social Council for Each Year from 1945 to 2002," data updated and originally published in P. Willetts, *"The Conscience of the World": The Influence of Non-Governmental Organisations in the UN System* (London: Hurst, and Washington: Brookings Institution, 1996), p. 38; online at: http://www.staff.city.ac.uk/p.willetts/NGOS/NGO-GRPH .HTM, accessed 7 June 2005.

2. Muslim Brotherhood Movement website, http://www.ummah.org.uk/ ikhwan/, accessed 23 June 2005.

3. Ibid.

4. Hizb ut-Tahrir official website, http://www.hizb-ut-tahrir.org/english/ english.html, accessed 23 June 2005.

5. Paul Gilroy, "Diving into the Tunnel: The Politics of Race Between the Old and New Worlds," OpenDemocracy, 31 January 2002, http://www.open democracy.net/debates/article-2-49-138.jsp, accessed 22 June 2005.

6. Scott Long (n.d.), "Anatomy of a Backlash: Sexuality and the 'Cultural' War," Human Rights Watch, http://www.hrw.org/wr2k5/anatomy/3.htm, accessed 22 June 2005.

7. Ibid.

8. "Anger Across the Arab World," BBC News Online, 12 October 2000, http://news.bbc.co.uk/1/hi/world/middle_east/968941.stm, accessed 21 June 2005.

9. "Protests Spread in the Arab World," BBC News Online, 6 October 2000, http://news.bbc.co.uk/1/hi/world/middle_east/960170.stm, accessed 21 June 2005.

10. Paul Schemm, "Sparks of Activist Spirit in Egypt," *Middle East Report Online,* 13 April 2002, http://www.merip.org/mero/mero041302.html, accessed 20 June 2005; Asef Bayat, "The 'Street' and the Politics of Dissent in the Arab World," *Middle East Report Online,* no. 226 (spring 2003), http://www.merip .org/mer/mer226/226_bayat.html, accessed 20 June 2005; "Anti-Israeli Protests Spread," BBC News Online, 7 April 2002, http://news.bbc.co.uk/1/hi/world/ middle_east/1915507.stm, accessed 21 June 2005.

11. Amira Huweidy, "Solidarity in Search of a Vision," *Al-Ahram Weekly Online,* 11–17 April 2002, http://weekly.ahram.org.eg/2002/581/eg4.htm, accessed 21 June 2005; Fatemah Farag, "The Many Faces of Solidarity," *Al-Ahram Weekly Online,* 2–8 May 2002, http://weekly.ahram.org.eg/2002/584/ eg5.htm, accessed 21 June 2005.

12. Dahlia Hammouda, "Border March," *Al-Ahram Weekly Online,* 2–8 May 2002, http://weekly.ahram.org.eg/2002/584/eg4.htm, accessed 21 June 2005.

13. "Anti-Israeli Anger Sweeps the Arab World," BBC News Online, 5 April 2002, http://news.bbc.co.uk/1/hi/world/middle_east/1910850.stm, accessed 21 June 2005.

14. "Bringing the Intifada to Egypt," *Al-Ahram Weekly Online,* 26 Sept.–2 Oct. 2002, http://weekly.ahram.org.eg/2002/605/sup113.htm, accessed 26 May 2005.

15. Amira Huweidy, "Continuing Solidarity," *Al-Ahram Weekly Online,* 16–22 May 2002, http://weekly.ahram.org.eg/2002/586/eg3.htm, accessed 21 June 2005; "Solidarity Squeeze," *Al-Ahram Weekly Online,* 5–11 September 2002, http://weekly.ahram.org.eg/2002/602/eg3.htm, accessed 21 June 2005.

16. ISM website, http://www.palsolidarity.org, accessed 21 June 2005.
17. Ibid.
18. Ibid.
19. For example, Ewa Jasciewicz, "A Personal Bias," *The Guardian Online,* 26 August 2004, http://www.guardian.co.uk/comment/story/0,,1290869,00 .html, accessed 22 June 2005.
20. Adam Shapiro, "Freedom Summer," *The Nation,* 17 July 2003, http:// www.thenation.com/doc/20030804/shapiro, accessed 22 June 2005.
21. "Israeli Officers Announce Refusal to Serve in Occupied Territories," originally printed in Ha'aretz and reproduced on the *Palestine Monitor* website, http://www.palestinemonitor.org/Special%20Section/Israeli%20resistance/56_ israeli_officers_announce__refusal.htm, accessed 22 June 2005.
22. Veronique Dudouet, "Heading in the Right Direction," PeaceNews #2454, March-May 2004, http://www.peacenews.info/issues/2454/2454122.htm, accessed 12 July 2006.
23. Zeina Abu Rizk, "Globalising Opposition," *Al-Ahram Weekly Online,* 8–14 November 2001, http://weekly.ahram.org.eg/2001/559/re2.htm, accessed 26 May 2005; "Anti-Capitalists Meet in Beirut," *Socialist Worker,* 17 November 2001, http://www.socialistworker.co.uk/1775/sw177513.htm, accessed 26 May 2005.
24. Ibid.
25. Abu Rizk,"Globalising Opposition."
26. "Anti-Capitalists Meet in Beirut."
27. Abu Rizk,"Globalising Opposition."
28. "Anti-Capitalists Meet in Beirut."
29. Fatemah Farag, "Another World Is Possible," *Al-Ahram Weekly Online,* 17–23 October 2002, http://weekly.ahram.org.eg/2002/608/eg3.htm, accessed 26 May 2005.
30. Ibid.
31. Anti-Globalization Egyptian Group website, "What is AGEG?" http://www.ageg.net/About_us_English.htm, accessed 15 June 2005.
32. Fatemah Farag, "Palestinian Flag over the Nile," *Al-Ahram Weekly Online,* 19–25 October 2000, http://weekly.ahram.org.eg/2000/504/pal62.htm, accessed 15 June 2005.
33. Omayma Abdel-Latif, "Raising a Voice," *Al-Ahram Weekly Online,* 26 December 2002–1 January 2003, http://weekly.ahram.org.eg/2002/618/sc1.htm, accessed 15 June 2005.
34. Cairo Declaration (2002), http://www.stopwar.org.uk/Resources/cairo .pdf, accessed 26 May 2005.
35. Abdel-Latif, "Raising a Voice."
36. Cairo Declaration (2002).
37. Amira Huweidy, "A Rickety Bridge?" *Al-Ahram Weekly Online,* 18–24 December, 2003, http://weekly.ahram.org.eg/2003/669/eg8.htm, accessed 26 May 2005.
38. Ibid.
39. Ibid.
40. Wael Gamal, "Uniting the Struggles," *Al-Ahram Weekly Online,* 24–30 March 2005, http://weekly.ahram.org.eg/2005/735/eg12.htm, accessed 26 May 2005.

41. Gihan Shahine, "It Starts at Home," *Al-Ahram Weekly Online,* 31 March-6 April 2005, http://weekly.ahram.org.eg/2005/736/eg6.htm, accessed 26 May 2005.

42. Luke Stobart, "Among Men and Women of Steel," 18 April 2005, *Znet/Activism,* http://www.zmag.org/, accessed 18 June 2005. For further details of these struggles, see Human Rights Watch, "Egypt: Attacks by Security Forces in Sarando," letter to the Egyptian minister of the interior, 17 March 2005, http://hrw.org/english/docs/2005/03/17/egypt10334.htm, accessed 18 June 2005; Aaron Glantz, "Egyptian Asbestos Workers Dying of Cancer," 13 January 2005, *CorpWatch,* http://www.corpwatch.org/article.php?id=11791, accessed 18 June 2005.

43. President Hosni Mubarak, cit. in Gary C. Gambill, "Has Saddam Lost the Arab Street?" *Middle East Intelligence Bulletin,* January 2003, http://www.meib.org/articles/0301_ir1.htm, accessed 31 May 2005.

44. For estimated numbers of protesters in the Arab world, see Gary Leupp, "The Weekend the World Said No: Notes on Numbers," *CounterPunch,* 25 February 2003, http://www.counterpunch.org/leupp02252003.html, accessed 31 May 2005.

45. *BBC News Online,* "Millions Join Global Anti-War Protests," 17 February 2003, http://news.bbc.co.uk/2/hi/europe/2765215.stm, accessed 31 May 2005.

46. "Appeal: Demonstrate Against Egypt Govnt Human Rights Abuses," 21 February 2003, distributed through Birmingham University Stop the War list; Amira Howeidy, "Preempting Activism," *Al-Ahram Weekly Online,* 27 February-5 March 2003, http://weekly.ahram.org.eg/print/2003/627/eg3.htm, accessed 26 May 2005.

47. Aziza Sami, "The Sound of Civil Silence," *Al-Ahram Weekly Online,* 6–12 March 2003, http://weekly.ahram.org.eg/print/2003/628/eg2.htm, accessed 26 May 2005.

48. "New Round of Protests in the Middle East and the World," *Revolutionary Worker Online,* 16 March 2003, http://rwor.org/a/v24/1191-1200/1191/awtwns-protests.htm, accessed 31 May 2005.

49. "World Erupts Against the US," *Socialist Review,* April 2003, http://pubs.socialistreviewindex.org.uk/sr273/ashford.htm, accessed 31 May 2005.

50. Human Rights Watch, "Egypt: Crackdown on Antiwar Protestors," press release, 24 March 2003, http://hrw.org/press/2003/03/egypt032403.htm, accessed 17 June 2005.

51. "Arab World on the March Against War," iafrica.com news, 24 March 2003, http://iafrica.com/news/worldnews/221646.htm, accessed 17 June 2005.

52. "World Erupts Against the US," *Socialist Review,* April 2003.

53. Sami, "The Sound of Civil Silence."

54. "Enough Is Not Enough," *Al-Ahram Weekly Online,* 24 February-2 March 2005, http://weekly.ahram.org.eg/2005/731/eg10.htm, accessed 20 June 2005.

55. "Space to Say 'No' to the President," *Al-Ahram Weekly Online,* 16–22 December 2004, http://weekly.ahram.org.eg/2004/721/eg4.htm, accessed 20 June 2005.

56. Mona Salem, "Reform Groups Mushroom in Egypt to Shake off State Grip," Agence France Presse, 6 June 2005.

# 7

## Conclusion

THROUGHOUT THIS BOOK I HAVE examined the dynamics of authoritarianism in order to understand the potential for democratization. I have argued that the Arab world has failed to experience a transition to democracy not because civil-society actors do not support democracy but because there does not exist a consensus that challenges the postindependence hegemony underpinning authoritarianism. Chapter 1 illuminates the theory that authoritarianism represents not only a regime type but also a hegemonic system underpinned by a complex interplay of socioeconomic, ideological, and institutional structures. This system is reproduced not only by the actions of regimes but also by those of ordinary people. In particular, civil society plays an essential role in this process as the arena within which consent for hegemony is generated. On the other hand, this consent may break down and open the way for challenges to the status quo to emerge. However, opposition to authoritarian regimes cannot be equated with challenges to authoritarianism. In order for authoritarianism to be dismantled, it is necessary that civil society creates a new consensus that challenges the whole complex of socioeconomic, ideological, and institutional structures of authoritarianism. In other words, civil society must wage a "war of position" against authoritarianism. Such a process would enable democratization to proceed in a sustained manner. The remaining chapters of this book have investigated the way in which these processes have played out in the one-party states of Algeria, Egypt, Iraq, Syria, and Tunisia.

Chapter 2 demonstrates that authoritarianism was not imposed upon societies in the Arab world by authoritarian regimes but was the result of the interaction between the hopes and desires of civil-society actors and regime actions. That is not to say that civil-society activists wanted authoritarianism. On the contrary, many civil-society activists attempted to resist authoritarian rule by military regimes. However, they were unsuccessful for various reasons—one of which is that, within the hegemonic consensus that had developed under colonial rule, the policies of authoritarian regimes appeared legitimate, even if the means in which these policies were pursued were not. For example, the building of national popular coalitions was seen as necessary to mobilize against threats to national sovereignty (such as the Suez Crisis). Nationalization of the economy would enable the state to generate the economic growth for national modernization to occur. By supporting national unity, national sovereignty, and national modernization, civil-society actors contributed toward creating a consensus that normalized the socioeconomic, institutional, and ideological bases for authoritarianism. This consensus helped regimes to consolidate their control over civil society and to establish authoritarian systems, thereby stifling independent civil and political activism. Not only were civil-society activists hindered by the emergence of new restrictions on their autonomy. In addition, the consensus supporting the project of national modernization operated to ideologically disarm any potential opposition.

The hegemonic consensus began to break down as a result of problems inherent within the import-substitution industrialization (ISI) strategy. The crises experienced by regimes from the mid-1960s onward were more acute for Egypt, Tunisia, and Syria, which were not able to use massive oil revenues to mask structural problems within the economy. These problems were compounded by and linked to the military defeat of the Arab armies against Israel in 1967, which also represented a defeat of the Arab nationalism espoused by the Egyptian and Syrian regimes. Economic and ideological breakdown created opportunities for contentious politics to emerge in various forms. Yet Chapter 3 demonstrates that, despite these challenges to their rule, contentious politics did not move beyond the hegemonic consensus that normalized authoritarianism. In demonstrating their opposition to *infitah* policies, civil-society actors called for the restoration of regimes' commitment to national modernization, including the populist socioeconomic benefits and the anti-imperialist foreign policy that characterized postindependence politics. In this way, civil-society actors contributed toward reproducing the consensus normalizing authoritarianism. In Syria and

Iraq, and to some degree in Algeria, challenges to the regime were communal in nature and expressed opposition to the dominant construction of national identity (as Arab or secular) or to the identity of the regime. However, by promoting one essentialized identity (based on religion, sect, and/or ethnicity) against another essentialized identity (based on religion, sect, and/or ethnicity), these groups failed to articulate an alternative vision of the polity through which to mobilize support from other sections of civil society against authoritarian rule. Nevertheless, the emergence of human rights and women's rights groups, although rooted in the impulse to restore the postindependence hegemony, demonstrated the beginnings of a shift in thinking away from the dominant framework of the postindependence period.

While arguing that dissent does not necessarily challenge authoritarian regimes, nonetheless it represents the potential to do so. By creating new opportunities for the debate and discussion of alternative visions of the polity, contentious politics may develop into the formulation of counter-hegemonic projects that challenge authoritarianism. In light of this potential, authoritarian regimes have responded to contentious politics by attempting to reestablish their control over civil society. The implementation of economic liberalization programs, which aim to dismantle regime control over the economy, has provided an additional hurdle to regimes' ability to hold onto power. Rather than embarking on political liberalization to accommodate new political and economic pressures, Chapter 4 presents the idea that regimes have attempted to reformulate authoritarian rule through a combination of coercion and consent. Coercion, through various legal and extralegal mechanisms, has been aimed at controlling civil-society activity and, in particular, in attempting to prevent activism that is independent of the regime. In addition, regimes have sought to bolster their authority through ideological means and, in particular, through interventions in the increasingly contested realm of public culture. Attempts to reformulate public culture have, to different degrees, enabled regimes to neutralize opposition, build new constituencies, and/or play off different factions of civil society against one another. This suggests the ability of authoritarianism to renew itself, despite adverse economic and political conditions. Culture plays a significant part in this process—not as a static resource upon which regimes may draw to legitimize their actions but rather because culture is continually being (re)constructed with political effects.

In Chapter 5 I focused on the responses of civil-society actors to authoritarian rule. The emergence of contentious politics studied in Chapter 3 gave rise to a diverse and assertive range of civil-society actors from the late 1980s onward. Among these actors, there has developed a consensus in favor of democracy. Yet, there exists no consensus over which type of polity is needed to sustain democracy. In deciding upon these questions, civil-society actors articulate different visions of the nature of political institutions, national identity, and citizenship. Chapter 5 categorized these different positions within a continuum ranging between accommodation of and resistance to the postindependence hegemonic project. The accommodation of the hegemonic consensus entails subscribing to certain elements that have underpinned or normalized authoritarianism, such as hierarchies of social relations based on gender, class, religion, or ethnicity, essentialized notions of national identity, and a willingness to work within corporatist structures. Islamists, as well as many secular-oriented activists, tend toward accommodation of the hegemonic consensus. On the other hand, resistance to hegemony is expressed as positions that challenge existing social relations, essentialized notions of national identity, and corporatist institutions. In particular, human rights and women's rights organizations have gone furthest in developing counter-hegemonic positions. This represents an important element in the development of a war of position against authoritarianism. While there is no guarantee that a consensus in support of such counter-hegemonic positions will evolve, the maintenance of civil society as an arena of debate is essential for such a consensus to develop.

Chapter 6 examines the potential for democratization to be strengthened by links between activists within Arab civil societies and those beyond. On the one hand, transnational links displace the authority of the nation-state and challenge assumptions that link particular national identities to particular political/ideological positions. This runs counter to the notions of essentialized national identity that normalize authoritarianism. In particular, transnational links challenge the representation of the West as a monolithic bloc with opposed interests to the Arab world, thereby confronting a dichotomous world view. Moreover, transnationalism opens up new spaces for civil-society actors to debate different visions of the polity and, possibly, to advance alternatives to the postindependence hegemony. These spaces are strengthened by the participation of actors beyond Arab countries, who are able to bring international pressure to bear upon authoritarian governments to refrain from arresting or harassing activists within Arab countries. Indeed, the above factors contributed to the significant growth of the prodemocracy movement in Egypt from 2003 onward. Despite this, as I argue in Chapter 6, it is also necessary to evaluate the degree to which the framing of transnational movement objectives reproduces or challenges the normalization of authoritarianism. The objectives of those movements examined here may be incorporated within the hegemonic consensus of the postindependence period, in that they may reproduce the dichotomy of "us" and "them." While transnational movements include activists who seek to challenge such dichotomies, equally they include those who seek to maintain such dichotomies because of their political and ideological positions. Transnational movement activity may strengthen those groups whose politics help to reproduce authoritarianism, rather than to dismantle it.

Studies of democratization have created three major dichotomies in explaining democratic transitions: institutions versus actors; political economy versus political culture; and domestic versus external factors.[1] The following sections explore the implications for these established dichotomies as posed by this book.

## Institutions vs. Actors

The "institutions versus actors" dichotomy mirrors, to a large degree, the debate over structure versus agency (Pripstein Posusney 2005: 3). Institutions refer to the macro structures that shape politics, that is, the rules that give rise to and regulate political conduct, such as periodic elections, a multiparty system, or corporatism. Actors refer to the individuals that shape politics, including government officials, members of political parties and civil-society groups, workers, peasants, and any other individual or group of individuals who participates in the political system.

The dominant "transitions paradigm" tends to focus on the significance of actors in initiating the process. It contends that democratic transitions are triggered by splits within the ruling regime, which enable democratic forces to come to the fore. Institutions (the establishment of a multiparty system and free and fair elections) are significant in that they consolidate democracy. In other words, at certain historical moments, actors are able to escape authoritarian institutions in order to introduce democratic institutions. Once in place, democratic institutions shape actions in order to maintain democracy. In other words, while institutional factors (namely, the division within the ruling regime) create an appropriate context, it is the process of certain individuals choosing to push for democracy that is the significant factor in enabling democratic transitions.

Observation of countries experiencing political transitions demonstrates that this paradigm applies to only a minority of cases. In most countries, regime splits have not led to democratization but to a "grey zone" in which countries occupy a diversity of positions between authoritarianism and democracy (Carothers 2002: 9ff). Indeed, this book has demonstrated that Arab regimes have managed a number of political crises by renewing authoritarianism rather than eschewing it. The empirical cases refute the implicit assumption of the transitions paradigm that political transformation entails a linear progression from authoritarianism to democracy.

In response to these limitations of the transitions paradigm, Thomas Carothers proposes that democracy promoters should target their efforts according to "a penetrating analysis of the particular core syndrome that defines the political life of the country in question" (2002: 19). The core syndrome relates to the institutional context in which politics is conducted. In those cases where polities are dominated by a single power (for example, one political party), Carothers suggests a need to develop other political parties as "alternative centers of power" and to reduce the concentration of economic resources that sustain "dominant-power systems" (p. 19). Several authors have highlighted the role of institutional design in hindering democratic transitions in Arab/Middle East countries. For example, the nature of the rules governing electoral competition have enabled regimes to manipulate elections in order to return parliaments that are loyal and, simultaneously, lack the legitimacy that would inspire citizens to push for greater parliamentary powers to counterbalance the executive (Herb 2005; Pripstein Posusney 2005). Meanwhile, the rules governing political parties in Middle Eastern countries prevent the political mobilization and aggregation of preferences that may lead to democratization (Herb 2005; Langohr 2004 and 2005). In addition, regimes have built up huge coercive apparatuses that they have used on a number of occasions to quash popular uprisings that threaten them (Bellin 2004 and 2005; Brownlee 2005).

I have attempted to demonstrate that agential and institutional factors cannot be separated out as causal factors in explaining the failure of democratic transitions to take root. As others have argued, institutions and agency (or structure and agency) are mutually dependent and mutually constitutive (for example, Giddens 1984). While institutions play a role in structuring actors' behavior, simultaneously, actors construct institutions. In the cases examined here, civil-society actors and regimes constructed corporatist institutions in the initial postindependence state-building phase. This process was largely influenced by the legacy of colonial rule. These institutions, in turn, structured the behavior of actors in ways that normalized authoritarianism. Yet actors were also able to adjust and resist these structures in response to the breakdown in the national modernization project. *Infitah* and "deliberalization" were policies pursued by regimes that involved reforming corporatist institutions. Simultaneously, the rise of contentious politics and the emergence of transnational movements have represented a challenge not only to regimes but also to corporatist structures.

In other words, both structure (institutions) and agency can account for the emergence and maintenance of authoritarianism. However, this does not enable us to understand the reasons why, when, and how democratic transitions take off. As argued by Colin Hay, this sort of "substantive empirical dispute" is not resolved by an understanding that politics unfolds as a result of the interaction between actors and structures (2002: 93). In attempting to understand democratic transitions, it is necessary to examine why actors choose certain courses of action and how these relate to the context in which they find themselves. Here, I examine this question in terms of the debate between political economy and (political) culture.

## Political Economy vs. Political Culture

The debate over democratization in the Arab world/Middle East has been largely shaped by the debate over political economy versus political culture. On the one side, some scholars have argued that Arab-Muslim culture is incompatible with democracy (Kedourie 1994; Lewis 1993). Put crudely, actors within the Arab-Muslim cultural context have not chosen democracy because it does not correspond with their (culturally determined) preferences and/or political traditions. A variation of the culturalist argument is that the diversity in ethnic and religious identities in the region has prevented democratic transitions because polities are fragmented along sectarian lines. For example, in the case of post-Ba'th Iraq, it is argued that a democratic transition is threatened by violence and instability fueled by ethnic and religious cleavages (for example, Byman 2003).

The absence of democracy in Arab-Muslim countries may be used to substantiate such claims. For example, a statistical analysis found a high incidence of correlation between authoritarianism and countries that are Arab-Muslim in character (Stepan and Robertson 2003). However, correlation does not prove causation. Culturalist explanations have been criticized on a number of grounds. It is possible to argue that factors other than culture, such as low economic growth rates or the failure to achieve full national sovereignty, may be considered causal explanations for the absence of democracy (Anderson 1995). In addition, culturalist explanations tend to represent identities within the region (whether Arab, Muslim, or some other ethnic or religious affiliation) as immutable and monolithic, thereby ignoring that culture is a social process rather than an inherent attribute.

As I have demonstrated, culture is constantly being constructed and contested, thereby rendering propositions based on essentialized identities (not only within the Arab world but beyond) empirically indefensible. Rather, identities have been constructed by actors within the Arab world as natural and unchanging for *political and strategic* reasons. The expression of a monolithic pan-Arab or territorial national identity has represented a means of challenging derogatory Western representations of Arab/Middle Eastern people in order to politically resist Western intervention in the region (Pratt 2005). Chapter 2 demonstrated how the construction of national identity represented an important element in building anticolonial nationalist movements. In the postindependence period, events such as the Suez Crisis triggered an upsurge in support for Arab nationalism across the region, as a mechanism for opposing Western aggression.

Simultaneously, the construction of essentialized identities has operated to suppress social differences within the nation, in particular, non-Arab/non-Muslim identities, and to posit certain roles for social groups based on class and gender. In this way, nationalism has structured social relations in ways that subordinate certain social groups and facilitated the exercise of authority by regimes and other elites. This was illustrated here by the process of constructing Algerian national identity in the initial postindependence period and other regimes' efforts to control the sphere of public culture in order to renew authoritarianism in the context of economic recession and economic liberalization.[2] In addition, various civil-society actors have contested dominant representations of culture in order to advance their visions of the polity. For example, Islamists have attempted to "Islamize" public culture as a means of promoting their political agenda. On the other hand, rights activists have engaged in attempts to break down the dichotomy of the West versus the Arab world in order to reformulate national identities. Indeed, I have argued that civil society's war of position against essentialized national identities is necessary for the advancement of human rights and women's rights.

On the other side, various authors have argued that it is the interplay of economics and politics that has contributed to the endurance of authoritarianism. I have contended that state control of the economy has given regimes access to revenues to finance the means to stay in power. A state-led economic development strategy was supported by civil-society actors as a means of compensating for the legacy of colonialism and ensuring national modernization. Regimes have used their access to revenues, greatly expanded by income from oil exports (in the case of Iraq and Algeria), to fund the distribution of socioeconomic benefits in order to build support for their rule and maintain corporatist structures (Ayubi 1995; Owen 2004). Meanwhile, revenues have also been invested in building the state's control functions, including their security apparatuses, in order to suppress opponents (Bellin 2004 and 2005). Moreover, the involvement of regimes in control of the economy and the benefits derived from this has made it unlikely that they will surrender power voluntarily (Bromley 1994: 166–169).

In addition, the nature of the political economy has influenced how regimes have managed economic recession and how civil-society actors have responded to it. When the problems of the ISI strategy threatened the socioeconomic gains of the postindependence period, civil-society actors demanded their restoration. In recognition that *infitah* policies and austerity measures contravened the "terms of the moral economy," regimes initiated political decompression in order to manage (and hopefully defuse) dissent. The fighting of wars may also be considered another means for regimes to shore up faltering support due to economic problems. The Egyptian and Syrian regimes were propelled toward the 1967 war due to their rivalry over leadership of the Arab world, which, itself, was partly attributable to the need to deflect domestic attention away from economic problems by asserting Arab nationalist credentials.

Yet (like political culture) it is possible to criticize political economy approaches to democratization on various grounds. It is difficult to make empirical claims about the influence of political economic factors on (the absence of) democratic transitions given that regimes have initiated both political openings and political closures in response to economic difficulties. This suggests that other factors are also at work in shaping political outcomes (namely, the strategic decisions of actors). Moreover, a focus on political economic factors alone suggests that democratic transitions (or their absence) may be reduced to an effect of the economy (the nature of the distribution of economic ownership and economic outputs). Such economic determinism has been heavily critiqued in relation to certain variants of Marxism.

While culture and political economy are aspects shaping the context in which individuals act, these do not determine the absence or presence of democratic transitions. Rather, it is the strategic decisions taken by actors in relation to changing contexts that are significant in shaping political outcomes (Jessop 1990; Hay 2002: 126–129). For example, regime decisions about how to manage economic difficulties resulted in political decompression during the 1970s and 1980s and in political "deliberalization" in the 1990s. These different approaches appear to have been influenced by the qualitative increase in the assertiveness of civil-society actors operating beyond corporatist institutions, in addition to the ability of regimes to maintain or reduce their control over the economy, respectively. Meanwhile, civil-society actors have also changed their demands over time. During the 1970s, there existed a consensus in favor of restoring the elements contributing to the postindependence hegemony (namely, socioeconomic benefits and an anti-imperialist foreign policy). By the 1990s, the consensus in support of the existing hegemony was beginning to break down, largely due to continuing economic crises, thereby helping to fuel demands for human rights, women's rights, and democracy.

Hegemony represents the context within which actors have taken strategic decisions. As argued in Chapter 1, hegemony comprises economic, institutional, and moral-ideological elements and thereby indicates the significance of both political economic and (political) cultural factors, as well as institutions, in shaping the political system. More generally, I have argued that, in pursuit of the objective of national modernization, regimes and civil-society actors have constructed a state-dominated economy, corporatist institutions, and a nationalist-populist ideology. This has been underpinned by a particular hierarchy of social relations, in turn constructed through essentialized conceptions of national identity and culture.

Actors orient themselves within the context of the hegemonic project. The strategic decisions of civil-society actors are identified as key to either maintaining/accommodating or resisting hegemony. It is through their strategic decisions, expressed as political demands, stated objectives, and ways of operating, that hegemony is either reproduced or breaks down. Chapter 3 demonstrates that civil-society actors' demands for a restoration of the postindependence hegemony, despite their opposition to regime policies of *infitah,* contributed to maintaining the consensus normalizing authoritarianism. Meanwhile, Chapter 5 demonstrates that the consensus in favor of hegemony has been breaking down, thereby allowing space for counter-hegemonic positions to emerge, such as new demands with regard to women's rights and human rights and the establishment of groups beyond corporatist institutions. These positions represent attempts at formulating a counter-hegemonic project. While the expression of counter-hegemonic positions is regarded as essential to the development of a "war of position" against authoritarianism, this process is not linear. There exist actors within civil society whose demands, objectives, and methods of operating continue to accommodate the hegemonic project. In particular, Islamist movements operate within corporatist structures, while their demands are framed in terms of essentialized cultural constructions related to Islam. Moreover, Chapter 6 demonstrates that the position of these actors may be reinforced by the dynamics of transnational movements, as well as in response to the actions of international governments.

## Internal vs. External Factors

The transitions paradigm has privileged domestic factors in determining democratization (namely, the role of elites). However, scholars of Middle East politics have also noted the importance of external factors "in either undergirding or undermining authoritarian rule" (Pripstein Posusney 2005: 15). In particular, some have focused on the role of Western governments and the nature of the international political economy in providing Arab regimes with economic resources with which to bolster control of their societies. The strategic importance of the region has led to a situation in which the US and European governments have provided support to authoritarian regimes rather than risk instability that may usher in governments that are not conducive to Western interests.

In this regard, Eva Bellin notes that military aid from Western governments plays a role in sustaining robust coercive apparatuses that are used to suppress internal dissent (Bellin 2004 and 2005). Western governments have provided military aid, in addition to development aid (which, due to its fungibility, may be allocated for security purposes), in order to maintain regional allies. In the case of Ba'thist Iraq, external support was certainly a factor in enabling Saddam to build up the military and to execute a war against Iran (Khalidi 2004: 42–43). Similarly, maintaining Egypt as an ally has constituted an important element of US and European foreign policies toward the region (particularly in the context of the "war on terror"). Toward this end, Egypt was one of the largest recipients of foreign aid in the world[3] and the largest recipient of US aid (ahead of Iraq, in third place) in 2003.[4]

It is not only government aid that has provided regimes with revenues that could be used in maintaining authoritarian rule. The ability of regimes to generate large external revenues in foreign currency from a number of sources, including the export of oil, foreign tourism, and from Suez Canal fees, are also seen to be contributing factors in preventing democratization. The reliance on external as opposed to internally de-rived revenues has enabled governments to maintain their autonomy from domestic constituencies and, therefore, to resist demands for de-mocratization (Beblawi and Luciani 1987). Moreover, ensuring the flow of these external rents depends, to a certain degree, on the maintenance of political stability and suppression of domestic discontent.

Western governments may have contributed to buttressing authori-tarianism by their failure to sufficiently condemn human rights abuses perpetrated by Arab regimes, from the arrest of political opponents across the region to the mass killing of civilians in Ba'thist Iraq during the 1980s (Paul and Stork 1987). This is particularly pertinent regarding the relative inaction of the US government in relation to widespread human rights abuses within the region. As Rashid Khalidi notes, "Before the president's sudden embrace of democracy in the Middle East, the actions of [allies such as Egypt, Saudi Arabia, Turkey, and Israel] rarely provoked the ire of the Bush administration, or indeed of earlier Amer-ican administrations" (2004: 44). While Western governments fail to condemn their allies, simultaneously they possess limited leverage over regimes that are not allies (such as Syria), since the latter are not depen-dent upon their direct support (Brownlee 2005).

However, even in pushing for democratic reforms and respect for human rights, Western governments and agencies may indirectly con-tribute to the continuation of authoritarianism. This is due to the failure of Western actors to sufficiently understand the contexts in which they attempt to intervene. Western democracy promoters have operated according to the assumptions of the dominant transitions paradigm. As noted above, Thomas Carothers has critiqued this paradigm for present-ing a "one size fits all" solution to the issue of democratization (2002). A particular focus has been the provision of support for elections, with the aim of consolidating democratic transitions. In addition, support for civil-society groups has also been a prevalent form of democracy pro-motion, based on the assumption, discussed in Chapter 4, that a prolif-eration of such organizations will contribute to pluralizing the polity and providing a counterbalance to regime power. As discussed here, rather than undermining authoritarianism, elections have enabled regimes to consolidate their power. Meanwhile, support for civil-society groups has been critiqued on a number of bases (see Chapter 4 for further discus-sion). With respect to the argument presented here, civil society plays a role in democratization in that it represents the arena in which a counter-hegemonic project, challenging authoritarianism, is mobilized and diffused. However, that is not to say that support for civil society should be equated with support for democratization, given that civil society has also played a role in normalizing authoritarianism in the postindependence period. It is the nature of ideological contestation within civil society, rather than the number of civil-society groups, that influences the ability of these actors to contribute toward a democratic transition. In this respect, a significant aspect of the West's influence over democratization lies in its relationship to these ideological struggles.

Here, I have attempted to demonstrate that the West's ideological influence over democratization in the Arab world is not only a result of the attempts by governments and various organizations to diffuse democratic and human rights norms within Arab countries. More significantly, democratization in the Arab world is shaped by its historical relationship to the West, which includes the West's political, economic, and military domination, in one form or another, of the Arab region from the period of colonialism until today. Consequently, the West represents a source of domination that must be resisted, and resistance to this domination has been principally located on the ideological level. Actors in the Arab world have constructed certain imaginings about national identity and culture in opposition to the West.[5] In an attempt to mobilize domestic support for the idea of nation-states and to affirm the nation's political sovereignty, various actors have engaged in constructing an "authentic" national identity and culture that is *different from* the West. This difference is located in the sphere of culture (for example, language, religion, gender relations), rather than the "outer domains" of technology, the economy, or the military (Chatterjee 1993). Attempts at creating "authentic," or essentialized, national identities necessarily entail the construction of monolithic representations of the nation. This in turn constructs the political and social hierarchies that underpin authoritarian politics by excluding or subbordinating individuals and groups on the basis of their failure to comply with the norms of behavior, belief, or even ethnic and religious affiliation that are deemed "authentic."

The influence of the West on democratization is also linked to the processes of national identity and culture construction in that it is often actions by Western actors that trigger efforts to reaffirm national identity. This is clearly demonstrated by the upsurge in Arab nationalism that occurred in response to the Suez Crisis in 1956. Similarly, the 1967 and 1973 wars against Israel also led to an upsurge in nationalist fervor.

In more recent times, regimes and certain civil-society actors have re-affirmed authentic national identities and cultures in response to various international events, including Israeli attacks on Palestinians, the UN imposition of sanctions on Iraq, the US-led war against Iraq, and the general threat posed to national sovereignty by growing transnational links between civil-society actors in the Arab world and beyond (Pratt 2004).

The process of reaffirming national identity necessarily implies a process of excluding or suppressing those actors who challenge this identity. This provides a justification for regimes to clamp down on domestic dissent, as well as the human rights of individuals. Toward this end, the concept of national security is invoked and underpinned by notions of authentic national identities that must be policed or secured against Western infiltration. For example, domestic human rights and prodemocracy activists have experienced periodic harassment and even arrest, on the grounds that they threaten national security due to their links to civil-society actors in the West (for example, Pratt 2004 and 2005). The objective of protecting national security against the West was also used to justify the harassment and arrest of gay men in Egypt in 2001 (Pratt, forthcoming). In other words, claims of protecting national security against the West represent a normalization of authoritarian politics and practices. In this context, attempts by Western governments and international organizations to call Arab regimes to account for their human rights abuses and other antidemocratic practices act to reaffirm the perception of Western interference, as well as contribute to the continual hardening of the so-called cultural differences between the Arab world and the West. Given that Western intervention indirectly supports authoritarianism by eliciting efforts at policing national cultural boundaries, what place is there for Western support for democratization?

On the one hand, a solution to the Israel-Palestine conflict and the exit of Western military forces from the region could help to break down Arab images of the West as inherently opposed to the Arab region. However, this does not prevent future foreign-policy actions by Western governments that seek to intervene in the region. To a large degree, these foreign policies are predicated on the construction of notions of Western "national interests" that, in turn, are supported by concepts of "Western" identity and culture as distinct from the identity and culture of "the Rest." In this respect, those seeking to promote democratization in the Arab region must reformulate imaginings of Western nations and their interests that go beyond geographic location or "cultural" belonging. Such a process may occur within the realm of opposition to certain foreign policies—for example, through the antiwar and Palestinian solidarity movements. However, as I argue in Chapter 6, such transnational movements do not necessarily engage in the dismantling of essentialized cultural differences. Therefore, there is also a need to directly address the sources of those ideas that maintain notions of inherent difference between "us" and "them." These ideas are located within the realm of intellectual and cultural production, such as Samuel Huntington's "clash of civilizations" thesis, as well as particular representations of people from the Arab/ Muslim world in news media, among other sources.

Simultaneously, the logic of essentialized identity construction will not disappear within the Arab world simply because Western governments change their foreign policies. In this respect, it is necessary to demonstrate solidarity with those actors that seek to challenge the logic of identity construction within the hegemony of authoritarianism, as a means of clearing the way for democratization. This challenge includes current attempts by civil-society actors to break down monolithic representations of national or subnational communities by promoting the rights of individuals, regardless of their class, gender, religion, or ethnicity. In addition, this process is represented in efforts to reformulate the agenda for women's rights and the rights of working people in order to escape the instrumentalization of their rights for the purpose of national modernization. The process of challenging current national identities does not mean that people must escape from identity. Rather, it will be necessary to formulate alternative identities that recognize diversity and fluidity. Such identities may provide a coherent context in which actors can make strategic decisions to reject the structures underpinning authoritarianism and to support democratization.

In this respect, current attempts to impose liberal democratic institutions on the Arab world, predominantly through US pressure, are counterproductive to democratization. Multiparty elections do not, in and of themselves, constitute a route out of authoritarianism. Within a context in which authoritarianism retains its hegemony, elections may serve to consolidate the power of groups who do not have an interest in supporting the long-term process of democratization—as the case of post-Ba'th Iraq demonstrates. There, different political leaders utilize the "democratic" political process to capture state resources for themselves and their constituencies at the expense of building a state that guarantees universal citizen rights. Consequently, the state is unable to protect the rights of individuals, which are sacrificed for the sake of communal political agendas.

Rather, the path toward greater democracy lies in a war of position against authoritarianism. Toward this end, it is essential that a space is

5

maintained in which civil-society actors are able to debate and discuss the future polity, in the hope that this will enable the formulation of a counter-hegemonic project in support of democratization. This signifies that a minimum guarantee of liberal rights is necessary. These rights may be obtained through the establishment of procedural democracy. However, prodemocracy actors must be aware that procedural democracy does not necessarily lead to sustained democratization. Without a consensus that challenges authoritarianism, the liberal rights that sustain civil-society activism may be rapidly eroded—as the immediate post-independence period demonstrates, as well as the situation in post-Ba'th Iraq. External actors have a role to play in helping to maintain autonomous spaces for civil society—not through imposition but through transnational solidarity.

## Notes

1. These categories are taken from Marsha Pripstein Posusney (2005).

2. Similarly, with regard to Iraq, Eric Davis demonstrates how the restructuring of historical memory, as an element in identification processes, was essential to the Ba'th Party's efforts at consolidating power (2005). Meanwhile, Lisa Wedeen argues that the Syrian regime's promotion of a culture of leadership cult, surrounding the late Hafez al-Assad, has produced political compliance among the country's citizens (1999).

3. In 2003, Egypt ranked seventh in the world, ahead of Mozambique and Afghanistan. Organisation for Economic Cooperation and Development, Development Assistance Committee (OECD DAC), "Aid at a Glance: All DAC Members," 2004, http://www.oecd.org/dataoecd/17/39/23664717.gif, accessed 14 November 2005.

4. OECD DAC, "Aid at a Glance: the US," 2004, http://www.oecd.org/dataoecd/42/30/1860571.gif, accessed 14 November 2005.

5. The logic of identification processes is that they occur in relation to an "Other" (Connolly 1991: 9). The Arab world is not unique in this respect. Historical experience has rendered the West the Arab world's "Other."

# Bibliography

'Abbas, Kamal, Sabr Barakat, and Rahma Rif'at (1997). *Intikhabat fi muftaraq al-turuq* (Cairo: Centre for Trade Union and Workers' Services).

Abd al-Jabbar, Faleh (1992). "Why the Uprisings Failed," *Middle East Report,* no. 176 (May-June), pp. 2–14.

Abdalla, Ahmed (1985). *The Student Movement and National Politics in Egypt* (London: Saqi Books).

——— (1993). "Egypt's Islamists and the State: From Complicity to Confrontation," *Middle East Report,* no. 183 (July-August), pp. 28–31.

Abd-Allah, Umar F. (1983). *The Islamic Struggle in Syria* (Berkeley: Mizan Press).

Abdela, Lesley (2005). "Iraq's War on Women," *openDemocracy,* 18 July.

Abdel-Fadil, Mahmoud (1975). "Development in Income Distribution and Social Changes in Rural Changes in Rural Egypt, 1952–1972," University of Cambridge Department of Applied Economics Occasional Papers, no. 45 (Cambridge: Cambridge University Press).

——— (1980). *The Political Economy of Nasserism: A Study of Employment and Income Distribution Policies in Urban Egypt, 1952–1972* (Cambridge: Cambridge University Press).

Abdel-Malek, Anouar (1962). *Egypte Société Militaire* (Paris: Editions du Seuil).

Abdelrahman, Maha M. (2001). "State–Civil Society Relations: The Politics of Egyptian NGOs," doctoral thesis submitted to the Institute of Social Studies, The Hague.

Abdel-Rahman, Maha (2002). "The Politics of un-Civil Society in Egypt," *Review of African Political Economy* 29, no. 91, pp. 21–40.

Abu 'Ila, Abu 'Ila Madi, Rafiq Habib, and Karim al-Gawhary (1996). "'We Are a Civil Party with an Islamic Identity': An Interview with Abu 'Ila Madi Abu 'Ila and Rafiq Habib," *Middle East Report,* no. 199 (April-June), pp. 30–32.

'Adli, Huwayda (1993). *al-'ummal w-al-siyasa: al-dawr al-siyasi li-l-haraka al-'ummaliya fi misr: 1952–1981* (Cairo: Kitab al-Ahali).

Ahmad, Eqbal (1966)."Trade Unionism," in L. Carl Brown (ed.), *State and Society in Independent North Africa* (Washington, D.C.: The Middle East Institute), pp. 146–191.

Ahmed, Leila (1982)."Feminism and Feminist Movements in the Middle East, A Preliminary Exploration: Turkey, Egypt, Algeria, People's Democratic Republic of Yemen," in Azizah Al-Hibri (ed.), *Women and Islam* (Oxford: Pergamon Press), pp. 153–168.

Ahsan, Syed Aziz al- (1984). "Economic Policy and Class Structure in Syria: 1958–1980," *International Journal of Middle East Studies* 16, no. 3 (August), pp. 301–323.

Ajami, Fouad (1992). *The Arab Predicament: Arab Political Thought and Practice Since 1967* (Cambridge: CUP).

Alavi, Hamza (1972). "The State in Post-Colonial Societies: Pakistan and Bangladesh," *New Left Review* 74 (July-August), pp. 59–81.

Alexander, Christopher (1996). "State, Labor, and the New Global Economy in Tunisia," in Dirk Vandewalle (ed.), *North Africa: Development and Reform in a Changing Global Economy* (New York: St. Martin's).

Ali, Nadje Al- (2000). *Secularism, Gender, and the State in the Middle East: The Egyptian Women's Movement* (Cambridge: Cambridge University Press).

———. (2005). "Reconstructing Gender: Iraqi Women Between Dictatorship, War, Sanctions, and Occupation," *Third World Quarterly* 26, no. 4, pp. 733–752.

Ali, Nadje Al-, and Nicola Pratt (2005). "Women in Iraq: Beyond the Rhetoric," *Middle East Report,* no. 239 (summer).

Allen, Chris (1997). "Who Needs Civil Society?" *Review of African Political Economy* 73, no. 24, pp. 329–337.

Alport, E. A. (1967). "Socialism in Three Countries: The Record in the Maghrib," *International Affairs* 43, no. 4 (October), pp. 678–692.

*Al-Wafd* 1996. 18 October.

Anderson, Lisa (1995). "Democracy in the Arab World: A Critique of the Political Culture Approach," in Rex Brynen, Bahgat Korany, and Paul Noble (eds.), *Political Liberalization and Democratization in the Arab World,* vol. 1 (Boulder, Colo., and London: Lynne Rienner Publishers), pp. 77–92.

*Arab Human Development Report* (2002). (New York: UNDP, 2002).

Aulas, Christine (1982). "Sadat's Egypt: A Balance Sheet," *Middle East Report and Information Project,* no. 107 (July), pp. 6–18, 30–31.

Ayubi, Nazih (1980). *Bureaucracy and Politics in Contemporary Egypt* (London: Ithaca Press).

——— (1991). *Political Islam: Religion and Politics in the Arab World* (London: Routledge).

——— (1995). *Over-Stating the Arab State: Politics and Society in the Middle East* (London: I. B. Tauris).

Aziz, T. M. (1993). "The Role of Muhammad Baqir al-Sadr in Shii Political Activism in Iraq from 1958 to 1980," *International Journal of Middle East Studies* 25, no. 2 (May), pp. 202–222.

Aziz Chaudhry, Kiren (1991). "On the Way to Market: Economic Liberalization and Iraq's Invasion of Kuwait," *Middle East Report,* no. 170 (May-June), pp. 14–23.

Baaklini, Abdo, Guilain Denoeux, and Robert Springborg (1999). *Legislative Politics in the Arab World: The Resurgence of Democratic Institutions* (Boulder, Colo.: Lynne Rienner Publishers).

Babal, Mubejel (2006). Unpublished paper presented during a panel discussion on women's rights and issues in Iraq, organized by Act Together, SOAS, UK, 17 July.

Badie, Bertrand, and Pierre Birnbaum (1986). *Les deux états: pouvoir et société en Occident et an terre d'Islam* (Paris: Fayard).

Badran, Margot (1991)."Competing Agendas: Feminists, Islam and the State in 19th and 20th Century Egypt," in Deniz Kandiyoti (ed.), *Women, Islam and the State* (Philadelphia: Temple University Press), pp. 201–236.

——— (1993)."Independent Women: More Than a Century of Feminism in Egypt," in Judith E. Tucker (ed.), *Arab Women: Old Boundaries, New Frontiers* (Bloomington: Indiana University Press), pp. 129–148.

——— (1995). *Feminists, Islam, and Nation: Gender and the Making of Modern Egypt* (Princeton, N.J.: Princeton University Press).

Baer, Gabriel (1964). *Population and Society in the Arab East* (London: Routledge and Kegan Paul).

Bakr, Ayman, Elliott Colla, and Nasr Hamid Abu Zayd (1993). "Silencing Is at the Heart of My Case," *Middle East Report,* no. 185 (November-December), pp. 27–29, 31.

Baram, Amatzia (1991). *Culture and Ideology in the Making of Ba'thist Iraq, 1968–1989* (New York: St. Martin's Press).

——— (1997). "Neo-Tribalism in Iraq: Saddam Hussein's Tribal Policies, 1991–1996," *International Journal of Middle East Studies* 29, no. 1, pp. 1–31.

Barnett, Michael N. (1998). *Dialogues in Arab Politics* (New York: Columbia University Press).

Baron, Beth (1991)."Marital Bonds in Modern Egypt," in Nikki Keddie and Beth Baron (eds.), *Women in Middle Eastern History* (New Haven and London: Yale University Press), pp. 275–291.

Batatu, Hanna (1978). *The Old Social Classes and the Revolutionary Movements of Iraq* (Princeton, N.J.: Princeton University Press).

Beattie, Kirk J. (1994). *Egypt During the Nasser Years: Ideology, Politics, and Civil Society* (Boulder, Colo.: Westview Press).

Beblawi, Hazem, and Giacomo Luciani (eds.) (1987). *The Rentier State in the Arab World* (London: Croom Helm).

Beinin, Joel, and Zachary Lockman (1987). *Workers of the Nile: Nationalism, Communism, Islam, and the Egyptian Working Class, 1882–1954* (Princeton, N.J.: Princeton University Press).

Beinin, Joel (1994)."Will the Real Egyptian Working Class Please Stand Up?" in Zachary Lockman (ed.), *Workers and Working Classes in the Middle East* (New York: State University of New York Press), pp. 247–270.

——— (1998). *The Dispersion of Egyptian Jewry* (Berkeley: University of California Press).

——— (2001). *Workers and Peasants in the Modern Middle East* (Cambridge: Cambridge University Press).

Belev, Boyan (2000). *Forcing Freedom: Political Control of Privatization and Economic Opening in Egypt and Tunisia* (Lanham, Md., and Oxford: University Press of America).

Bellin, Eva (1994). :Civil Society: Effective Tool of Analysis for Middle East Politics?" *PS: Political Science and Politics* 27, no. 3 (September), pp. 509–510.

——— (1995). "Civil Society in Formation: Tunisia," in A. R. Norton (ed.), *Civil Society in the Middle East,* vol. 1 (Leiden: E. J. Brill), pp. 120–147.

——— (2002). *Stalled Democracy: Capital, Labor, and the Paradox of State-Sponsored Development* (Ithaca and London: Cornell University Press).

——— (2004). "The Robustness of Authoritarianism in the Middle East: Exceptionalism in Comparative Perspective," *Comparative Politics,* special edition: "Enduring Authoritarianism: Lessons from the Middle East for Comparative Theory," 36, no. 2 (January), pp. 139–158.

——— (2005). "Coercive Institutions and Coercive Leaders," in Marsha Pripstein Posusney and Michele Penner Agrist (eds.), *Authoritarianism in the Middle East: Regimes and Resistance* (Boulder, Colo.: Lynne Rienner Publishers), pp. 21–42.

Bennoune, Mahfoud (1988). *The Making of Contemporary Algeria, 1830–1987* (Cambridge: Cambridge University Press).

Bianchi, Robert (1989). *Unruly Corporatism: Associational Life in Twentieth Century Egypt* (New York and Oxford: Oxford University Press).

Boggs, Carl (1976). *Gramsci's Marxism* (London: Pluto Press).

——— (1984). *The Two Revolutions: Antonio Gramsci and the Dilemmas of Western Marxism* (Boston: South End Press).

Botman, Selma (1988). *The Rise of Egyptian Communism, 1939–1970* (New York: Syracuse University Press).

Brand, Laurie (1998). *Women, the State, and Political Liberalization: Middle Eastern and North African Experiences* (New York: Columbia University Press).

Bromley, Simon (1994). *Rethinking Middle East Politics* (Cambridge: Polity Press).

Brown, Nathan J. (2005). "Constitution Drafting Update," Carnegie Foundation for International Peace, August.

Brownlee, Jason (2005). "Political Crisis and Restabilization: Iraq, Libya, Syria and Tunisia," in Marsha Pripstein Posusney and Michele Penner Agrist (eds.), *Authoritarianism in the Middle East: Regimes and Resistance* (Boulder, Colo.: Lynne Rienner Publishers), pp. 43–62.

Brynen, Rex, Bahgat Korany, and Paul Noble (1995a). "Introduction: Theoretical Perspectives on Arab Liberalization and Democratization," in Rex Brynen, Bahgat Korany, and Paul Noble (eds.), *Political Liberalization and Democratization in the Arab World,* vol. 1 (Boulder, Colo., and London: Lynne Rienner Publishers), pp. 3–27.

Brynen, Rex, Bahgat Korany, and Paul Noble (eds.) (1995b). *Political Liberalization and Democratization in the Arab World,* vol. 1 (Boulder, Colo., and London: Lynne Rienner Publishers).

Bulbeck, Chilla (1998). *Re-Orienting Western Feminisms: Women's Diversity in a Postcolonial World* (Cambridge: Cambridge University Press).

Bunch, Charlotte, et al. (2001). "International Networking for Women's Human Rights," in Michael Edwards and John Gaventa (eds.), *Global Citizen Action* (Boulder, Colo.: Lynne Rienner Publishers), pp. 217–230.

Byman, Daniel (2003). "Constructing a Democratic Iraq," *International Security* 28, no. 1 (summer), pp. 47–78.

Cairo Institute for Human Rights Studies (CIHRS), EOHR, and GDD (1998). *Min ajl tahrir al-'amal al-ahli* (Cairo: Cairo Institute for Human Rights Studies).

Carothers, Thomas (2002). "The End of the Transition Paradigm," *Journal of Democracy* 13, no. 1, pp. 5–21.

Centre for Human Rights Legal Aid (CHRLA) (1995). *Final Report on the Legislative Elections in Egypt 1995* (Cairo: CHRLA).

Centre for Trade Union and Worker Services (CTUWS) (n.d.). "Al-'amal 'ala ard al-waqa'" (Cairo: CTUWS).

Charrad, Mounira (2001). *States and Women's Rights: The Making of Postcolonial Tunisia, Algeria, and Morocco* (Berkeley and London: University of California Press).

Chatterjee, Partha (1986). *Nationalist Thought and the Colonial World—A Derivative Discourse* (London: Zed Books).

———— (1993). *The Nation and Its Fragments* (Princeton, N.J.: Princeton University Press).

———— (2001)."On Civil and Political Society in Postcolonial Democracies," in Sudipta Kaviraj and Sunil Khilnani (eds.), *Civil Society: History and Possibilities* (Cambridge: Cambridge University Press), pp. 165–178.

Cheriet, Boutheina (1992). "The Resilience of Algerian Populism," *Middle East Report,* no. 174, pp. 9–14, 34.

Childs, Peter, and Patrick Williams (1997). *An Introduction to Post-Colonial Theory* (Hemel Hempstead, England: Prentice Hall Europe).

Choueiri, Youssef M. (2000). *Arab Nationalism: A History* (Oxford: Blackwell Publishers Ltd.).

Clarke, John, Stuart Hall, Tony Jefferson, and Brian Roberts (1976). "Subcultures, Cultures and Class," in Stuart Hall and Tony Jefferson (eds.), *Resistance Through Rituals: Youth Subcultures in Post-War Britain* (London: Hutchinson), pp. 9–74.

Clawson, Patrick (1981). "The Development of Capitalism in Egypt," *Khamsin* 9, pp. 77–116.

Cohen, Jean L., and Andrew Arato (1994). *Civil Society and Political Theory* (London: MIT Press).

Collins, Carole J. L., Zie Gariyo, and Tony Burdon (2001). "Jubilee 2000: Citizen Action Across the North-South Divide," in Michael Edwards and John Gaventa (eds.), *Global Citizen Action* (Boulder, Colo.: Lynne Rienner Publishers), pp. 135–148.

Connolly, William E. (1991). *Identity/Difference: Democratic Negotiations of Political Paradox* (Ithaca and London: Cornell University Press).

Constitution of the Arab Republic of Egypt (1971) after the Amendments Ratified in the 22 May 1980 Referendum (Cairo: State Information Service, n.d.).

Cooper, Mark (1979). "Egyptian State Capitalism in Crisis: Economic Policies and Political Interests, 1967–1971," *International Journal of Middle East Studies* 10, no. 4 (November), pp. 481–516.

———— (1982). *The Transformation of Egypt* (Baltimore: Johns Hopkins University Press).

Darwish, Yusif, 'Abd al-Ghafar Shukr, and Fathi Mahmud (1997). "Ma'ziq al-niqabat al-'ummaliyya wa khiyar al-ta'addudiyya," *al-Musa'ada* (May), pp. 15–19.

Davis, Eric (1983). *Challenging Colonialism: Bank Misr and Egyptian Industrialization, 1920–1941* (Princeton, N.J.: Princeton University Press).

—— (1991). "Theorizing Statecraft and Social Change in Arab Oil-Producing Countries," in Eric Davis and Nicolas Gavrielides (eds.), *Statecraft in the Middle East* (Miami: Florida International University Press), pp. 1–35.

—— (1994). "History for the Many or History for the Few? The Historiography of the Iraqi Working Class," in Zachary Lockman (ed.), *Workers and Working Classes in the Middle East* (New York: State University of New York Press), pp. 271–302.

—— (2005). *Memories of State: Politics, History, and Collective Identity in Modern Iraq* (Berkeley: University of California Press).

Davis, Eric, and Nicolas Gavrielides (eds.) (1991). *Statecraft in the Middle East* (Miami: Florida International University Press).

Diamond, Larry (1999). *Developing Democracy: Toward Consolidation* (Baltimore and London: Johns Hopkins University Press).

Diamond, Larry, Marc F. Plattner, and Daniel Brumberg (eds.) (2003). *Islam and Democracy in the Middle East* (Baltimore: Johns Hopkins University Press).

Dickey, Christopher (2005). "An Arabian Spring," *Newsweek,* 14 March, pp. 26–33.

Disney, Nigel (1978). "The Working Class Revolt in Tunisia," *MERIP Reports,* no. 67 (May), pp. 12–14.

Dodge, Toby (2003). *Inventing Iraq: The Failure of Nation Building and a History Denied* (London: Hurst & Co.).

Dwyer, Kevin (1991). *Arab Voices: The Human Rights Debate in the Middle East* (London: Routledge).

Eagleton, Terry (1991). *Ideology: An Introduction* (London: Verso).

*Economist, The* (2005). "The Muslim Brothers: Getting Stronger?" (4–10 June), pp. 62–63.

Egset, Willy (2000). "Poverty in the Middle East and North Africa: A Survey of Data and Recent Trends," MENA-projektet, Delstudie 12.

Egyptian human rights NGOs (1999). "Press release," Cairo, 18 May.

Egyptian Organization for Human Rights (EOHR) (1988). "Birnamij al-'amal li-l-munathama al-misriya li-huquq al-insan," unpublished document.

—— (1990, onward). *The Human Rights Situation in Egypt: Annual Report* (Cairo: EOHR).

—— (1994). Appendix no. 2 to "Taqrir majlis al-umana' ila-l-jama'iya al-'umumiya al-khamisa, 28 January 1994" (Cairo: EOHR), pp. 18–19.

—— (1996). *Democracy Jeopardised—Nobody Passed the Elections* (Cairo: EOHR).

Egyptian Popular Committee in Solidarity with the Palestinians (EPCSP) (2004). "Press Release: Arrest of Activists of the Palestine Solidarity Committee," Cairo, 27 February.

Eickelman, Dale F., and James Piscatori (2004). *Muslim Politics* (Princeton, N.J.: Princeton University Press).

Entelis, John (1980). *Comparative Politics of North Africa* (Syracuse, N.Y.: Syracuse University Press).

Eschle, Catherine (2005). "Constructing 'the Anti-Globalisation Movement'," in Catherine Eschle and Bice Maiguashca (eds.), *Critical Theories, International Relations, and the "Anti-Globalisation Movement"* (London: Routledge), pp. 17–35.

Falk, Richard (1999). *Predatory Globalization: A Critique* (Cambridge: Polity Press).

Farouk-Sluglett, Marion, and Peter Sluglett (1983). "Labor and National Liberation: The Trade Union Movement in Iraq, 1920–1958," *Arab Studies Quarterly* 5, no. 2, pp. 139–154.

―――― (1987). *Iraq Since 1958: From Revolution to Dictatorship* (London: Routledge and Kegan Paul).

―――― (1990). "Iraq Since 1986: The Strengthening of Saddam," *Middle East Report,* no. 167 (November-December), pp. 19–24.

―――― (1991). "The Historiography of Modern Iraq," *The American Historical Review* 96, no. 5 (December), pp. 1408–1421.

―――― (2001). *Iraq Since 1958: From Revolution to Dictatorship,* 3rd ed. (London: I. B. Tauris).

Femia, Joseph (2001). "Civil Society and the Marxist Tradition," in Sudipta Kaviraj and Sunil Khilnani (eds.), *Civil Society: History and Possibilities* (Cambridge: Cambridge University Press), pp. 131–146.

Fergany, Nader (1994). "The Human Rights Movement in Arab Countries: Problems of Concept, Context, and Practice," in *Human Rights and the Arab World—Proceedings of the Fourth Annual Symposium of the Cairo Papers in Social Science* 17, no. 3, pp. 24–31.

Fisher, Julie (1998). *Nongovernments: NGOs and the Political Development of the Third World* (West Hartford, Conn.: Kumarian Press).

Fisk, Robert (2003). "A Million March in London But, Faced with Disaster, the Arabs Are Like Mice," *The Independent,* 18 February.

Flores, Alexander (1988). "Egypt: A New Secularism?" *Middle East Report* (July-August), pp. 27–30.

―――― (1993). "Secularism, Integralism, and Political Islam: The Egyptian Debate," *Middle East Report* (July-August), pp. 32–38.

Forgacs, David (ed.) (1999). *The Antonio Gramsci Reader: Selected Writings 1916–1935* (London: Lawrence & Wishart).

Freedom House (2005). "Algeria Amnesty Provides Neither Truth nor Justice," press release, New York, 28 September.

Fuccaro, Nelida (1997). "Ethnicity, State Formation, and Conscription in Postcolonial Iraq: The Case of the Yazidi Kurds of Jabal Sinjar," *International Journal of Middle East Studies* 29, no. 4 (November), pp. 559–580.

Garon, Lise (2003). *Dangerous Alliances: Civil Society, the Media, and Democratic Transition in North Africa* (London: Zed).

Gelvin, James L. (1997). "The Other Arab Nationalism: Syrian/Arab Populism," in James Jankowski and Israel Gershoni (eds.), *Rethinking Nationalism in the Arab Middle East* (New York: Columbia University Press), pp. 231–248.

George, Alan (2003). *Syria: Neither Bread nor Freedom* (London: Zed Books).

Gershoni, Israel (1997)."Rethinking the Formation of Arab Nationalism in the Middle East, 1920–1945: Old and New Narratives," in James Jankowski and Israel Gershoni (eds.), *Rethinking Nationalism in the Arab Middle East* (New York: Columbia University Press), pp. 3–25.

Ghalyun, Burhan (1992)."Bina' al-mujtama' al-madani al-'arabi: dawar al-'awamil al-dakhiliya wa-l-kharijiya," in *Al-mujtama al-madani fi-l-watan al-'arabi wa dawruhu fi tahqiq al-dimuqratiya* (Beirut: Centre for Arab Unity Studies), pp. 733–782.

Giddens, Anthony (1984). *The Constitution of Society* (Cambridge: Polity).

Gordon, Joel (1992). *Nasser's Blessed Movement: Egypt's Free Officers and the July Revolution* (Cairo: AUC Press).

——— (2000). *"Nasser 56/*Cairo 96: Reimagining Egypt's Lost Community," in Walter Armbrust (ed.), *Mass Mediations: New Approaches to Popular Culture in the Middle East and Beyond* (Berkeley: University of California Press), pp. 161–181.

Graham-Brown, Sarah (1999). *Sanctioning Saddam: The Politics of Intervention in Iraq* (London: I. B. Tauris).

Gramsci, Antonio (1971). *Selections from the Prison Notebooks,* trans. and ed. by Quinton Hoare and Geoffrey Nowell-Smith (London: Lawrence and Wishart).

Gross, Joan, David McMurray, and Ted Swedenburg (1992). "Rai, Rap, & Ramadan Nights: Franco-Maghribi Cultural Identities," *Middle East Report,* no. 178 (September-October), pp. 11–16, 24.

Hafez, Sabry (2000). "The Novel, Politics, and Islam," *New Left Review,* no. 5 (September-October), pp. 117–141.

Haim, Sylvia G. (ed.) (1974). *Arab Nationalism: An Anthology* (Berkeley: University of California Press).

Hall, Stuart (1996). "Introduction: Who Needs Identity?" in Stuart Hall and Paul du Gay (eds.), *Questions of Cultural Identity* (London: Sage), pp. 1–17.

Halliday, Fred, and Hamza Alavi (eds.) (1988). *State and Ideology in the Middle East and Pakistan* (New York: Monthly Review Press).

Halliday, Fred (1987). "1967 and the Consequences of Catastrophe," *Middle East Report and Information Project,* no. 146 (May), pp. 3–5.

——— (1990). "Tunisia's Uncertain Future," *MERIP,* no. 163 (March-April), pp. 25–27.

——— (2000). *Nation and Religion in the Middle East* (London: Saqi Books).

——— (2005). *The Middle East in International Relations* (Cambridge: Cambridge University Press).

Hamzawy, Amr (2005). "The Key to Arab Reform: Moderate Islamists," Policy brief # 40, Carnegie Endowment.

Handoussa, Heba (1991). "Crisis and Challenge: Prospects for the 1990s," in Heba Handoussa and Gillian Potter (eds.), *Employment and Structural Adjustment: Egypt in the 1990s* (Cairo: AUC Press), pp. 3–24.

Harik, Iliya (1987). "The Origins of the Arab State System," in Ghassan Salamé (ed.), *The Foundations of the Arab State* (London: Croom Helm).

——— (1992a). "Privatization: The Issue, the Prospects, and the Fears," in Iliya Harik and Dennis Sullivan (eds.), *Privatization and Liberalization in the Middle East* (Bloomington: University of Indiana Press), pp. 1–23.

——— (1992b). "Privatization and Development in Tunisia," in Iliya Harik and Dennis Sullivan (eds.), *Privatization and Liberalization in the Middle East* (Bloomington: University of Indiana Press), pp. 210–232.

Harik, Iliya, and Dennis Sullivan (eds.) (1992). *Privatization and Liberalization in the Middle East* (Bloomington: University of Indiana Press).

Hatem, Mervat (1992). "Economic and Political Liberation in Egypt and the Demise of State Feminism," *International Journal of Middle East Studies* 24, no. 2 (May), pp. 231–251.

——— (1993). "Toward the Development of Post-Islamist and Post-Nationalist Feminist Discourses in the Middle East," in Judith E. Tucker (ed.), *Arab Women: Old Boundaries, New Frontiers* (Bloomington: Indiana University Press), pp. 29–64.

Hawthorne, Amy (2004). "Middle Eastern Democracy: Is Civil Society the Answer?" Paper no. 44, Carnegie Endowment.

Hay, Colin (2002). *Political Analysis: A Critical Introduction* (Basingstoke, England: Palgrave).

Heggoy, Alf Andrew, and Paul J. Zingg (1976). "French Education in Revolutionary North Africa," *International Journal of Middle East Studies* 7, no. 4 (October), pp. 571–578.

Held, David, and Anthony McGrew (2000). "The Great Globalization Debate," in David Held and Anthony McGrew (eds.), *The Global Transformations Reader: An Introduction to the Globalization Debate* (Cambridge: Polity Press), pp. 1–45.

Henry, Clement M. (1997). *The Mediterranean Debt Crescent: Money and Power in Algeria, Egypt, Morocco, Tunisia, and Turkey* (Cairo: AUC Press).

Henry, Clement M., and Robert Springborg (2001). *Globalization and the Politics of Development in the Middle East* (Cambridge: Cambridge University Press).

Herb, Michael (2005). "Princes, Parliaments, and the Prospects for Democracy in the Gulf," in Marsha Pripstein Posusney and Michele Penner Agrist (eds.), *Authoritarianism in the Middle East: Regimes and Resistance* (Boulder, Colo.: Lynne Rienner Publishers), pp. 169–192.

Hetata, Sherif (1997). "Mutilation, Identity, and Aid," unpublished article, Cairo.

Hewitt de Alcántara, Cynthia (1998). "Uses and Abuses of the Concept of Governance," *International Social Science Journal* 155 (March), pp. 105–113.

Hibri, Azizah al- (ed.) (1982). *Women and Islam* (Oxford: Pergamon Press).

Hijab, Nadia (1988). *Womanpower: The Arab Debate on Women at Work* (Cambridge: Cambridge University Press).

Hinnebusch, Raymond (1990). *Authoritarian Power and State Formation in Ba'thist Syria: Army, Party, and Peasant* (Boulder, Colo.: Westview Press).

——— (2001). *Syria: Revolution from Above* (London: Routledge).

——— (2003). *The International Politics of the Middle East* (Manchester: Manchester University Press).

Hopwood, Derek (1988). *Syria 1945–1986: Politics and Society* (London: Unwin Hyman).

Hourani, Albert (1983). *Arabic Thought in the Liberal Age, 1798–1939* (Cambridge: Cambridge University Press).

——— (1991). *A History of the Arab Peoples* (London: Faber & Faber).

——— (2002). *A History of the Arab Peoples,* 2nd ed. (London: Faber & Faber).

Hudson, Michael (1977). *Arab Politics: The Search for Legitimacy* (New Haven, Conn., and London: Yale University Press).

Human Rights Watch (HRW) (1991). *Syria Unmasked: The Suppression of Human Rights by the Asad Regime* (New Haven, Conn.: Yale University Press).

Huntington, Samuel (1991). *The Third Wave: Democratization in the Late Twentieth Century* (London: University of Oklahoma Press).

—— (1993). "The Clash of Civilizations?" *Foreign Affairs* 72, pp. 22–49.

Hussein, Mahmoud (1973). *Class Conflict in Egypt, 1945–1970* (New York: Monthly Review Press).

Ibrahim, Saad Eddin (1995). "Civil Society and Prospects of Democratization in the Arab World," in A. R. Norton (ed.), *Civil Society in the Middle East*, vol. 1 (Leiden: Brill), pp. 27–54.

International Crisis Group (ICG) (2003). "Unrest and Impasse in Kabylia," *Middle East/North Africa*, no. 15, Cairo/Brussels, 10 June.

—— (2004a). "Islamism in North Africa: The Legacies of History," Cairo/Brussels, 20 April.

—— (2004b). "Islamism, Violence, and Reform in Algeria: Turning the Page," *Middle East Report*, no. 29, Cairo/Brussels, 30 July.

Ismael, Jacqueline (1980). "Social Policy and Social Change: The Case of Iraq," *Arab Studies Quarterly* 2, no. 3, pp. 235–248.

Ismael, Tareq Y. (1976). *The Arab Left* (New York: Syracuse University Press).

—— (2005). *The Communist Movement in the Arab World* (London: Routledge Curzon).

Ismael, Tareq Y., and Rifa'at el-Sa'id (1990). *The Communist Movement in Egypt, 1920–1988* (New York: Syracuse University Press).

Ismail, Salwa (1995). "Democracy in Contemporary Arab Intellectual Discourse," in Rex Brynen, Bahgat Korany, and Paul Noble (eds.), *Political Liberalization and Democratization in the Arab World*, vol. 1 (Boulder, Colo., and London: Lynne Rienner Publishers), pp. 93–112.

—— (2003). *Rethinking Islamist Politics: Culture, the State, and Islamism* (London: I. B. Tauris).

Jabra, Jabra (1996). "Modern Arabic Literature and the West," in Issa J. Boullata (ed.), *Critical Perspectives on Modern Arabic Literature* (Boulder, Colo.: Lynne Rienner Publishers).

Jankowski, James, and Israel Gershoni (eds.) (1997). *Rethinking Nationalism in the Arab Middle East* (New York: Columbia University Press).

Jayawardena, Kumari (1986). *Feminism and Nationalism in the Third World* (London: Zed Books).

Jessop, Bob (1990). *State Theory: Putting Capitalist States in Their Place* (Cambridge: Polity).

—— (1997). "Capitalism and Its Future: Remarks on Regulation, Government, and Governance," *Review of International Political Economy* 4, no. 3 (autumn), pp. 567–591.

Johnson, Peter (1972). "Egypt Under Nasser," *MERIP Reports*, no. 10 (July), pp. 3–14.

—— (1973). "Egyptian Student Revolt Moves from Street to Chambers," *MERIP Reports*, no. 15 (March), p. 28.

Jones, Linda (1988). "A Portrait of Rashid al-Ghannoushi," *Middle East Report*, no. 153 (July-August), pp. 19–22.

Joseph, Suad (1991). "Elite Strategies for State Building: Women, Family, Religion and the State in Iraq and Lebanon," in Deniz Kandiyoti (ed.), *Women, Islam and the State* (Philadelphia: Temple University Press), pp. 176–200.

Kabbani, Rana (1986). *Europe's Myths of Orient* (Bloomington: Indiana University Press).

Kaminer, Reuven (1996). *The Politics of Protest: The Israeli Peace Movement and the Palestinian Intifada* (Brighton: Sussex Academic Press).

Kandiyoti, Deniz (1991)."Identity and Its Discontents: Women and the Nation," *Millenium: Journal of International Studies* 20, no. 3, reprinted in Patrick Williams and Laura Chrisman (eds.), *Colonial Discourse and Post-Colonial Theory: A Reader* (New York: Harvester Wheatsheaf, 1993), pp. 376–391.

Karsh, Efraim, and Inari Rautsi (1991). *Saddam Hussein: A Political Biography* (London: Brassy's UK).

Kassem, May (1999). *In the Guise of Democracy: Governance in Contemporary Egypt* (Reading, Pa.: Ithaca Press).

Katz, Sheila Hannah (1996). *"Adam* and *Adama, 'Ird* and *Ard:* En-gendering Political Conflict and Identity in Early Jewish and Palestinian Nationalisms," in Deniz Kandiyoti (ed.), *Gendering the Middle East* (New York: Syracuse University Press), pp. 85–106.

Kaufman, Ilana (1997). *Arab National Communism in the Jewish State* (Gainesville: University of Florida Press).

Kaviraj, Sudipta (2001). "In Search of Civil Society," in Sudipta Kaviraj and Sunil Khilnani (eds.), *Civil Society: History and Possibilities* (Cambridge: Cambridge University Press), pp. 287–323.

Kazziha, Walid (1990)."The Impact of Palestine on Arab Politics," in Giacamo Luciani (ed.), *The Arab State* (London: Routledge), pp. 300–318.

Keck, Margaret E., and Kathryn Sikkink (1998). *Activists Beyond Borders: Advocacy Networks in International Politics* (Ithaca and London: Cornell University Press).

Kedourie, Elie (1994). *Democracy and Arab Political Culture* (London: Frank Cass).

Kepel, Gilles (1997). "Islamic Groups in Europe: Between Community Affirmation and Social Crisis," in Steve Vertovec and Ceeri Peach (eds.), *Islam in Europe: The Politics of Religion and Community* (Houndmills, Basingstoke, England: Macmillan Press Ltd.), pp. 48–58.

Khafaji, Isam el- (1988). "Iraq's Seventh Year: Saddam's Quart d'Heure?" *Middle East Report,* no. 151 (March), pp. 35–39.

Khalidi, Rashid (2004). *Resurrecting Empire* (Boston: Beacon Press).

Khalil, Samir al- (1991a). "Kuwaiti Rights Are the Issue," *Middle East Report,* no. 168 (January–February), pp. 14–16.

——— (1991b). *The Monument: Art, Vulgarity, and Responsibility in Iraq* (London: Andre Deutsch).

Khater, Akram F. (2004). *Sources in the History of the Modern Middle East* (Boston: Houghton Mifflin).

Khawaga, Dina el- (1997). "Les droits de l'homme en Égypte: Dynamiques de relocalisation d'une référence occidentale," *Egypte/Monde arabe* 30–31, pp. 231–249.

Khoury, Philip S. (1987). *Syria and the French Mandate: The Politics of Arab Nationalism, 1920–1945* (Princeton, N.J.: Princeton University Press).

Kienle, Eberhard (2001). *A Grand Delusion: Democracy and Economic Reform in Egypt* (London: I. B. Tauris).

King, John (1997). "Tablighi Jamaat and the Deobandi Mosques in Britain," in Steve Vertovec and Ceeri Peach (eds.), *Islam in Europe: The Politics of Religion and Community* (Houndmills, Basingstoke, England: Macmillan Press Ltd.), pp. 129–146.

Kodmani, Bassma (2005). "The Dangers of Political Exclusion: Egypt's Islamist Problem," Carnegie Papers, no. 63, October.

Kramer, Gudrun (1992). "Liberalisation and Democracy in the Arab World," *Middle East Report,* no. 174 (January-February), pp. 22–25, 35.

——— (1993). "Islamist Notions of Democracy," *Middle East Report* (July-August), pp. 2–8.

——— (1995). "Islam and Pluralism," in Rex Brynen, Bahgat Korany, and Paul Noble (eds.), *Political Liberalization and Democratization in the Arab World,* vol. 1 (Boulder, Colo., and London: Lynne Rienner Publishers), pp. 113–128.

Lalor, Paul (1991). "Report from Baghdad," *Middle East Report,* no. 169 (March–April), pp. 11–13, 36.

Langohr, Vickie (2004). "Too Much Civil Society, Too Little Politics: Egypt and Liberalizing Regimes," *Comparative Politics,* special edition: *Enduring Authoritarianism: Lessons from the Middle East for Comparative Theory* 36, no. 2 (January), pp. 181–204.

——— (2005). "Too Much Civil Society, Too Little Politics? Egypt and Other Liberalizing Arab Regimes," in Marsha Pripstein Posusney and Michele Penner Agrist (eds.), *Authoritarianism in the Middle East: Regimes and Resistance* (Boulder, Colo.: Lynne Rienner Publishers), pp. 193–220.

Lawson, Fred (1992). "Divergent Modes of Economic Liberalization in Syria and Iraq," in Iliya Harik and Denis J. Sullivan (eds.), *Privatization and Liberalization in the Middle East* (Bloomington and Indianapolis: Indiana University Press), pp. 123–144.

Lawson, Stephanie (1991). *The Failure of Democratic Politics in Fiji* (Oxford: Clarendon).

——— (1998). "The Culture of Politics," in Richard Maidment and Colin Mackerras (eds.), *Culture and Society in the Asia-Pacific* (London: Routledge), pp. 231–252.

Layachi, Azzedine (2005). "The Berbers in Algeria: Politicized Ethnicity and Ethnicized Politics," in Maya Shatzmiller (ed.), *Nationalism and Minority Identities in Islamic Societies* (Montreal and Kingston: McGill-Queen's University Press), pp. 195–228.

Lazreg, Marnia (1990). "Gender and Politics in Algeria: Unraveling the Religious Paradigm," *Signs* 14, no. 4 (summer), pp. 755–780.

——— (1994). *The Eloquence of Silence: Algerian Women in Question* (New York and London: Routledge).

Leftwich, Adrian (1994). "Governance, the State, and the Politics of Development," *Development and Change,* no. 25, pp. 363–386.

Lenczowski, George (1966). "Radical Regimes in Egypt, Syria, and Iraq: Some Comparative Observations on Ideologies and Practices," *The Journal of Politics* 28, no. 1, pp. 29–56.

Lewis, Bernard (1993). "Islam and Liberal Democracy," *Atlantic Monthly* 271, no. 2 (February), pp. 89–98.

Liauzu, Claude (1996). "The History of Labor and the Workers' Movement in North Africa," in Ellis Goldberg (ed.), *The Social History of Labor in the Middle East* (Boulder, Colo.: Westview Press), pp. 193–221.

Linz, Juan (2000). *Totalitarian and Authoritarian Regimes,* new edition (Boulder, Colo.: Lynne Rienner Publishers).

Lobmeyer, Hans Gunter (1994). "Al-dimuqratiyya hiyya al-hall? The Syrian Opposition at the End of the Asad Era," in Eberhard Kienle (ed.), *Contemporary Syria: Liberalization Between Cold War and Cold Peace* (London: British Academic Press), pp. 81–96.

Longuenesse, Elizabeth (1985). "The Syrian Working Class Today," *Middle East Report,* no. 134 (July-August), pp. 17–24.

——— (1996). "Labor in Syria: The Emergence of New Identities," in Ellis Goldberg (ed.), *The Social History of Labor in the Middle East* (Boulder, Colo.: Westview Press), pp. 99–130.

Loomba, Ania (1991). "Overworlding the 'Third World,'" *Oxford Literary Review* 13, no. 1–2, reprinted in Patrick Williams and Laura Chrisman (eds.), *Colonial Discourse and Post-Colonial Theory: A Reader* (New York: Harvester Wheatsheaf, 1993), pp. 305–323.

Luethold, Arnold (2004). "Security Sector Reform in the Arab Middle East: A Nascent Debate," in SSR yearbook; online at: http://www.dcaf.ch/publications/e-publications/SSR_yearbook2004/Chapter5_Luethold.pdf, accessed 11 July 2005.

Luizard, Pierre-Jean (1995). "The Iraqi Question from Inside," *Middle East Report,* no. 193 (March-April), pp. 18–22.

Mabro, Robert (1974). *The Egyptian Economy 1952–1972* (Oxford: Oxford University Press).

Mandaville, Peter (2004). *Transnational Muslim Politics: Reimagining the Umma* (London: Routledge).

Marshall, Susan E., and Randall G. Stokes (1981). "Tradition and the Veil: Female Status in Tunisia and Algeria," *Journal of Modern African Studies* 19, no. 4, pp. 625–646.

Masri, Sanna' al- (1998, 1999). *Tatbia' wa tamwil: qissa al-jama'iyat ghayr al-hukumiya,* vols. 1 and 2 (Cairo: Markaz al-Nadim li-l-bhath wa-l-ma'lumat).

Matthews, Jessica T. (1997). "Power Shift," *Foreign Affairs* 76, no. 1 (January-February), pp. 50–66.

McClintock, Anne (1992). "The Angel of Progress: Pitfalls of the Term 'Post-Colonialism,'" *Social Text* (spring), reprinted in Patrick Williams and Laura Chrisman (eds.), *Colonial Discourse and Post-Colonial Theory: A Reader* (New York: Harvester Wheatsheaf, 1993), pp. 291–304.

MERIP Reports (1973). "Interview with Egyptian Student Leaders," no. 17 (May), pp. 6–10.

——— (1974). "Open Door in the Middle East," no. 31 (October), pp. 3–28.

——— (1975). "Egyptian Demonstrations Hit Sadat's Political, Economic Policies," no. 34 (January), pp. 28–29.

——— (1976). "Popular Opposition to Sadat's Economic Policy," no. 53 (December), p. 23.

——— (1977). "How Life and Scandal Rocked Sadat," no. 54 (February), pp. 19–20.

—— (1979). "Sadat's 'New Democracy': Fresh Rounds of Arrests and Detentions," no. 80 (September), pp. 14–15.

—— (1987). "Israel Cracks Down on Jewish Peace Activists," no. 145 (March–April), p. 42.

—— (2000). "Critiquing NGOs: Assessing the Last Decade," 30, no. 1 (spring), p. 1.

Mezhoud, Salem (1993). "Glasnost the Algerian Way: The Role of Berber Nationalists in Political Reform," in George Joffe (ed.), *North Africa: Nation, State, and Region* (London: Routledge), pp. 142–169.

Milton-Edwards, Beverly (2004). *Islam & Politics in the Contemporary World* (Cambridge: Polity).

Milton-Edwards, Beverly, and Peter Hinchcliffe (2001). *Conflicts in the Middle East Since 1945* (London: Routledge).

Minces, Juliette (1978). "Women in Algeria," in Lois Beck and Nikki Keddie (eds.), *Women in the Muslim World* (Cambridge, Mass.: Harvard University Press), pp. 159–171.

Mishra, Vijay, and Bob Hodge (1991). "What Is Post(-)Colonialism?" *Textual Practice* 5, no. 3, reprinted in Patrick Williams and Laura Chrisman (eds.), *Colonial Discourse and Post-Colonial Theory: A Reader* (New York: Harvester Wheatsheaf, 1993), pp. 276–290.

Mitchell, Timothy (1991). "The Limits of the State: Beyond Statist Approaches and Their Critics," *American Political Science Review* 85, no. 1 (March).

Moghadam, Valentine (1993). *Modernizing Women: Gender and Social Change in the Middle East* (Boulder, Colo.: Lynne Rienner Publishers).

Mohi El Din, Khaled (1995). *Memories of a Revolution—Egypt 1952* (Cairo: American University in Cairo Press).

Mojab, Shahrzad (2004). "No 'Safe Haven': Violence Against Women in Iraqi Kurdistan," in Wenona Giles and Jennifer Hyndman (eds.), *Sites of Violence: Gender and Conflict Zones* (Berkeley: University of California Press), pp. 108–133.

Moore, Clement Henry (1965). *Tunisia Since Independence* (Berkeley: University of California Press).

Murphy, Emma (1999). *Economic and Political Change in Tunisia* (Houndsmills, England: Macmillan).

Mustafa, Hala (1995). "The Egyptian Regime and the Opposition in 1994," in Al-Ahram Centre for Political and Strategic Studies (ed.), *The Arab Strategic Report: 1994* (Cairo: ACPSS), pp. 95–123.

Mustafa, Tamir (2003). "Law Versus the State: The Judicialisation of Politics in Egypt," *Law and Social Enquiry* 28, no. 4, pp. 883–930.

Na'ana, Hamida (1999). "The Cultural Impact of the Left in Syria and Palestine: A Personal View," in Roel Mijer (ed.), *Cosmopolitanism, Identity and Authenticity in the Middle East* (London: Curzon), pp. 61–70.

Nederveen Pieterse, Jan (1995). "Globalization as Hybridization," in Mike Featherstone et al. (eds.), *Global Modernities* (London: Sage), pp. 45–68.

Nelson, Cynthia (1996). *Doria Shafik, Egyptian Feminist* (Gainesville: University of Florida Press).

New Woman Research and Study Centre (NWRC) (1996). *The Feminist Movement in the Arab World: Intervention and Studies from Four Countries* (Cairo: Dar al-Mustaqbal al-Arabi).

Niva, Steve (1990). "US Organizations and the Intifada," *Middle East Report*, no. 164–165 (May-August), pp. 72–74.

Norton, Augustus Richard (ed.) (1995). *Civil Society in the Middle East*, vol. 1 (Leiden: E. J. Brill).

———— (1996). *Civil Society in the Middle East*, vol. 2 (Leiden: E. J. Brill).

Nouschi, Andre (1993). "The FLN, Islam, and Arab Identity," in Alec G. Hargreaves and Michael J. Heffernan (eds.), *French and Algerian Identities from Colonial Times to the Present* (Lewiston and Lampeter: Edwin Mellen), pp. 111–128.

O'Brian, Robert, Anne Marie Goetz, Jan Aart Scholte, and Marc Williams (2000). *Contesting Global Governance: Multilateral Economic Institutions and Global Social Movements* (Cambridge: Cambridge University Press).

O'Donnell, Guillermo (1973). *Modernization and Bureaucratic Authoritarianism: Studies in South American Politics* (Berkeley, Calif.: Institute of International Studies).

O'Donnell, Guillermo, and Philippe C. Schmitter (1986). *Transitions from Authoritarian Rule: Tentative Conclusions About Uncertain Democracies* (Baltimore: Johns Hopkins University Press).

Ottaway, David, and Marina Ottaway (1970). *Algeria: The Politics of a Socialist Revolution* (Berkeley: University of California Press).

Owen, Roger (1981). *The Middle East in the World Economy, 1800–1914* (London and New York: Methuen).

———— (2004 [1992]). *State, Power, and Politics in the Making of the Modern Middle East* (London and New York: Routledge).

Pappé, Ilan (2005). *The Modern Middle East* (London: Routledge).

Paul, James, and Joe Stork (1987). "The Middle East and Human Rights," *Middle East Report*, no. 149 (November-December), pp. 2–5.

Perthes, Volker (1992). "Syria's Parliamentary Elections: Remodelling Asad's Political Base," *Middle East Report* (January-February), pp. 15–18, 35.

Peteet, Julie M. (1991). *Gender in Crisis: Women and the Palestinian Resistance Movement* (New York: Columbia University Press).

Pfeifer, Karen (1999). "How Tunisia, Morocco, Jordan, and Even Egypt Became IMF 'Success Stories' in the 1990s," *Middle East Report*, no. 210 (spring), pp. 23–27.

Philipp, Thomas (1978). "Feminism and Nationalist Politics in Egypt," in Lois Beck and Nikki Keddie (eds.), *Women in the Muslim World* (Cambridge, Mass.: Harvard University Press), pp. 277–294.

Pipes, Daniel (1988). "Radical Politics and the Syrian Social Nationalist Party," *International Journal of Middle East Studies* 20, no. 3 (August), pp. 303–324.

Piscatori, James (1986). *Islam in a World of Nation States* (Cambridge: Cambridge University Press).

Pratt, Nicola (1998). "The Legacy of the Corporatist State: Explaining Workers' Responses to Economic Liberalisation in Egypt," *Durham Middle East Papers*, no. 60 (November).

———— (2000/2001). "Maintaining the Moral Economy: Egyptian State-Labor Relations in an Era of Economic Liberalization," *Arab Studies Journal* 8, nos. 2 and 9 (fall/spring), pp. 111–129.

——— (2002). "Globalisation and the Post-Colonial State in Egypt: Human Rights NGOs and the Prospects for Democratic Governance in Egypt," unpublished Ph.D. thesis, University of Exeter.

——— (2004a). "Bringing Politics Back In: Examining the Link Between Globalization and Democratization," *Review of International Political Economy* 11, no. 2 (May), pp. 311–336.

——— (2004b). "Understanding Political Transformation in Egypt: Advocacy NGOs, Civil Society and the State," *Journal of Mediterranean Studies* 14, no. 1–2, pp. 237–262.

——— (2005). "Identity, Culture, and Democratization: The Case of Egypt," *New Political Science* 27, no. 1 (March), pp. 69–86.

——— (forthcoming). "Sexuality, National Identity and State Sovereignty: The Queen Boat Case in Egypt," *Review of International Studies.*

Pripstein Posusney, Marsha (1997). *Labor and the State in Egypt* (New York: Columbia University Press).

——— (1998). "Behind the Ballot Box: Electoral Engineering in the Arab World," *Middle East Report,* no. 209 (winter), pp. 12, 15, 42.

——— (2005). "The Middle East's Democracy Deficit in Comparative Perspective," in Marsha Pripstein Posusney and Michele Penner Angrist (eds.), *Authoritarianism in the Middle East: Regimes and Resistance* (Boulder, Colo.: Lynne Rienner Publishers), pp. 1–20.

Pripstein Posusney, Marsha, and Michele Penner Angrist (eds.) (2005). *Authoritarianism in the Middle East: Regimes and Resistance* (Boulder, Colo.: Lynne Rienner Publishers).

Progressive Assembly of National Unionists (1979). "No to the Egyptian-Israeli Treaty," MERIP Reports, no. 80 (September), pp. 14–18.

Przeworski, Adam (1991). *Democracy and the Market: Political and Economic Reforms in Eastern Europe and Latin America* (Cambridge: Cambridge University Press).

Putnam, Robert (1993). *Making Democracy Work. Civic Traditions in Modern Italy* (Princeton, N.J.: Princeton University Press).

——— (2000). *Bowling Alone: The Collapse and Revival of American Community* (New York: Simon & Schuster).

Rabinovich, Itamar (1972). *Syria Under the Ba'th 1963–66* (Jerusalem: Israel Universities Press).

Rai, Shirin M. (2002). *Gender and the Political Economy of Development* (Cambridge: Polity).

Reid, Donald (1981). *Lawyers and Politics in the Arab World, 1880–1960* (Chicago: Bibliotheca Islamica, Inc.).

Richards, Alan (1995). "Economic Pressures for Accountable Governance in the Middle East and North Africa," in A. R. Norton (ed.), *Civil Society in the Middle East,* vol. 1 (Leiden: E. J. Brill), pp. 55–78.

Richards, Alan, and John Waterbury (1990). *A Political Economy of the Middle East* (Boulder, Colo.: Westview Press).

——— (1996). *A Political Economy of the Middle East,* 2nd ed. (Boulder, Colo.: Westview Press).

Risse, Thomas, Stephen C. Ropp, and Kathryn Sikkink (eds.) (1999). *The Power of Human Rights: International Norms and Domestic Change* (Cambridge: Cambridge University Press).

Roberts, Hugh (1992). "The Algerian State and the Challenge of Democracy," *Government and Opposition* 27, no. 4, pp. 433–456.

Rose, Ben (1986). "Cairo's Long Summer," *Middle East Report* (September–October), pp. 41–42.

Rosefsky Wickam, Carrie (2004). "Strategy and Learning in the Formation of Egypt's Wasat Party," *Comparative Politics* 36, no. 2 (January), pp. 205–228.

Ruedy, John (2005). *Modern Algeria: The Origins and Development of a Nation,* 2nd ed. (Bloomington: Indiana University Press).

Saadawi, Nawal El (1977). *The Hidden Face of Eve* (London: Zed Books).

———— (1988). "The Political Challenges Facing Arab Women at the End of the 20th Century," in Nahid Toubia (ed.), *Women of the Arab World: Papers of the Arab Women's Solidarity Association Conference* (London and New Jersey: Zed Books), pp. 8–26.

———— (1997). *The Nawal El-Saadawi Reader* (London: Zed Books).

Sadiki, Larbi (1997). "Towards Arab Liberal Governance: From the Democracy of Bread to the Democracy of the Vote," *Third World Quarterly* 18, no. 1, pp. 127–148.

———— (2004). *The Search for Arab Democracy: Discourses and Counter-Discourses* (New York: Columbia University Press).

Sadiqi, Fatima (2005). "Political-Social Movements: Revolutionary: North Africa," in Suad Joseph et al.(eds.), *Encyclopedia of Women and Islamic Cultures,* vol. 2 (Leiden: Brill), pp. 653–655.

Said, Edward (1978). *Orientalism* (London: Penguin Books).

Salah Tahi, Mohand (1992). "The Arduous Democratisation Process in Algeria," *Journal of Modern African Studies* 30, no. 3, pp. 397–419.

Salamé, Ghassan (1988). "Integration in the Arab World: The Institutional Framework," in G. Luciani and G. Salamé (eds.), *The Politics of Arab Integration* (London: Croom Helm).

Salamé, Ghassan (ed.) (1994). *Democracy Without Democrats? The Renewal of Politics in the Muslim World* (London: I. B. Tauris).

Salem, Amir (1991). *In Defense of the Freedom of Association* (Cairo: Legal Research and Resource Centre for Human Rights).

Sayed Said, Mohamed el- (1994). "The Roots of Turmoil in the Egyptian Organization for Human Rights: Dynamics of Civil Institution-Building in Egypt," in *Human Rights and the Arab World—Proceedings of the Fourth Annual Symposium of the Cairo Papers in Social Science* 17, no. 3, pp. 65–87.

———— (1997). "Problems of the Arab Human Rights Movement," in Cairo Institute for Human Rights Studies, *Rowaq Arabi* (Cairo: Cairo Institute for Human Rights Studies), July, pp. 13–24.

———— (1998a). "Hisham Mubarak: al-mufakir w-al-bahith 'an al-ma'arifa," in Centre for Human Rights Legal Aid, *Hisham Mubarak: al-faris w-al-rihla* (Cairo: Centre for Human Rights Legal Aid), pp. 11–21.

———— (1998b). "Phantom of the Foreigner Reigns over Debates Concerning Private Associations," *Sawasiah* 23–24 (newsletter of CIHRS), pp. 6–9.

———— (1999). "Cosmopolitanism and Cultural Autarky in Egypt," in Roel Meijer (ed.), *Cosmopolitanism, Identity, and Authenticity in the Middle East* (Richmond: Curzon), pp. 183–196.

Sayed, Mustapha K. el- (1989). "Egyptian Popular Attitudes Toward the Palestinians Since 1977," *Journal of Palestine Studies* 18, no. 4 (summer), pp. 37–51.

Sayyid, Mustapha Kamil al- (1995a). "The Concept of Civil Society and the Arab World," in Rex Brynen, Bahgat Korany, and Paul Noble (eds.), *Political Liberalization and Democratization in the Arab World,* vol. 1 (Boulder, Colo., and London: Lynne Rienner Publishers), pp. 131–148.

—— (1995b). "A Civil Society in Egypt?" in A. R. Norton (ed.), *Civil Society in the Middle East,* vol. 1 (Leiden: E. J. Brill), pp. 269–294.

Scott, James (1990). *Domination and the Arts of Resistance: Hidden Transcripts* (New Haven, Conn.: Yale University Press).

Scott, Matthew J. O. (2001). "Danger—Landmines! NGO-Government Collaboration in the Ottawa Process," in Michael Edwards and John Gaventa (eds.), *Global Citizen Action* (Boulder, Colo.: Lynne Rienner Publishers), pp. 121–133.

Seale, Patrick (1965). *The Struggle for Syria* (Oxford: Oxford University Press).

—— (1988). *Asad: The Struggle for the Middle East* (Berkeley: University of California Press).

Seddon, David (1986). "Riot and Rebellion: Political Responses to Economic Crisis in North Africa," Discussion paper no. 196, School of Development Studies, University of East Anglia, October.

Seitz, Charmaine (2003). "ISM at the Crossroads: The Evolution of the International Solidarity Movement," *Journal of Palestine Studies* 32, no. 4 (summer), pp. 50–67.

Shafei, Omar el- (1995). "Workers, Trade Unions, and the State," *Cairo Papers in Social Science* 18, monograph 2 (summer).

Sharabi, Hisham (1966). *Nationalism and Revolution in the Arab World* (Princeton, N.J.: D. Van Nostrand Company Inc.).

Sha'rawi, Hilmi (1994). "Mafahim wa harakat huquq al-insan fi-l-watan al-'arabi," in Issa Shivji and Hilmi Sha'rawi, *Huquq al-insan fi afriqiya w-al-watan al-'arabi* (Cairo: Arab Research Centre), pp. 195–336.

Sharoni, Simona (1998). "The Myth of Gender Equality and Limits of Women's Political Dissent in Israel," *Middle East Report,* no. 207 (summer), pp. 24–28.

Sid-Ahmed, Mohamed (1991). "The Gulf Crisis and the New World Order," *Middle East Report,* no. 168 (January-February), pp. 16–17.

Silverstein, Paul (1996). "Realizing Myth: Berbers in France and Algeria," *Middle East Report,* no. 200 (July-September), pp. 11–15.

—— (1998). "'The Rebel Is Dead. Long Live the Martyr!': Kabyle Mobilization and the Assassination of Lounes Matoub," *Middle East Report,* no. 208 (fall), pp. 3–4.

Simon, Reeva S. (1986). *Iraq Between the Two World Wars* (New York: Columbia University Press).

Singerman, Diane (1995). *Avenues of Participation: Family, Politics, and Networks in Urban Quarters of Cairo* (Princeton, N.J.: Princeton University Press).

—— (n.d.). "Civil Society in the Shadow of the Egyptian State: The Role of Informal Networks in the Construction of Public Life," in James Gelvin (ed.), *The Civil Society Debate in Middle Eastern Studies,* UCLA Near East Center Colloquium Series, pp. 63–105.

Sivan, Emmanuel (1976). *Communisme et nationalisme en Algérie, 1920–1962* (Paris: Presses de la Fondation Nationale des Sciences Politiques).

*Socialist Worker* (2003). "Arab Street Marches in Step with Global Street," no. 517 (6 June), p. 3.

Stepan, Alfred, and Graeme B. Robertson (2003). "An 'Arab' More Than a 'Muslim' Electoral Gap," *Journal of Democracy* 14, no. 3, pp. 30–44.

Stevens, Janet (1978). "Political Repression in Egypt," MERIP Reports, no. 66 (April), pp. 18–21.

Stewart, Sheelagh (1997). "Happy Ever After in the Marketplace: Non-Government Organisations and Uncivil Society," *Review of African Political Economy,* no. 71, pp. 11–34.

Sullivan, Denis J. (1990). "The Political Economy of Reform in Egypt," *International Journal of Middle East Studies* 22, pp. 317–334.

Sullivan, Denis, and Sana Abed-Kotob (1999). *Islam in Contemporary Egypt* (Boulder, Colo.: Lynne Rienner Publishers).

Tarrow, Sidney (1998). *Power in Movement: Social Movements and Contentious Politics* (Cambridge: Cambridge University Press).

Tessler, Mark (1993). "Alienation of Urban Youth," in I. William Zartman and William Mark Habeeb (eds.), *Polity and Society in Contemporary North Africa* (Boulder, Colo.: Westview Press), pp. 71–101.

Thabit, Ahmad (1996). "Taghayur tabi'at wa dawr al-dawla al-misriya fi daw' al-numu al-tabi' wa siyasat sanduq al-naqd al-dawli," in Samir Amin (ed.), *Al-mujtam'a w-al-dawla fi-l-watan al-'arabi* (Cairo: Maktabat Madbuli).

Thompson, E. P. (1971). "The Moral Economy of the English Crowd in the 18th Century," *Past and Present* 50 (February), pp. 76–136.

Thompson, Elizabeth (2000). *Colonial Citizens: Republican Rights, Paternal Privilege and Gender in French Syria and Lebanon* (New York: Columbia University Press).

Tibi, Bassam (1981). *Arab Nationalism: A Critical Enquiry,* trans. M. and P. Sluglett (London: Macmillan).

———— (1997). *Arab Nationalism: Between Islam and the Nation State* (London: Macmillan).

Tignor, Robert L. (1984). *State, Private Enterprise and Economic Change in Egypt, 1918–1952* (Princeton, N.J.: Princeton University Press).

Tlemcani, Rachid (1986). *State and Revolution in Algeria* (London: Zed).

———— (1990). "Chadli's Perestroika," *Middle East Report,* no. 163 (March-April), pp. 14–18.

Toubia, Nahid (ed.) (1988). *Women of the Arab World: Papers of the Arab Women's Solidarity Association Conference* (London and New Jersey: Zed Books).

Tripp, Charles (2000). *A History of Iraq* (Cambridge: Cambridge University Press).

Tucker, Judith E. (1999). "Women in the Middle East and North Africa: The Nineteenth and Twentieth Centuries," in Guity Nashat and Judith E. Tucker, *Women in the Middle East and North Africa: Restoring Women to History* (Bloomington and Indianapolis: Indiana University Press), pp. 73–131.

Vatikiotis, P. J. (1969). *The History of Modern Egypt* (London: Weidenfeld & Nicolson).

——— (1991). *The History of Modern Egypt,* 4th ed. (London: Weidenfeld & Nicolson).

Vatin, Jean-Claude (1983). "Popular Puritanism Versus State Reformism: Islam in Algeria," in James Piscatori (ed.), *Islam in the Political Process* (Cambridge: Cambridge University Press).

Verges, Meriem (1995). "'I Am Living in a Foreign Country Here': A Conversation with an Algerian Hittiste," *Middle East Report,* no. 192 (January-February), pp. 14–17.

Walton, John, and David Seddon (1994). *Free Markets and Food Riots: The Politics of Global Adjustment* (Oxford: Blackwell).

Waltz, Susan (1995). *Human Rights and Reform* (Berkeley and Los Angeles: University of California Press).

Waterbury, John (1983). *The Egypt of Nasser and Sadat: The Political Economy of Two Regimes* (Princeton, N.J.: Princeton University Press).

Weber, Max (1946/1958). *From Max Weber,* trans. and ed. by H. H. Gerth and C. Wright Mills (New York: Galaxy).

Wedeen, Lisa (1999). *Ambiguities of Domination: Politics, Rhetoric, and Symbols in Contemporary Syria* (Chicago: University of Chicago Press).

Williams, Raymond (1977). *Marxism and Literature* (Oxford: Oxford University Press).

Yapp, M. E. (1996). *The Near East Since the First World War: A History to 1995* (Harlow, Essex: Longman).

Yapp, Malcolm (1987). *The Making of the Modern Near East 1792–1923* (London: Longman).

Yildiz, Kerim (2004). *The Kurds in Iraq* (London: Pluto).

Yuval-Davis, Nira, and Floya Anthias (eds.) (1989). *Women–Nation–State* (Basingstoke and London: Macmillan).

Zakaria, Fareed (2005). "What Bush Got Right," *Newsweek* (14 March), pp. 22–26.

Zaki, Moheb (1995). *Civil Society and Democratization in Egypt, 1981–1994* (Cairo: Ibn Khaldoun Centre and Konrad-Adenauer Stiftung).

Zartman, I. William (1963). *Government and Politics in Northern Africa* (London: Methuen).

——— (1990). "Opposition as Support of the State," in Giacamo Luciani (ed.), *The Arab State* (London: Routledge), pp. 220–246.

Zubaida, Sami (1989). *Islam, the People, and the State* (London: Routledge).

——— (1999). "Cosmopolitanism and the Middle East," in Roel Meijer (ed.), *Cosmopolitanism, Identity, and Authenticity in the Middle East* (Richmond, UK: Curzon).

——— (2003). "The Rise and Fall of Civil Society in Iraq," *openDemocracy,* 5 February; online at: www.openDemocracy.net, accessed 26 July 2005.

# Index

Abbas, Ferhat, 46
Abbas, Mahmoud, 4
'Abduh, Muhammad, 161
Abu 'Ila, Abu 'Ila Madi, 135
Abu Seada, Hafez, 150, 159
Abu Shadi, Ali, 109
Abu Zayd, Nasr Hamid, 107
Act Together—Women's Action for Iraq, 146
Adonis, 67
Afghani, al-, Jamal al-Din, 161, 166
Aflaq, Michel, 17, 33
Ahmad, Kamal Mazhar, 81
Ahrar party, 72
Ait Ahmed, Hocine, 114
Alawites, 17, 58n.3, 66, 78
Algeria, Arabic language, 17, 47–48; Arabization, 47–48, 114–115; austerity measures, 92; autogestion, 45; bureaucracy, 46; civil society, 46, 103; civil war, 97, 99–100, 103, 104; economic recession, 92; elections, 14, 72, 93–94, 96, 97, 99; French occupation, 26, 27; human rights movement, 85, 100–101, 103; ISI, 45, 61–62; independence, 39, 122 n.45; introduction of multiparty system, 72, 94; Islam, 46–48; Islamic reformism, 46; Islamists, 78, 96, 97, 99–100, 115–117, 167; land reform, 45–46; landownership, 28; military coup, 96, 99; national identity, 46–48, 113–117, 191; national reconciliation, 4, 117; nationalism, 46–48; nationalization, 45; oil, 61; peasants, 45–46; political reforms, 93–94; populism, 45–48; schools, 17, 47–48, 114–115, 116; 'specific socialism', 46–48; sufism, 46,, 48; Tripoli Programme, 45; urban protests, 92, 93; war of independence, 36, 39; women in, 36–37, 78, 83, 103, 115; workers in, 45–46, 62, 74, 78, 97; *see also* Berbers, Front de Libération Nationale
Algerian League for Human Rights (LADH), 85, 103, 140
Algerian League of Human Rights, later becomes Algerian League for the Defense of Human Rights (LADDH), 85
Ali Yahia, Abdennour, 85, 140
Allawi, Iyad, 146
Amazighité, *see* Berbers
Amin, Qasim, 36
Amin, Samir, 177
Amnesty International, 159
Ansar al-Islam, 147
ANSWER (Act Now to Stop War and End Racism), 178

225

# About the Book

WHAT EXPLAINS THE ENDURING RULE of authoritarian regimes in the Arab world? Nicola Pratt offers an innovative approach to this recurring question, shedding light on the failure of democratization by examining both the broad dynamics of authoritarianism in the region and the particular role of civil society.

Pratt appraises the part that civil society actors played in the normalization of authoritarianism in the Middle East, the challenges that new organized groups now pose to entrenched Arab regimes, and the varying ways in which those regimes are responding. She also explores the diversity of conceptions of democracy among nonstate actors. Arguing against the idea that Arab culture is inherently incompatible with democracy—the concept of Middle East "exceptionalism"—she assesses the realistic potential for democratization in the region.

**Nicola Pratt** is lecturer in comparative politics and international relations at the University of East Anglia and associate editor of the *British Journal for Middle Eastern Studies*.